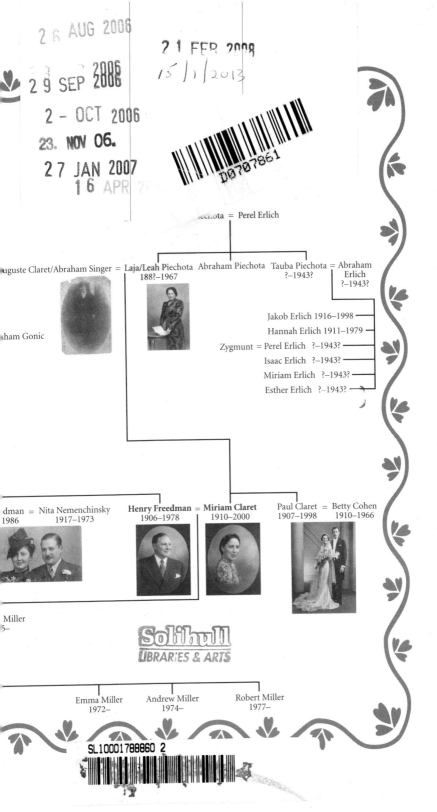

...echota = Perel Erlich

...uguste Claret/Abraham Singer = Laja/Leah Piechota   Abraham Piechota   Tauba Piechota = Abraham
                                      188?–1967                                  ?–1943?        Erlich
                                                                                               ?–1943?

...ham Gonic

Jakob Erlich 1916–1998
Hannah Erlich 1911–1979
Zygmunt = Perel Erlich  ?–1943?
Isaac Erlich  ?–1943?
Miriam Erlich  ?–1943?
Esther Erlich  ?–1943?

...dman = Nita Nemenchinsky      Henry Freedman = Miriam Claret      Paul Claret = Betty Cohen
1986            1917–1973         1906–1978       1910–2000         1907–1998    1910–1966

Miller
5–

Emma Miller        Andrew Miller        Robert Miller
1972–              1974–                1977–

# THE EARL OF PETTICOAT LANE

# The Earl of Petticoat Lane

by Andrew Miller

WILLIAM HEINEMANN: LONDON

Published in the United Kingdom in 2006 by William Heinemann

1 3 5 7 9 10 8 6 4 2

Copyright © Andrew Miller 2006

The right of Andrew Miller to be identified as the author of this work
has been asserted by him in accordance with the Copyright, Designs
and Patents Act, 1988

William Heinemann
The Random House Group Limited
20 Vauxhall Bridge Road, London, SW1V 2SA

Random House Australia (Pty) Limited
20 Alfred Street, Milsons Point, Sydney, New South Wales 2061, Australia

Random House New Zealand Limited
18 Poland Road, Glenfield
Auckland 10, New Zealand

Random House (Pty) Limited
Endulini, 5a Jubilee Road, Parktown, 2193, South Africa

The Random House Group Limited Reg. No. 954009
www.randomhouse.co.uk

A CIP catalogue record for this book is available from the British Library

Papers used by Random House are natural, recyclable products made
from wood grown in sustainable forests. The manufacturing processes
conform to the environmental regulations of the country of origin

Maps and family tree design copyright © ML Design, 2006

Typeset in Minion
Printed and bound in the United Kingdom by
Clays Ltd, St Ives plc

ISBN 0434013307

To Perry Keenlyside, in memoriam,

And for Emma Bell, in love

## Author's note

This book is a reconstruction. Some names have been changed, and some minor details inferred. All quotations are authentic.

# Contents

# Acknowledgements

First, last, and in the middle, I thank Emma Bell, for everything.

*The Earl of Petticoat Lane* also belongs to my grandparents' three children: my uncles Philip and Michael Freedman, and my mother Amelia. If Philip hadn't preserved the papers that Henry and Miriam accumulated, this book would not have been possible. Philip, Michael and Amelia have suffered many years of relentless and obscure questions with forbearance, trust and remarkable recall. I thank Philip for accompanying me to South Shields, and I thank him, his wife Brenda and Michael for a great weekend in Ukraine. I am forever in all of their debts. Thank you also to Brenda and Frances Freedman for their recollections and hospitality.

Thank you to my father Michael Miller for sharing his broad knowledge of Anglo-Jewry and the Jewish East End. Thanks to Huby Miller for helping to hunt for the elephant, and to David and Primrose Bell for their support. I am grateful to many other patient and kind members of my extended family: thanks to the suave Philip Newman; to Michel Troper, not least for sharing the memoir written by his father; Jake Claret, a fellow researcher; David and Rachel Freedman; Norman Feltz; Marilyn and Malcolm Murray; Raymond Claret; Mylene Perry; Diana Karznik; Carol Waxman; Leonard Freedman; and Sandra Conway. Posthumous thanks to Freda Freedman and Sally Skolnick, two sensational and beloved ladies. I thank my cousin Dr Jonathan Freedman for giving me the idea for this book at Miriam's *shiva*.

Also: Mr Alfred Dunitz JP, a gentleman; Sam Amiel of the Joint for his help in Ukraine; the encyclopaedic Professor Bill Fishman; the glorious Anna Tzelniker; Rabbi Kolesnik of Ivano-Frankivsk; William Frankel; the Jewish Museum, for letting me sift through their archives; Robert Podgursky of Saloman films, for information about the mines of Kopeysk; the Jewish Genealogical Society of Great Britain; Peter O'Meara of the Strand Palace Hotel; Miss Diana Parrott of Harpenden and District Local History Society; the Royal Archives; Murray Craig, clerk of the Chamberlain's court; Richard Wragg at the archives of Royal Holloway; Marcelle Adamson at the ILN archive; the Direction de la Mémoire, du Patrimoine et des Archives at the French Ministry of Defence; the *Jewish Chronicle*; Lewisham local studies library; Harpenden library; the London Metropolitan Archive; the National Archives; Senate House library; the Family Records Centre; the Guildhall library; the Imperial War Museum; Yad Vashem; the archivists of Scope, formerly the National Spastics Society; the Poulters' and Carmen's companies; the Polish State Archive in Kalisz; JRI-Poland; the Family History Library of the Church of the Latter Day Saints. Thanks to Andrew Fraser, Caroline Lambert and Polly Rossdale for help with French, and Mordechai Zucker for Yiddish. Thanks to Arkady, Becky and Petka Ostrovsky for their advice.

Of the many books that have helped, I would especially like to mention *The Alien Invasion* by Bernard Gainier; *The Alien Immigrant* by William Evans-Gordon; Jerry White's books about the East End; *A Social History of the Jewish East End in London* by Joseph Green; Norman Longmate's and Philip Ziegler's books about the Second World War; the Kalisz memorial book; *The History of Underclothes* by C.W. and P. Cunnington; Valerie Hope's *My Lord Mayor*; David Cannadine's

*The Decline and Fall of the British Aristocracy*; and S.E. Thomas's *Air Raid Warden Incident Cards*. Thanks to the Zoological Society of London (p. 239), Associated Newspapers Archive/ Solo Syndication (p. 256), the Illustrated London News Picture Library (p. 263), and the ITN Archive/Reuters/Gaumont Graphic (p. 301) for permission to reproduce photographs.

Thank you to Emma Duncan, Bill Emmott and Peter David at *The Economist* for giving me some time off to get started. Thanks to Gill Coleridge for her valuable encouragement, and for referring me to Zoe Waldie, who is a star. Thanks to my sensitive copy-editor Tamsin Shelton and, finally, to the wonderful Caroline Knight and the almost irresistible Ravi Mirchandani of William Heinemann.

Moscow, 2006

# List of Illustrations

THREE: 'I am in a whirl'

FOUR: 'Your friend, Walter'

FIVE: 'Living as in a dream'

SIX: 'Quite a success in society'

SEVEN: 'Identifying myself'

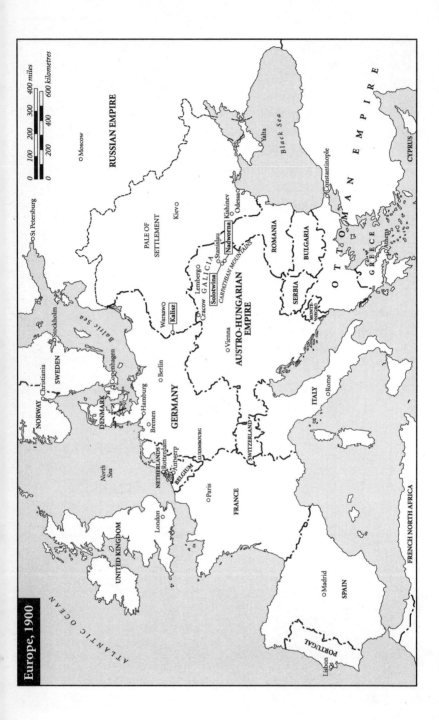

Europe, 1900

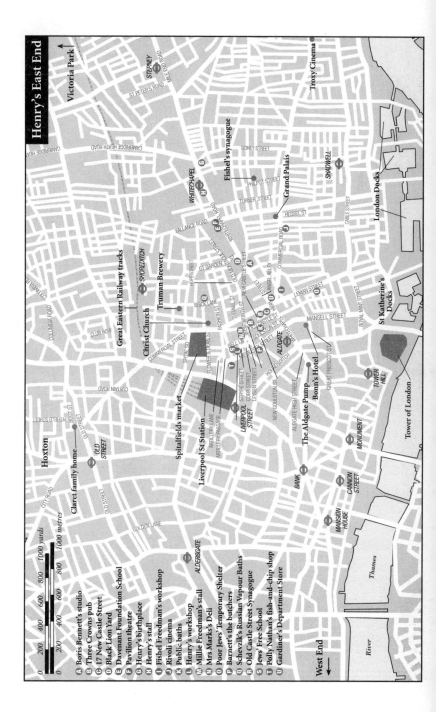

# Henry's East End

- Ⓐ Boris Bennett's studio
- Ⓑ Three Crowns pub
- Ⓒ 17 New Castle Street
- Ⓓ Black Lion Yard
- Ⓔ Davenant Foundation School
- Ⓕ Pavilion theatre
- Ⓖ Henry's birthplace
- Ⓗ Henry's stall
- Ⓘ Fishel Freedman's workshop
- Ⓙ Rivoli cinema
- Ⓚ Public baths
- Ⓛ Henry's workshop
- Ⓜ Millie Freedman's stall
- Ⓝ Mrs Marks's Deli
- Ⓞ Poor Jews' Temporary Shelter
- Ⓟ Barnett's the butchers
- Ⓠ Schevzik's Russian Vapour Baths
- Ⓡ Old Castle Street Synagogue
- Ⓢ Jews' Free School
- Ⓣ Polly Nathan's fish-and-chip shop
- Ⓤ Gardiner's Department Store

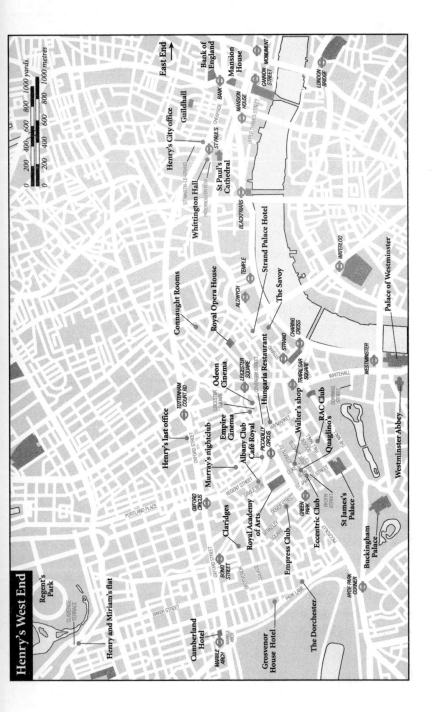

Henry's West End

# Prologue

When she was very old, and had forgotten nearly everything, there were a few memories that my grandmother clung to, disparate dots that she struggled to join up to keep hold of the life that she was losing. One that she kept almost to the end was the fact that the chandelier in my parents' suburban front room had belonged to her mother, my great-grandmother, who was born in Poland and brought up her children in a London slum. Every time she saw that chandelier, my grandmother would stop, stare and remember. Then in the cockney accent that re-emerged in her old age, finally overcoming the effects of the elocution lessons my grandfather had sent her to after the war, she would say, 'That was my mummy's, you know.' She would repeat this statement several times, with a mixture of pride and, still, astonishment at this unlikely provenance.

But most of her imperishable memories concerned Henry, her husband and my grandfather, and they were mainly from the tough but happy times before they were married. She told anyone who would listen about how, on the night they met in Spitalfields in 1929, when he was a barrow boy and she was a milliner's apprentice, Henry had danced all the way home, and the idea of him leapfrogging fire hydrants, dodging horses and twirling around lamp-posts would always make her beam. She had forgotten all the garden parties and glitzy balls that they eventually went to, but she remembered what she ate on their early dates in the West End, which, to them, was then both enemy territory and a sort of promised land. She would croak the refrains of inter-war ballads (especially 'If You Were the Only Girl in the World'), which had lodged in her fraying mind, in the way that song lyrics can, for over seventy years. My brother and I visited her in hospital when she no longer knew who we were, and she grabbed and stroked the red hair my brother has inherited from his grandfather as if he were Henry's ghost.

As tends to happen, while I had the chance I didn't ask my grandmother as much as I wish I had about her childhood, her courtship, her war, her husband and her life. Then when it was too late I wanted to know where she and Henry had come from, and how they had got from there to where they ended up. I was lucky. It turned out that Henry, who died too early for me to have known him properly when he was alive, had written copiously and kept everything: letters, diaries, photographs, address books, invitations, business ledgers and notes scribbled to himself on the backs of envelopes. So he left a musty record of how, with my grandmother, he escaped the poverty of his own immigrant's childhood; how he became an Englishman; and how he met the more commonplace challenges of love, friendship and ambition.

Looked at in one way, Henry's life was, like most lives, inconsequential, unfolding as it did on the margins of mass migrations, world wars and social upheavals. He fought in no famous battles, held no high office and was never quite successful enough in business to make headlines. Considered in another, closer way, it was, like most lives, extraordinary. It was harder and richer, both more foreign and more English than I had known – and the England it was lived in was a subtler and more fluid place than it is often thought to be. Henry and

Miriam, my grandmother, grew up in conditions that are still a living memory, but one that already seems scarcely credible. Their story spans three little worlds that have now all but vanished: the Jewish communities of Russian Poland and Galicia that their families came from; the immigrant Jewish colony that once occupied a part of London's East End; and the last encore of British high society in which, after the war, my grandparents played unlikely cameos. Henry almost died during the Blitz. But soon after he emerged from the chrysalis of his bandages he befriended a *bona fide* gentleman named Walter Sherman, who was drifting gently downwards in the world as Henry was clawing his way up. Their friendship – documented in correspondence that is, I discovered, as tender and intimate in its way as Henry's love letters to Miriam – revised my grandfather's ideas about what his life could become.

Soon after he and Walter met, Henry was frequenting the gentlemen's clubs of Pall Mall, where footmen boiled the coins and ironed the newspapers. In place of the chancers and sharks of his early acquaintance, he and Miriam, with her newly polished accent, would hobnob and do-good with aristocrats, American heiresses and the wives of prime ministers. They penetrated the rarefied scene of coming-out parties, presentations at Court and the London Season, just as the version of England that such diversions embodied was finally expiring. Instead of drinking lemon tea through a lump of sugar clenched between his front teeth, in the Russian style he had learned from his father, Henry would sip his coffee through cream as the English did. His conventional aspiration for a better life than his parents had managed was superseded by more extravagant quests. He would strive to become Lord Mayor of London; he would shake the hands of monarchs and pursue impossible proofs of gentility. He would exchange his immigrant's legacy for the birthright of a true-born Englishman. His less metamorphic siblings called him, half-mockingly, but half in admiration, the Earl of Hertfordshire.

This is not a story about the stoicism of poverty. The lives I have tried to put back together – Henry's, and my grandmother's life in his shadow – show what ingenuity and audacity and determination can do, even at a time when every dropped 'h' is supposed to have betrayed a person's origins and predetermined his fate. In the end, though, Henry and Miriam's story is also about the limits of what pluck and perseverance can achieve, and what they can transform. Henry was perpetually reminded of those limits by his mother-in-law and my great-grandmother, Leah Claret, a woman with an enigmatic, heroic, tragic story of her own, and a secret cache of letters that help to tell it. Walter Sherman was Henry's guide to the new world he set out to conquer; Leah Claret, seamstress and aficionado of chandeliers, was a breathing memento of the old world and Henry's old self, both of them incarnate and incessant in her uncompromising, big-boned flesh.

Leah almost wrecked my grandparents' romance. But before that, she tried to save it by abducting Henry's dog.

# ONE:

# 'Only a dreamer'

*17, New Castle Street*
*Aldgate, E.1.*
*London*

*August 1930*

*Dearest Miriam Darling,*
*As I saw the boat leaving the dock with you I do not think*
*I quite realised that you were going away from me and that*
*I should not see you perhaps for fourteen days and for*
*fourteen nights.*

*I waved you goodbye for as long as I could see the boat*
*and I immediately went to the hotel and up to bed. I slept*
*right on to half past four in the morning. When I awoke it*
*seemed to me that I could see you landing, and when you*
*and all were on land I went to sleep again. I slept until 8.30*
*when the thunder storm awoke me, and from then on I*
*kept thinking where you must be and how excited you were*
*gradually getting. Believe me darling I wished with all my*
*might that I was with you.*

*I walked back to the station and sat about until the train*
*came in. I don't know what was the matter but all I could do*
*was sleep all the way to London. You bet I had a dream! And it*
*was all about you. I thought you were by my side and holding*

*my hand and talking to me, and you can guess my disap-*
*pointment when I awoke at Liverpool Street Station, to find*
*I was only a Dreamer.*

*I don't think, Darling, that you know how much I am*
*missing you and how much I love you. I am longing for the*
*day when I should see you and hold you again. I want to see*
*those lovely eyes looking at me so tenderly and I want to kiss*
*your marvellous hair.*

*Sweetheart I love you with all my heart. I wish you were*
*here now so that I could tell you this instead of writing it.*

*Good night my Darling and God bless you. I hope you had*
*a pleasant crossing and are enjoying your journey onwards.*

*Goodnight sweetheart. xxxx*

Henry Freedman first took against his future mother-in-law when his dog disappeared. He had bought the dog, a Kerry Blue whom he named Teddy, when he was a teenager in the early 1920s, at the Sunday animal emporium in Club Row. Along with those on Whitechapel Road, Hessel Street, Columbia Road and the Mile End Waste, Club Row was one of the street markets that collectively formed the heart of east London and were the centre of my grandfather's early life. Among the winkles and whelks, live and jellied eels, the kippered, chopped and pickled herrings, the cursing bagel ladies, the dead and living fowl, the dyed canaries, tame mice and bird-warbler men, was a dog salesman. He barked his special offers with puppies nosing out of every pocket (all pedigrees, naturally). Like many people in Club Row, including the Irish hawkers and costermongers when they needed to, Henry and the dog man conducted their business in Yiddish.

After that, the dog went along when Henry did the rounds of Chatsworth Road market on Wednesdays and Caledonian Road market on Fridays, pushing a barrow laden with underwear, hosiery and socks. They trudged north together to Kingsland Waste in Hackney, and east to the Roman Road market and to Queen's Road in Upton Park. They went to Chrisp Street in Poplar, to White Horse Road and to White Cross Street. Teddy stood guard while Henry cried his wares at the underwear stall his mother ran in Wentworth Street. Along with Middlesex Street, Wentworth Street hosted the queen of all the East End markets, better known as Petticoat Lane. In local parlance, the two adjoining streets and their famous bazaar were just 'the Lane'.

Soon after they began walking out, in one of the letters Henry wrote to Miriam on the days when they couldn't see each other, he tells her how, after one expedition without his dog, Teddy 'jumped into my arms and absolutely cried . . . the poor thing did not know what to do to show how pleased he was to see me, and the least I could do was to take him out with me after I had some tea'. So Henry and Teddy went 'on the top of a bus to Epping Town. It was a beautiful ride; but the beauty I saw was not the countryside but your face, which I had in front of me all the time.' They went to an inn, Henry tells Miriam, with 'an old-fashioned fireplace, and old plates round the walls', where my grandfather ordered plaice and chips and 'everybody made a fuss of Teddy. You see I gave him a good comb and brush up before I took him out and he looked simply splendid.' Soon afterwards, the dog growled jealously at Miriam; her mother Leah Claret saw him; and then Teddy disappeared.

Henry never found out what had happened, but he had his suspicions. Leah had decided that he would do for Miriam, and he knew it. He was much less eligible than a master tailor or a cabinet-maker would have been, it was true; but there was something about my grandfather that suggested his troubles were only temporary. Maybe it was his superior market patter; perhaps it was the way he strolled around self-confidently as if he had a secret that nobody else was privy to: whatever it was, it was enough for Leah. The dog was in the way. When he vanished, Henry was certain that Leah had something to do with it. Yet in an extreme version of a paradox familiar to many suitors, Leah soon seemed as intent on driving Henry away as she had at first been on landing him for her daughter.

Henry Freedman met Miriam Claret in February 1929, when he was twenty-two and she eighteen. Photos of my grandmother from around that time portray a slender figure, perfectly suited to upmarket tubular twenties couture, the type she coveted but couldn't afford. Most of her clothes were made by Leah from cheap, unfashionable material, with decorous hemlines to keep her out of trouble in the ribald atmosphere of the East End workshops. Though they were otherwise unlike each other, Miriam had inherited her mother's dark brown eyes and hair, which my grandmother wore long until she followed fashion and cut it short in the mid-twenties. After she started an apprenticeship at a milliner's in Brick Lane – where Ida Freedman, one of Henry's sisters, was also an apprentice – Miriam took to wearing cloche hats that she had made herself. To begin with she was only allowed to tie the lace and ribbon trimmings onto the finished articles, and then deliver them by tram to shops that sold them to grand ladies at huge mark-ups. Then she was taught to make bandeaux and linings for the insides of the hats. Later she made up shapes in wire, felt and buckram, copied from magazine articles about Parisian fashion shows, and she eventually got to mould lace, velvet, velour and georgette onto the foundations.

Henry was short – a consequence, he and his equally diminutive brothers always liked to joke, of the low ceilings in his family's Whitechapel home. But he had a costermonger's compact muscularity and distinguished features, not dissimilar to the young Winston Churchill's. Beneath his hat (a cap for work; a trilby in the evenings) he had assiduously groomed, fine

reddish hair. He dressed as nattily as he could afford, with a carefully arranged breast-pocket handkerchief and a cheap watch chain strung across his waistcoat. As a young man he intermittently grew a thin moustache, of the kind made fashionable by American film stars of the twenties. It didn't suit him.

Their lives collided when Miriam went with Ida to meet Henry after work, at Polly Nathan's fish-and-chip shop in the Lane. By the time they left, charitably offering a few chips to the people in the queue as custom demanded, Henry had decided. He talked twenty to the dozen while Miriam ate the chips from the soggy newspaper. She didn't say much, entranced but inhibited by his way with words, and afterwards thought that everything she did say had been silly. She needn't have worried. 'It is no use trying to tell you in words how much I love you,' he wrote in one of his early love letters, 'as there are no words in all the world which can describe my feelings for you . . . I think I had better leave you now and go to bed and dream about when we shall be with each other again.' As he confided to her after they were married, on the night they met Henry danced all the way home. He danced down Wentworth Street and across Old Castle Street. He pirouetted into New Castle Street, a narrow cobbled turning off Whitechapel High Street, coming to rest at Number Seventeen, in which he lived in intimate indigence with his brothers Sid and Mick, his sisters Ida and Babs, and their widowed mother Millie.

Number Seventeen was a poky, two-up, two-down terrace that they shared with a family named Isaacs: the New Castle Street *loch* (hole), Henry and his siblings called it, in Yiddish, after they had escaped it. The Freedmans rented the two rooms at the front of the house, and the Isaacses occupied the two overlooking the yard and the outside toilet. They were divided by thin walls and flimsy ceilings, through which Ida once stamped a foot that dangled through the floorboards into the room below, where her brothers tickled it sadistically until it was extricated. The ground floor room was lit by a gas mantle, and the upstairs bedroom by candlelight: electricity

arrived just as the family left in 1936. Millie, Ida and Babs slept in one bed upstairs; the three boys shared one downstairs, which was used as a sofa during the day. The downstairs room was also the kitchen, dining and sitting rooms, and the storage room for whatever goods the Freedmans had acquired but had not yet been able to sell. Henry slept with his head at the top of the bed, alongside his two brothers' four feet, the dubious privilege of his seniority. In the winter, the bed also contained a brick heated in the fireplace. At four in the morning, as the fishmongers made their way to Billingsgate and the butchers to Smithfields, Henry got up to borrow his capital from the market-men's lender, then buy his stock from Atlas the hosiery specialists at the Aldgate, Kaye's in Houndsditch and the other piled-high apparel wholesalers on the edge of the City.

In good weather Number Seventeen smelled of carbolic and sulphur, which Millie ineffectually deployed against the bugs that emerged from cracks in the walls and the joints of bed-steads, depriving the children of sleep and leaving ugly little blood stains on the wallpaper when they were squished. There was also the smell of tea from the warehouse in Old Castle Street, the whiff of interminable fish-frying and soup-making, and the ineradicable odour of horses, which cars would not usurp in the poorer parts of London until the late forties.

So, before a date with Miriam, Henry worked on his perfume at the public baths around the corner in Goulston Street. For tuppence you got the bath, a piece of soap and a reasonably clean towel. Lined up on benches to wait for their turn, Henry and the other grubby traders, bootmakers, tailors and carpenters would chant the baths' unofficial theme song – '*Hot vater number twenty-two/Ooo, aaah, tanking you*' – to the tune of the soldiers' chorus from Gounod's *Faust*. Then, isolated in their numbered cubicles, the bathers would indeed beseech the gruff attendant for more hot water, and be subject to surprise scaldings if they didn't pay attention. Now and then

Henry ventured instead beneath the fine oriental ironwork outside Schevzik's Russian Vapour Baths in Brick Lane, and joined the bearded old men in its sweaty interior. He would emerge from his alchemic dip wearing his one good suit and a fashionable striped tie, the sort designed to make young men who weren't look like Varsity types, with precisely the right length of shirt-cuff protruding from his jacket.

When my grandparents began walking out, on the other side of town, in the Café de Paris, the Kit-Cat Club and the Embassy Club in Bond Street, young women with 'kiss' curls stuck to their cheeks were wearing lipstick and flapper dresses, drinking cocktails and smoking through long cigarette holders. They craned their necks and manipulated their dance partners to catch a glimpse of the playboy Prince of Wales, not yet entangled with Mrs Simpson. They raced around London in motor cars, and went on the arms of men swinging canes to the array of parties wearily catalogued by Evelyn Waugh in *Vile Bodies*: 'Masked parties, Savage parties, Victorian parties, Greek parties, Wild West parties, Russian parties, Circus parties, parties where one had to dress as somebody else, almost naked parties . . . '. Reliable contraception had just been invented, and well-heeled revellers, to whom the old rules did not apply, availed themselves of it.

Miriam, meanwhile, for months wouldn't let Henry kiss her, in case it made her pregnant. This was a largely irrelevant injunction, since, in accordance with a rule imported and imposed by Millie Freedman, Henry's immigrant mother, when they saw each other they always had a chaperone. Millie and her husband Fishel had grown up in what was then Galicia, a province of the Habsburg empire. Millie still thought court-ship was much less economical than the old-style marriage-brokers who furnished kosher matches in Whitechapel and Spitalfields for a modest percentage of the dowry. She worried that there would be nothing left to talk about after the wedding.

Still, if the young people must waste their time and money, God forbid that there should be any scandal. Ida, Henry's sister, must accompany them.

So my grandparents' relationship became a contradiction of infatuated correspondence and supervised encounters. Ida went with them to Victoria Park in Bethnal Green, on a tram known locally as the 'Polish Express', to listen to the band and eat ice creams and mess about on the boating lake. She accompanied them to the new, palatial Rivoli cinema on Commercial Road, where they were ushered in by a doorman dressed as a vampire or a gladiator or a cowboy, or whatever that evening's feature demanded. She haunted them, crunching peanuts and peeling oranges, while they sat in the dark, marvelling at the brand-new talkies and the vampish, fallen or falling women they portrayed. Or the three of them went to one of the picture-houses around Brick Lane, which had no orchestra or interval entertainers and had not yet been wired for sound, but only cost a penny. Here, Buster Keaton, Greta Garbo and the last silent pictures were holding out, stubborn but doomed, against Al Jolson and the talkie revolution. A pianist's busy feet were visible in a curtained-off recess, where she played impromptu overtures and melodramatic accompaniments. Whenever Polish-born parents, with only rudimentary English, whispered '*Vas sogt er?*' (Yiddish for 'what's he saying?') to their bilingual children, the pianist would play louder to drown out the children's translations of the titles, and the ensuing complaints. When the pianist played the national anthem at the end of the show, Henry, Miriam and Ida patriotically sang along, while the older people around them stood in respectful silence.

Mostly, though, they just paraded along Whitechapel Road, looking in shop windows with the other courting couples and prowling teenagers, or strolled down to the Tower of London or west to the Bank of England. Henry serenaded them in his fine tenor voice:

*If you were the only girl in the world*
*And I was the only boy,*
*Nothing else would matter in the world today,*
*We could go on loving in the same old way.*

– and 'Just a Little Piece o' Driftwood', and assorted sentimental Yiddish standards, all of which embarrassed Ida and enchanted Miriam. Sometimes he took along the scratched-up violin he had taught himself to play, and he fiddled while Miriam sang. 'I keep playing on the violin all the songs we sang together,' he wrote when they were separated for nearly two weeks in the summer of 1930, 'and my heart gets such an aching and longing for you that I have to put it down again.'

Finally, when he was determined to impress her, Henry took them all up West, on the Number Twenty-five bus from the Aldgate, to a tea dance at the Lyons Corner House in Coventry Street, between Piccadilly Circus and Leicester Square.

Henry had been brought up to view going up West as a shortcut to ruin. When his father Fishel had been alive, he and Millie Freedman had talked about the West End as if it were a gentile Gomorrah. They clung to their own neighbourhood like a rock of familiarity in a sea of alien godlessness. The colourful shawls that enlivened the Whitechapel women, the men's dark gabardines, and the familiar food that cluttered the markets and infused the atmosphere with its aromas almost let them pretend that they were still in Galicia, which they still talked about as if it were an adjacent region. Yiddish, their native tongue, filled the streets and sweatshops. Missionaries proselytised in it (not very successfully) and policemen policed in it. Yiddish versions of Molière, Ibsen, Strindberg, Verdi and Shakespeare ('translated and improved') were performed at the Pavilion Theatre in Whitechapel Road ('the Drury Lane of the East') and the Grand Palais in Commercial Road. After the actresses complained about their crummy parts, a local author knocked up a Yiddish *Queen Lear*; original drama contemplated the relative merits of Cracow and New York's Lower East Side, and the distress caused by wayward offspring. Henry overheard hushed gossip about neighbours' children who forsook this insular security to go prancing along the Strand and Piccadilly, frequent the theatreland musicals with their scantily clad chorus girls, and eke out drinks in the restaurants and fleshpots of Soho and Mayfair.

But, by 1929, my grandfather thought of the East End more as a forward staging-post than as a besieged enclave. Flexing the muscles of their freedom, he and his peers would ride the Number Twenty-five, or walk if they were especially skint, to explore the world to the west that wasn't yet theirs, but might be one day. The Lyons Corner House in Coventry Street was one of his first conquests. It had separate orchestras on each of its three floors – perhaps not as famous as the American jazz artistes who entertained the smart set in the flashy clubs, or as suave as the 'Savoy Orpheans', but wittily dressed to fit in with the Polynesian, Mexican and other ethnic themes of the dining rooms. The waitresses wore pristine black outfits and spotless white pinafores and called Henry 'sir', even though they had already sized him, Miriam and Ida up as 'one egg mayonnaise': the cheapest dish on the menu, and Corner House code for scrimping day-trippers. The walls and floors were beautified by mosaics, art deco fixtures, mahogany fittings and what looked like marble. Countless humble love stories reached their finales in this sumptuous yet affordable setting. It gave Henry and Miriam their first hint of what it might feel like to be posh.

The first time they went to Coventry Street, in July 1929, Miriam confessed that she had a sweet tooth and ordered a knickerbocker glory rather than an egg mayonnaise. Ida had a waffle; because the menu wasn't quite affordable enough, Henry said he wasn't hungry and didn't have anything. He and Miriam danced the foxtrot and the quickstep, and he waltzed attentively with Ida even though she told him he needn't. The second time they went to Coventry Street, they bought a brick of vanilla ice cream on their way out, which they ate stickily on the bus before it melted.

The third time they were due to go, at the beginning of August 1929, Henry told Ida she had a nasty cold, and she stayed at home. Miriam was anxious when he called for her alone and didn't talk much on the way; but when he said his piece as they sat out the Charleston, which always made her giggle, she understood why. Her childhood had been a training in patient acquiescence, and she might have found it difficult to refuse anyone who asked for her. But when Henry talked about her doing him the honour, and him striving with all his heart to please her, Miriam said 'yes' and meant it. Afterwards they took a stroll, and Henry gave her a bunch of violets from one of the flower girls under the statue of Eros at Piccadilly Circus, whose staple clientele were the couples in evening dress on their way to the latest Noel Coward in the Haymarket or Shaftesbury Avenue.

To be properly engaged, they needed two things: a ring – which, after his siblings chipped in, Henry bought for Miriam at one of the more modest jewellers in Black Lion Yard – and permission. Miriam had said that her father had been killed in the war, so it would have to come from her mother. To secure Leah Claret's say-so, Henry diligently observed all the proprieties that the cinema and newspaper Society columns had persuaded him were required of an English suitor. On Tuesday, 6 August 1929 he wrote to Leah to advise her of his plans. 'Dear Mrs Claret, I am coming round on Wednesday evening, at about 8.15, as I shall then be able to keep my promise to you, to pay you and Miriam a visit. I hope this will not be inconvenient to you . . . Please give my best regards to Miriam, and also yourself. I am', he assures her meaningfully, 'Your Very Sincere Friend, Henry Freedman.'

Leah Claret, Miriam and her elder brother Paul lived in the basement of Number Five, Boot Street, Hoxton, underneath a candle shop. Hoxton lies just to the north of the City of London, and just to the west of what most people considered the East End proper. Today, the area combines a nouveau trendiness with a resilient poverty. But between the two world wars, when the Clarets lived there, there was no suggestion of chic. Hoxton was one of the most overcrowded, deprived and depraved quarters of London. Men stood around on its corners during the day, even before they began to do so on corners across London and around the country after the crash of 1929. In the evenings, they packed the superabundant pubs; on pay day, rows of prams stood outside unattended, as abusive husbands and long-suffering wives buried their hatchets and drowned their sorrows.

Boot Street itself is now a cobbled alley that runs between a modern hotel on one side and, on the other, pleasantly land-scaped university halls of residence, with a sprinkling of art galleries and cafés. A clue to the street's former character can be found on the intricate maps of poverty in London prepared by Charles Booth, a pioneering sociologist, at the end of the nineteenth century. Boot Street appears as a slug of black with a border of dark blue, colours that, according to the maps' kaleidoscopic key, identify the street's turn-of-the-century residents as predominantly 'vicious' and 'semi-criminal'. A few of my grandmother's neighbours had ascended to the status defined by the maps as 'chronic want'. There were three or four families, plus a workshop or two, in each house. The base-ments had been built to store coal but, by the time the Clarets lived there, they instead helped to store the human fuel for the sweatshops and the docks. Decades of municipal efforts had failed to stop unscrupulous landlords renting and desperate tenants inhabiting these troglodytic hovels. Pubs stood at both ends of Boot Street like delinquent neighbourhood sentinels.

It was one of the first streets the bobbies from Old Street police station would target when they mustered up the courage to go looking for villains. It was the sort of place that a respectable boy from Whitechapel like Henry would ordinarily go the long way round to avoid, and that Leah would have avoided too if she could have helped it.

So on 7 August 1929 Henry had more than one reason to be apprehensive as he made his way to his appointment, wearing, as a mark of his high seriousness, the bowler hat that was almost all he had inherited from his father. The evening's unseasonal drizzle worked its way through his suit to mingle with his nervous perspiration. He dodged the horses and carts on Commercial Street, inhaling the tobacco smell that emanated from the cigarette workshops that lined it, and the sickly aroma of ripened fruit from Spitalfields market. He zig-zagged through the furniture stalls that cluttered Curtain Road, infecting the air with the whiff of linseed and turpentine. With his heart pummelling his waistcoat, he negotiated the narrow stairs to the Boot Street basement.

He and Ida had called for Miriam dozens of times, and he (and Teddy) had met Leah in the markets, but he hadn't yet crossed the Clarets' threshold. To do so would also mean cross-ing a Rubicon: where he came from, a young man generally intruded on a young lady's parents for only one reason. After the niceties, there would be businesslike questions about his prospects and their contribution to the cost of the wedding and the new household. If the answers were agreeable, hands would be shaken, cheeks kissed, backs slapped and the neigh-bours told. There might be a drop of cherry brandy; there would almost certainly be cake. Then the young lady's parents would contemplate the impending loss of a daughter – and the extra income she brought in – and the compensation of grandchildren. The young man would go away for a year or so to earn enough money to do things properly.

In this case, as it turned out, Henry didn't have much trouble getting Leah's permission, albeit delivered curtly, as if he were asking for a cup of tea rather than her daughter, and without the cake. But he had a lot of trouble getting the assurances about Miriam's lineage for which, in the name of another kind of decorum, he had been obliged delicately to ask.

In her own way my great-grandmother Leah Claret was a talented person. As a young woman, she had boasted the type of chiselled features that were described as handsome, though as she got older, along with her broad shoulders, sturdy legs and undisguisable bust, her natural grimace looked more and more as though it were designed to face down Eastern European winters. But along with the physiognomy, she had a peasant's gift for storytelling. When Henry met her in 1929 she was working as a needlehand, but there were several retail phases in her variegated career, and during them she used her narrative gift to enchant her customers, spinning seductive histories for the handbags or knick-knacks that she wanted them to buy. She also used it to soothe her children and grandchildren when she was bathing them or putting them to bed. The stories she told at bedtime ranged between autobiography and fantasy, but one way or another they all told of Poland and its privations. A tale about her father eluding homicidal highwaymen on his way home from market was one of the more credible ones. Another staple of her repertoire was a practical, Polish–Yiddish folktale on the *King Lear* theme. A king obliges his three daughters to compare their love for him to a substance of their choice; after the first two rhapsodise predictably about gold and silver, the third and favourite daughter incurs her banishment by saying that she loves her father just as she loves salt. A severe winter and subsequent famine persuade the king that salt is, after all, a rather valuable commodity, and he tracks down his most sensible offspring. Several of the stories in Leah's œuvre concerned the miraculous discovery of bars of gold and other lost or buried treasures, which are either returned to their owners, earning a reward in heaven, or kept, earning a move to London or New York. In one of these variants, Leah herself finds the loot. A nocturnal vision instructs her to dig beneath a tree, close to her father's house; in the morning she sneaks away, rummages beneath the tree and finds a bar of gold, which buys her passage to England.

She also had an impressive portfolio of violent curses, impugning their targets' ancestors and execrating their offspring. She had a propensity, on occasion, to plain violence, which instilled in her children a kind of canine devotion as well as fear. Her religious beliefs incorporated necromancy, and a variety of techniques for averting 'the Evil Eye'. Among her superstitions was an absolute refusal to sew up clothes while someone was wearing them, or to take them off and turn them round if they had been put on the wrong way. Her views on medicine were primitive: she would have applied leeches until she died if she had known where to find them. She had a sensitive eye for antiques, which she accumulated on instinct and loved and looked after like extra children. But, otherwise, she had no nose or palate for the finer things in life. She cooked sweet and stodgy Polish food and distilled borscht, never getting along with the pointless sophistication of less earthly cuisine. In her abrasive, feudal way, she loved Miriam powerfully. But she would never be refined; she would never be an English lady, which was what Henry was soon determined for his wife to become: survival, rather than self-improvement, was the limit of Leah's ambition for most of her hard, hard life. When he was striving to become something else, Henry couldn't forgive her for being and staying what she was. She would die in another basement, this one below what was to be my grandparents' most august address; but she always reminded him of that first cellar in Boot Street,

and the fact that he and Miriam would never entirely ascend from it.

However, long before the legibility of Leah's face and accent became a deep if unspeakable grievance, the mystery of her background, rather than its obviousness, infuriated my grandfather. More even than his dog's disappearance, this mystery set the tone for a relationship that, part duty, part love, part aversion, part self-aversion, would endure for most of Henry's life. When he went to Boot Street, in August 1929, he already knew that Leah had come to London from Poland, and that she was poor. He hadn't realised quite how poor, but he was in no position to regard that as a disqualifying fault. That she seemed to have raised Miriam and Paul by herself was also less than scandalous. Plenty of East End men had perished in the First World War fighting for King and country. After the British government obliged reluctant aliens to fight for somebody, some of his mother's male acquaintances had taken their chances on the eastern front rather than in the western trenches, and had died for the Tsar instead. A few had hurried back to Russia in the honeymoon optimism after the revolution, intending to send for their women and children later, as they had earlier summoned families left behind in Riga and Odessa when they found their feet in London. Many of them vanished. Other breadwinners met less cavalier ends through slaving year after year in boot-making and tailoring sweatshops. Hearts gave out and lungs became consumptive. In the slack periods, when there was no work, the strain of worry and debt could be just as corrosive. The fur trade was especially lethal: the perpetual inhalation of fibre and fur and too little air, shared by too many people in too small a space, sent platoons of sweatshop furriers wheezing to premature graves – including Fishel Freedman, Henry's father, whose death in 1915 had dispatched his family to the squalor of New Castle Street. My grandfather knew how punishing life could be for single mothers and their children, and he didn't expect a dowry or a fancy wedding.

What he wanted, along with her permission, was for Leah to convince him that the rumours he had heard about her weren't true. The source of these rumours was Harry Perlmutta, who sold oilcloths in the Lane from a pitch opposite the Freedmans. Perlmutta had a daughter, and both he and she, listening to Henry's patter and observing his profitably winning smile, thought he would make a useful addition to the family. Perlmutta also observed Miriam's frequent visits, and the way she and Henry looked at each other. So one afternoon in July 1929 he ambled over to the delicatessen run by the Marks family.

The Marks deli was a famous, fragrant heaven of pickles and smoked salmon. Along with Barnett's the butcher's – which had sawdust on the floor, a stuffed bull's head on the wall known to local children as Uncle Mannie, and whose hot salt beef sandwiches were universally agreed to be incomparable – the deli was one of the Lane's twin gastronomic landmarks.

Mrs Marks herself was an honorary member of the Freedman family: she had been an unofficial godmother to Henry ever since death and desperation had brought Millie Freedman to her stall in the Lane in 1917. Perlmutta found Mrs Marks on the pavement outside the shop, surrounded by barrels that, with her rotund form, she herself closely resembled. Each was filled with minutely differentiated varieties of cucumbers and herrings (*shmaltz*, pickled, chopped and marinated), which favoured customers were allowed to fish out for themselves after rolling up their sleeves. Perlmutta muttered something about Miriam, and Mrs Marks duly went to look for Mrs Freedman. She waded through the discarded fish heads and apple cores that carpeted Wentworth Street, nipped down Old Castle Street, crossed New Castle Place and knocked on the Freedmans' door.

The gist of the muttering was that Leah lacked the only thing Henry needed her to bequeath to her daughter: that mother and therefore daughter were not, as my grandfather was and needed them to be, Jewish. Mrs Claret (and Perlmutta also cast aspersions on her marital status and the origins of her French surname) had pretended to be Jewish because it suited her. It meant she could take advantage of the array of East End Jewish charities and philanthropists, like the temporary shelter for Hebrew immigrants in Leman Street, and free wine at Passover time from Frumkin's the kind-hearted vintner on the corner of Cannon Street Road. It would also broaden her children's options in the marriage market. Living among the Jews in Poland had taught her enough to carry it off.

It was a terrible accusation. It confirmed all Millie Freedman's worst fears about the strange city and demented modern world she found herself in; and it dismayed Henry when, between her sobs and her God-forbids, his mother managed to tell him. The imperative to marry someone of his own faith had been impressed on him, as on millions of Jews before and since, as if it were an unwritten eleventh commandment, and one that was far less flexible than several of the official ten. Although, by 1929, partly out of choice and partly out of necessity, he had forsaken more of the dictates of his religion than his father would have thought possible, marrying a gentile was still as unimaginable to him as marrying a mermaid.

Still, when he went to Boot Street in August 1929, Henry had assured himself that Leah would clear things up, and even kept his bowler hat on when he descended to the basement, in deference to the religious orthodoxy that he hoped would prevail inside. He hadn't told Miriam about the rumours. If true, they meant disaster; but since he was convinced that it was all trivial slander, why upset her?

Alas, there was little evidence of religion amid the jumble of oddments that Leah had brought back, the spoils of her bartering wars, from the stalls among the jugglers and sword-swallowers on the Mile End Waste. The basement had been divided into two squat rooms: a back one for sleeping in, and a front one for everything else. There was also a hypothermic outside toilet, furnished with cut-up bits of newspaper and shared with three other families, and a little coal hutch where Leah sometimes kept disgruntled chickens. There was one cold-water tap on the ground floor for the whole house; if Miriam wanted more than a strip wash, she nipped up to the public baths in Pitfield Street. Leah couldn't afford the linoleum that covered the floors in New Castle Street, and the bare stone, cold all year round, gave Miriam a lifelong reverence for carpets. She could never understand the appeal of polished floorboards, which to her were always shaming proofs of poverty that should be covered up at once. By the green gaslight that provided the front room's only illumination, Henry made out the carcass of a foot-treadle sewing machine, exuding its oily odour, and the disassembled pieces of an improbable chandelier. Leah showed Henry some pillows that she claimed were covered with the same material as those in a boudoir in Buckingham Palace, and he got the feeling that she wanted him to buy them. But there were no weathered daguerreotypes of austere male relatives, with serious brows and pious beards, that were reverentially displayed, like household gods, in most of the homes Henry knew. There was no *menorah*, the eight-branched candelabra lit on *Chanukah*, the winter festival of lights, and no *mezuzah* – a small, symbolic capsule that Jews affix to the door-posts of their homes, a totem of the Jewish faith that even the minimally observant would have possessed, and an absence that hardship alone could not excuse.

As Henry sat sweating into his hat, Leah only made things worse. True, there was some circumstantial evidence in her favour. As well as Polish and some Russian she knew Yiddish, the hybrid language once spoken by Jews across Central Europe and the Pale of Settlement (the western and southern provinces of Russia into which, from 1791, Catherine the Great and her successors had corralled their Jewish subjects). Leah was especially familiar, Henry discovered, with the plentiful stock of Yiddish expletives. But that hardly proved my grandmother's genealogy, and would certainly not satisfy the rabbinical authorities who would determine whether she was eligible for a synagogue wedding ceremony. Who were Leah's father and mother? Who was the father of her children? In short, who were the Clarets?

It was a hard question for Henry to ask and, as it turned out, an even harder one for Mrs Claret to answer. She sighed, contradicted herself, changed the subject and lost her temper. In the course of several strained, subterranean interviews, she claimed that her husband was a Frenchman; a Pole; and a Pole with a French pseudonym. His name was Claret, or Singer, and sometimes both. They had married in either France or London. He had died in Paris of natural causes just before the First World War; perished during the fighting soon after; succumbed to the pestilent post-war flu epidemic; or simply disappeared in the chaos of the war. She herself, Leah said, had been driven by curiosity to travel from Poland to London for the coronation of Edward VII – a tall story that might, just about, have placated any officials who accosted her when she got off the boat at the London docks, but didn't impress Henry. She had no London relatives who could corroborate anything she said, and there was no rabbi in England or, as Henry was patiently to ascertain, France, who could verify her supposed marriage. She had no documentary evidence to prove her stories. As he walked home to New Castle Street, passing the lamplighters who still made their nightly rounds, Henry was desolate.

Confirming Miriam's religious pedigree cost Henry more time than he had and more money than he could afford. It involved him in long and trying correspondences with civic and religious authorities in disparate corners of Europe, which he had to have translated from and into various languages by a down-at-heel scholar in Artillery Passage. When the replies to his inquiries from rabbis and registrars in Poland and Paris arrived in New Castle Street, Henry would rush round to Artillery Passage, only to learn that, no, his correspondents had never officiated at Leah Claret's wedding and had no record of her birth. It meant enduring the whispers and niggling inquiries of his acquaintances in the markets ('have you cracked it already, Henry?' and 'hope she's worth it, Henry'). It meant retreating back into the foreign hinterland of his life when, like many of his second-generation peers, he wanted to be pushing on and up into an English future.

On the other hand, Henry was in love. His mother Millie's generation mostly thought being in love was a faddish affectation, no likelier to endure than the sudden East End popularity of all-in wrestling. Were they to have been privy to it, to Millie and her peers the kind of language that filled my grandfather's

letters would have seemed *meshugah*, crazy. 'Dearest love,' Henry wrote to Miriam on the eve of her birthday in June 1930, 'I miss you terribly tonight.' He hadn't packed up his stall until 9.30 in the evening – it had been a record trading day, though 'it was really too hot today, wasn't it dear?' – and so hadn't managed to visit her as he had hoped to. But 'in every waking moment you are always in my thoughts . . . I hope tomorrow your twentieth birthday will be one of many which you and I will share with each other . . . I love you with all my heart and life.' Miriam herself had encountered this sort of talk in the cinema, but she had never expected to have it said to or written about her. She was brought up by Leah to think of marriage as, at best, an economic convenience rather than a source of happiness. So when she read Henry's rhapsodies she felt a furtive exhilaration, tempered by a sense that she must be eavesdropping on someone else's life. 'Why me?' she thought, and sometimes said, with an unaffected humility that only made him love her more; 'what's so special about me?'

Henry applied to the London *Beth Din* – the Jewish religious court that investigates questions of genealogy – but even it could not solve the mystery. By July 1930 there was only one thing for it: somebody would have to go to Kalisz, in western Poland, where Leah claimed to have grown up, to bring back some evidence of her parentage.

There were two problems with this solution. The first was deciding who should go. Citing the memory of her seasickness thirty years before, when as a lonely emigrant from Poland she had made the same journey but in the opposite direction, and the grave dangers involved in surprising her family, and other still less convincing arguments, Leah was adamant that she was staying put. But she was even more adamant that Henry was as well.

The second problem was money. Although more expensive than Leah's original passage to London three decades earlier, trips to the Continent were still within the means of many working people. The ships were also more seaworthy and sanitary than the one Leah remembered, and this time there would be only half a dozen other people in the cabin. But Henry and Leah had no savings, and at the end of each day only possessed the cash that they had earned during it. Whichever of them gave up work to go to Poland would struggle to cover the rent. In the end, Leah went to Kalisz, pretending it was a long-planned visit and taking along her two children as alibis, and Henry helped to pay, borrowing some money, settling with the Boot Street landlord and securing three berths on a steamer from Harwich to Hamburg.

Leah had brought her daughter up without much religion, as well as without a father. Miriam couldn't read Hebrew, and beyond the requirement to lay on chicken soup and fried fish on Friday night, her knowledge of Jewish ritual was always sketchy. She didn't really understand why Henry, whom she loved, and her mother, whom she also loved, had fallen out. If her mother said she was Jewish, then she was. Still, the Polish adventure was some compensation. Her only previous holidays had consisted of outings to Epping Forest, and once, on August Bank Holiday, a boisterous day-trip on a charabanc to Southend: in season, Southend became a beery and leery outpost of the East End, where visitors played on the water chutes and flying machines at the famous Kursaal pleasure park. Miriam's excitement about Poland (and the cost to Henry) grew when Leah insisted that they stay in a hotel, which my grandmother had never done before, rather than with Leah's family. Leah herself said nothing to Henry when he accompanied them on the train from Liverpool Street station to Harwich. He explained again to Miriam's brother Paul exactly what he wanted, running through every bureaucratic permutation: if the rabbi can't help, go to the town hall; if that doesn't resolve it, go to the regional procurator. He stayed on the boat with them for as long as he could, running along the gangplank as the foghorn sounded and Miriam sailed away, on the evening of 31 July 1930, on a journey that would either eventually unite them or separate them altogether.

There was no late train to London that night, so Henry spent it in a Harwich boarding house. Loneliness was now added to the list of grievances that he held and stored against Leah. Writing to Miriam, as he did every day that she was away, made it worse as well as better. He wrote even before he knew where to send his letters, hoarding them until she gave him an address for a stopover on the journey home ('It is a pity I do not know yet where to send my letters,' he tells her, 'but I will keep on writing until I do.'). Then he sent them in a bundle, and for as long as he thought they would reach her before she got back to him. The last few he kept, to give to her when she came home. His correspondence resounds with the sort of sonorous repetitions and rotund phrasing that autodidacts of his generation picked up from Gibbon's *Decline and Fall of the Roman Empire* and Macaulay's *History of England*, which Henry had found on one of the stalls in the Lane in flaking old editions and kept under his bed with an incomplete set of encyclopaedias. In the evenings, before the gaslight was turned out, Henry would lie in bed, reading his second-hand tomes and devouring the sherbet sweets that were then his only sensual indulgence, while his brothers read *Punch* and *The Strand* and other fashionable magazines at the other end of the mattress. But along with these influences, in his writing there is a vibrant idiom that is Henry's own.

'As I saw the boat leaving the dock with you,' Henry began his first letter, 'I do not think I quite realised that you were going away from me and that I should not see you perhaps for fourteen days and for fourteen nights.' He went back to the boarding house and 'slept right on to half past four in the morning. When I awoke it seemed to me that I could see you landing, and when you and all were on land I went to sleep again.' In some of his letters, he wants to tell Miriam about everything that has happened to him, as if such second-hand intimacy could cancel the distance between them. So his idolatry is often punctuated by quotidian information about food (bread, butter and marmalade for his breakfast; fish and chips for lunch) and the (lousy) weather. But in this first letter, he sticks to his main theme: 'I don't know what was the matter but all I could do was sleep all the way to London. You bet I had a dream! And it was all about you. I thought you were by my side and holding my hand and talking to me, and you can guess my disappointment when I awoke at Liverpool Street Station, to find I was only a Dreamer.' There is a mildly risqué passage: 'I don't think, Darling, that you know how much I am missing you and how much I love you. I am longing for the day when I should see you and hold you again. I want to see those lovely eyes looking at me so tenderly and,' he writes, adding a little detail of desire that helps to make this love his own, and not only an emulation of the silver screen, 'I want to kiss your marvellous hair.' And there is a reminder that such letters are no substitute for the real thing: 'I wish you were here now so that I could tell you this instead of writing it.'

Henry wrote some of the encomiums that he sent to Miriam as she travelled across Europe on paper headed 'Freedman and Sons; Wholesale Import and Export; Shirt and Pajama Manufacturers; Hosiery and Underwear Specialists'. This grand-sounding enterprise seems never to have progressed very far from page to reality. In the summer of 1930 Henry was working in the Lane and in the markets across east London. He watched the wide boys selling 'surprise packages', most of which surprised their purchasers by being empty, and the 'pound-note man' hawking stockings, his hat decorated with pound and ten-shilling notes. He heard the famous racing tipster Prince Monolulu, with his crazy feather headdress and all-weather umbrella, delivering his trademark cry of 'I gotta horse!' He listened to the poetic bagel man declaim his bagel-poems in a thick Polish accent: *Bagels for you, Takes away the flu, When you feel hungry don't feel blue, Bagels is waiting for you.*

Despite these distractions, whenever there was a lull in trade, as well as when he woke up and just before he went to sleep, Henry conjured his own brand of lyricism. Late and lonely on 6 August, he doesn't 'know what I've been doing all day, and to-night I went to the Empire [a music hall] but I left in the middle of the show, just like I was in a trance, and I had to come right home as fast as I could . . . Business has not been bad, but I somehow do not seem to care what happens, until I see you back safely home again . . . Dearest darling sweetheart I hope you are enjoying yourself and that Mother and Paul are too. They must excuse me if I do not write so much for them, as I have not much else in my mind except how lovely you looked when I said au Revoir to you on the ship.' Two days later, he senses that what he feels for Miriam is beyond compare: 'Dearest Love,' he writes, 'I am sure nobody could imagine how much we miss each other. You are the Light of my Eyes and I have no life without you.' But he also betrays the insecurity that sometimes lurks within such passion, complaining that Miriam has neglected him: 'I have waited for every post and so far I have not had word of you.' Was there any news?

He was being unfair. On Monday, 4 August Miriam had written to him hurriedly from Berlin (too hurriedly for Henry's taste: 'I awoke this morning and my first thought was whether there was a letter from you. I rushed downstairs and you can imagine how glad I was . . . but I am sorry you did not have time to write a few more lines'). 'We have arrived safely,' she tells him, 'and, while waiting for a connection, I am writing this very small letter.' Phrase-making and declarations of love came less easily to Miriam, and in Berlin she falls back on the sort of sentence that people were supposed to write in letters from foreign places: 'We are enjoying ourselves ever so much, and would love to have you with us.' This was not entirely true. She had never been to sea before, and the storm that had woken Henry during his night in Harwich, combined with the proximity of the ship's engines to her cabin, persuaded her that she never wanted to go back. Finally they arrived in Germany, which was febrile with unemployment and swelling extremism. Hitler's National Socialists would come a sensational second in the Reichstag elections of the following month, taking five and a half million more votes than they had in the poll two years before. They and the communists were regularly clashing on the streets of Berlin, which in October would witness the first attacks on Jews and their businesses. It wasn't a place for the Clarets to linger. They went straight through Berlin's Lichtenberg station, and east towards Poland in a cigar-smoke-stained train carriage.

When they arrived in Kalisz on the following day, 5 August, Miriam wrote conscientiously and at greater length to her lover. 'Thank God, at last I have received a letter from you,' Henry jubilates when it arrives. 'It seems like ten years since I saw you or heard from you.' (But 'please write me another long letter as I want to know all about everything you do . . . My Darling Love, How I miss you! I am longing for you so . . . I love you with all my heart.') 'My Darling Henry,' Miriam's letter begins, and then she tells him what he wanted to hear. 'It is only Tuesday, and I am miles and miles away from you . . . Dear Henry it seems Ive been away for weeks. I am thinking of you all the time, Don't forget darling that I love you, and I am looking forward to seeing you again. I have such a lot to tell you, when I see you.'

Before she signs off ('Your Love, For Ever'), she gives him a brisk preview. 'We only stopped in Berlin a little while, as mother was anxious to go to Poland . . . How strange everything is, especially the way the people talk. I would like to understand them.' She particularly enjoys 'going through the streets in a droshky', a sort of low, small open carriage. Though native to Leah, the time-warped countryside and Polish language were as foreign to Miriam as would then have been the drawing rooms of Belgravia and the pages of *Tatler*, both of which, later in her life, she would frequent. She gawped at the forests of western Poland, through which the train raced on its way to Kalisz, and was shocked by the mean wooden house, with an adjoining, dilapidated stable, in which Leah had grown up. Her family probably lived near Zlota (Gold) Street, better known as the Street of the Jews, which stretched between the town's main square and the pastures of the Maikow Fields. With its narrow pavement that obliged pedestrians to walk in the road, and its rickety two-storey wooden dwellings, the street's official name had long seemed ironic. Water spluttered from a communal standpipe. The sanitary arrangements seemed grotesque, even in comparison to those of Boot Street: a man came intermittently in the dead of night, ladling the contents of the outhouse pit into the back of his wagon, gathering fertiliser for the peasants and terrifying the children who heard him draw up and scrape around outside. The hotel was much nicer, though Miriam couldn't quite get the hang of it, bemusing the staff by clearing away her breakfast things and scrubbing the communal bath.

After the Second World War, Jakob Erlich, one of Miriam's cousins in Kalisz, wrote nostalgically to her about their 1930 meeting. 'I remember, dear cousin,' he writes, 'when you were in Kalisz. And I was so lucky to speak with you.' But Miriam herself didn't recall much in the way of pleasant conversation. She soon realised that, rather than being anxious to get to Poland, her mother had simply been keen to have done with the whole palaver as quickly as possible. Leah's parents were both dead, and the rest of her family seemed less than pleased to see her back again. Miriam went swimming with her cousins, leaping off the jetties and pontoons behind the houses that backed onto the River Prosna, in the part of town known locally as the 'Polish Venice'. They went for a walk in the park, which, with its ruined medieval palace, waterfalls, statues, acacia-lined avenues and orangery, compared favourably to Victoria Park. But Jakob and the others spoke no English, and spent most of the time either working or praying in the town's main synagogue, with its ornate Byzantine dome. Miriam gathered that there had been trouble with the Polish nationalists, which had made business and life difficult. Just how difficult is clear from a desperate letter that Tauba, Leah's sister, sent to London in December of the same year. 'That money what you have send me, I shall have for bred for my [six] children,' Tauba says. 'You keep me by my life, if not I could die for hunger. I beg you don't forget about me.' She concludes with a prayer that 'God should give you health and richness, that you should be able to do goodness, to your poor sister'.

The other main topic of conversation in Kalisz was Miriam's brother Paul. Leah explained to her children that Tauba wanted Paul to marry her eldest daughter Perel, and take her back with him to London. Paul was unimpressed; what Perel thought of the plan wasn't clear. He was three years older than Miriam, so more than old enough to marry, but had brought with him sophisticated anglicised views about the virtues of waiting before he settled down. He also had a newfangled objection to arranged marriages. That he objected at all was considered a grave impertinence by his relatives. Leah, who could and ordinarily would have cajoled him into submission, seemed to take a vicarious delight in her son's irreverence. Tauba pleaded; Leah shrugged. There was a lot of sulking, broken up by interludes of Yiddish vituperation. During the sulking, they peeled potatoes. Tauba made soup from water, onions and fish heads.

In the end they stayed only three days, which was long enough to do what had to be done. Paul escaped unmarried and Perel remained in Kalisz (though Tauba didn't give up: 'Perel has written a letter to Paul, she asks him to answer her,' she advised her sister in December). Leah left on even worse terms with her family than when she had arrived, shaking hands rather than kissing them goodbye, and without any promises to meet again. She didn't turn round to wave from the droshky as it drove them back to the station, and she didn't cry. They went straight back through Berlin to Hamburg, and were at Liverpool Street before Henry's fourteen days had elapsed, their ears still buzzing with the thrum of the ship's engines.

When he hurried round to Boot Street, Henry found his eventual mother-in-law even more morose than usual. Perhaps she was aggrieved at having been hustled into this embassy to the old country. Or perhaps she was less than certain that her new life was, after all, preferable to the one she had once again left behind. She did, however, hand over a certificate that Paul had obtained in Kalisz: Leah's birth, the document confirmed, had been registered in Kalisz in 1886. She was the daughter of Yakov Piechota, and she was Jewish.

*

My grandfather still had to wait nearly another year and a half. Local custom dictated that a brother remain single until his eldest sister was married. In this case, that part didn't take too long. During the summer of 1930 Ida got engaged to Solly Nemenchinsky, a Lithuanian immigrant and another habitué of the markets, who had also had a spell delivering kosher wine in a horse-drawn cart. Henry walked Ida down the aisle to marry Solly on New Year's Eve, 1930. The party was at Stern's hotel and restaurant at the Aldgate ('Indoor and outdoor catering at moderate prices'). Afterwards Ida and Solly moved up to Stoke Newington; Sid and Mick, Henry's brothers, later moved in with them too. But the festivities delayed Henry's marriage, as well as permitting it. Given Leah's poverty, he and his mother would have to lay on his own wedding as well; but the bill for Ida's party ('Carnival: £4.0.0 . . . Cigars: £1.8.0') deepened the debt he had already taken on to subsidise the Polish mission. He couldn't safely finance any more blow-outs until he had paid some of the money back. So Henry didn't become a husband until 6 January 1932, by which time the Depression was on, long hair was back in fashion for women, and Miriam's ban on kissing had been revoked.

As *The Times* noted on 7 January 1932, on the previous day, the day of my grandparents' wedding, the wind was strong enough to keep ships in their Channel ports, and the rain heavy enough to flood several British towns. In the grey morning, all the male guests – family, neighbours from the Lane and from New Castle Street, and old friends of Henry's father from the fur trade – gathered for breakfast in the Freedmans' two rooms. Their wives, plus some of Miriam's fellow apprentices and a few of Leah's acquaintances from the tailoring sweatshops, cooed over Miriam in Boot Street. Then they all trooped stoically down to the Philpot Street Synagogue, where Fishel Freedman had worshipped after he came to London from Galicia. The synagogue in Philpot Street was one of the grander of the Jewish temples that were once as thick on the ground as pubs in Whitechapel and Spitalfields. Like those in Dunk Street, Cannon Street Road, Great Garden Street, Duke Street, Old Montague Street, Artillery Lane, Fashion Street and many others that were once the fulcrum and consolation of wearisome immigrant lives, the Philpot Street Synagogue is now long gone.

As Jewish tradition required, Henry visited Miriam in a little ante-room before the ceremony, lifting her veil to check that he had the correct bride. His youngest sister Babs carried Miriam's train as she walked to the wedding canopy on brother Paul's arm. A small choir sang psalms. 'Be thou my wife according to the law of Moses and of Israel,' Henry declared in Hebrew. In accordance with an ancient choreography, Miriam walked around him seven times in small, symbolic circles. The rabbi gave her the ornate marriage contract, written, as is customary, in Aramaic. Then Henry stamped on a glass to commemorate the destruction of the temple in Jerusalem. Everyone shouted '*mazel tov*', the all-purpose Jewish congratulation, and sweets and raisins rained down on the new Mr and Mrs Freedman. Immediately afterwards, the couple processed down to Boris Bennett's photographic studio on Whitechapel Road, Henry holding onto his shiny top hat and Miriam to her veil, while Babs trotted behind them, grimacing through the rain.

Boris Bennett had been born in Poland and made his way to London via Paris, where he acquired his passions for photography and glamour. His art had been entirely self-taught. He started out by inveigling the florists of the East End to leak him the details of impending weddings, then went knocking on the doors of the brides and grooms to offer his services. By 1932 his studio on Whitechapel Road was so popular that on busy days a policeman would have to marshal the flotilla of hired bridal cars jostling for position outside it. Spectators would congregate to watch the brides going inside, and dressmakers assembled to sketch their gowns. The giant, electrified replica of Boris's signature later placed above the shopfront became the East End's closest equivalent to the Hollywood sign. Having a nuptial photograph displayed in the window under it was a coveted accolade. Boris kept his prints for as long as it took his customers (years, in some cases) to find the money to pay for them. As a hobby, he made after-dinner speeches at wedding parties, which he described as his revenge. In his photograph of Henry and Miriam it is impossible to tell that Miriam's dress was made by Leah from satin and muslin of obscure origin, or that the groom's suit was on twenty-four-hour hire. It is

possible to tell that Henry had grown his moustache for the occasion. It still didn't suit him.

The celebrations were held at Bonn's Hotel in Great Prescot Street. It wasn't as smart a venue as Shoreditch Town Hall, or the La Bohème ballrooms in the Mile End Road. Still, with its waiters in dicky-bows and the mirrors hung on the walls to make the dining room look bigger, it wasn't so bad. The even more impoverished Jewish residents of the tenement blocks in Flower and Dean Street made their weddings at home, rounding up buskers from the streets and invading the other flats on their landings. At Bonn's, there was a buffet luncheon after the service, which included a 'full herring bar' and such old-time delicacies as stuffed neck, chopped liver and chicken soup. After recovering at home during the afternoon, the guests changed

and returned for dinner, most of the men improvising dress trousers by sticking a black satin stripe onto the seams of ordinary ones. The evening menu's cover depicts a couple who seem dressed for a ball in pre-Revolutionary Paris; inside, a daunting catalogue of dishes is printed in questionable French. On the facing page is a summary of the eclectic music with which a pianist and a pair of game violinists were to accompany the meal. Beginning with a wedding march and moving on to the 'Glory of Russia' and 'Waltzes from Vienna', the playlist progresses through an 'operatic selection' and 'king of jazz' to a 'selection of community songs', several of which Henry sang himself, stretching out his short arms like an opera star.

After the 'Pouding Glace' and the 'Gateau Francaise', the two long dining tables, and the flowers and candelabras that decorated them, were cleared away to make room for the dancing.

Over the next few hours, the guests stepped across Europe and across time. A one-step was followed by a dizzying routine in which the men and women whirled in concentric circles, performed exactly as it would have been in Kalisz. A foxtrot led into an acrobatic, all-male *kazatzkeh*: the dancers competed to crouch down the lowest and kick out their legs the furthest, while the children chaotically tried to emulate them. Between the waltzes, Miriam and Henry were seated on chairs and carried aloft by their friends, a handkerchief stretched between them as a symbol of their union. There were lots of speeches, which nobody listened to. The old men played cards and smoked. Exhausted children fell asleep on piles of coats. At the end, everybody tipped the caterer, a convention that spread the cost of the party so that it wouldn't be prohibitive for the bride's family, or in this case the groom's.

It would have been nice for Henry and Miriam, and for those looking back on the struggle of their early lives, if this one evening had ended pleasantly, and the groom had carried the bride across a threshold before whisking her off to an exotic destination the following morning. Unfortunately, at midnight, two hours before the party was due to end, Leah put on her coat and insisted that Miriam go home with her, as if the ceremony and a knees-up were all Henry had wanted, and all that he was going to get. After an embarrassing wrangle she got her way: Miriam left early, Henry put a brave face on it, and he and his wife spent their first night together apart. This climactic act of wilfulness would also never be forgiven. But it would not have been much of a night anyway, because two hours after he arrived home Henry got up as usual to go to work. After packing away his remaining socks, petticoats and camisoles at the end of the day, he marched to Boot Street, demanded his wife, and took Miriam back with him to New Castle Street, where he squeezed her into the two rooms with his mother and still-resident sister Babs.

Eventually, in June, he and Miriam managed a kind of honeymoon. Like white weddings (another recent invention) honeymoons were becoming an obligatory ritual for those who could afford one. The fashionable destination for Whitechapel newlyweds was Torquay, but that was beyond Henry's budget. So, from a jetty near Tower Bridge, he and Miriam caught a Southend steamer, which had an onboard pianist and several bars. From Southend they made their way to Canvey Island.

Canvey was one of the myriad seaside towns that erupted in the Edwardian era and flourished until 1939, only to be strangled by the allure of mass air travel after the war. In their heyday, they offered working people with a little money to burn some relief from the smokestacks of the city, if only (and often only) for a day. Of all these seaside utopias, Canvey was reputed to be the very cheapest. Its accommodation consisted of old buses, defunct railway carriages, and bungalows jerry-built on land sold to holiday-makers by entrepreneurial farmers. Henry knew a man who knew a man who had a hospitable beach hut.

In 1932 Canvey was poised between the bathing hut and the bikini: bare flesh was both fashionable and outrageous. Tanned skin, not long before a mark of agricultural poverty, was coming to signify health, and the wealth required to spend time sunbathing. Miriam had a modest one-piece, which showed off her shapely legs, and both she and Henry had tight rubber swimming caps. But they were unlucky with the weather, so they didn't have to worry too much about the nuanced manners of exposure. Instead, they meandered up and down the pier and on the seafront, playing in the shooting galleries and looking at the waxworks. They rode the ponies on the beach, and were serenaded by a wandering troupe of musicians in Pierrot costumes, carrying a folding piano. They strolled around the Winter Gardens, admiring the exotic birds and fish. They gorged themselves on ice-cream, and danced and danced and danced. After four days Henry ran out of cash, and cabled his brothers to ask them to send down the money for the fare home.

# TWO:

# 'Better times is coming'

*Poste restante Bureau 21*
*Rue de la Bastille Paris*

*My Dear Love.*

*I am very most surprice that I have no news from you. I would like to Know aoh are the two poor childrens and my poor Paul what does he say and you Dear aoh are you doing in this mesirable time.*

*My Poor Love in my side I have been very unlooky, but I have certain in a few days then I will be able to barrow some money and come in aide to you, As I hope that you still beleive in me; Love it as not been my fault you see I add to run away from London without a penny and I have loste every thing, it is really a new life that I have to beguine again. After a small time you will be happy and our two little loves.*

*I give you the poste office as adresse, because I have to go to friend to friend time to time that is the raison, believe Dear and not a storie as you thinks. I will never forgette you and the two little Dears –, Love kiss them for me and say to Paul that he will see me very soon – Kiss my little girl for the 5th month of age.*

*I finish sending you my Love and believe in me Dear*
*AC*

The same turn of European history, but two very different women, brought my grandparents into the world in London and ultimately together in its East End. Henry's mother Millie and Miriam's mother Leah were both born in Eastern Europe, then deposited in Britain by one of the world's great mass migrations. They were both left to raise their children alone while tightrope-walking on London's breadline. But while Leah embraced almost all of the exigencies of poverty, Millie clung zealously to her honour, so that their children's backgrounds were at once identical and opposite. Millie never knew quite how Leah had become what she was; but what she did know ensured that the common hardships that ought to have brought them together instead kept them at a suspicious distance.

My wayward great-grandmother Leah came into the world in Kalisz as Laja Piechota. Anyone born between the Baltic and the Black Sea in the eighteenth or nineteenth centuries could live their lives in several different countries without ever leaving home: the Prussians, Russians and Austrians fought over and across this territory for hundreds of years, dividing and redividing its lands and populations. Kalisz epitomised this vicissitudinous history. After Poland was partitioned by Prussia, Austria and Russia in 1772, the town belonged briefly to the Prussians. From 1815, and throughout Laja's childhood, it found itself on the western border of the Russian empire. As a girl, she learned hymns of loyalty to the almighty Tsar, emperor of all the Russias. Her birth certificate (now stored in a Polish state archive) is written in Russian, and gives its dates according to both the Gregorian calendar and the Julian one, then still used across the Tsar's lands:

The registration took place in Kalisz on the fifth (seventeenth) of November 1886 at 4 p.m. Yakov Piechota, a merchant, fifty-eight years of age, resident of Kalisz, in the presence of the witnesses, Markus Vartsky, a church clerk, fifty years of age and Izek Orlinsky, a church attendant, forty-three years of age, both residents of Kalisz, brought a girl, declaring that she was born in Kalisz on the seventh (nineteenth) of March 1883 from his lawful wife, Perel née Erlich, forty years old, that his daughter was named Laja Piechota, and that this act was not made in due time because of forgetfulness. This act was read and signed by those present, apart from the father due to his illiteracy.

Yakov also registered Laja's older sister Tauba and younger brother Abraham on the same day. Perhaps he really did forget to declare Laja for nearly four years after she was born, and Tauba for even longer; perhaps he had been trying to hide them from the authorities. But other documents suggest that Laja was born in 1886, the year that she was registered, and Yakov may have seen some advantage in exaggerating her age. Her true birth date is impossible to establish.

After the First World War, Poland and Kalisz regained their sovereignty, though the Germans had flattened much of the town and most of its Jewish quarter soon after hostilities commenced in 1914. When Laja lived in that quarter at the end of the nineteenth century, and when Leah returned to it in 1930 to find the town rebuilt, and the Tsarist street names changed to patriotic Polish ones, Jewish Kalisz and gentile Kalisz were entwined but discrete entities. Each community had its own hospital, schools, libraries and cemeteries. Their generally peaceable, if wary, co-existence periodically turned violent. On 26 June 1876 the absence of the Russian garrison on manoeuvres enabled a mob of peasants to murder thirteen Jews. Another massacre was narrowly avoided on 3 July 1878, when an enlightened Russian colonel of the Hussars ordered his mounted men to snatch imperilled Jewish children onto their saddles. Both

Jews and gentiles depended on the lace-making industry for which Kalisz was renowned, and which was sustained by a combination of clean water from the River Prosna and cambric imported from England. As in many towns across the Tsars' Pale of Settlement, the two communities were thrust together on market days (in Kalisz, Tuesdays and Fridays).

'Piechota' is Polish for foot-soldier, and the name was probably bestowed on the family when one of Laja's ancestors was conscripted into the Russian army. Her father Yakov was not an infantryman but a horse-trader – an impecunious and, like many latter-day second-hand car dealers, not entirely reputable conduit between Russian wholesalers and their German clients. By the time Laja was born he was already becoming too old for the work, and later she, Abraham or Tauba were often taken along to market to keep the horses tethered and fed. She watched the peasants lay out their butter, cheese and eggs, and smoke their long pipes filled with *machorka* (a pungent, home-grown tobacco), and the customers weigh up live geese and chickens, and the frequent rumpuses over shoddy goods and dodgy measures. She and her siblings played hide-and-seek in the portico of Kalisz's Italianate town hall, on the broad market square, affectionately remembered in the memorial book produced after the Second World War by the town's surviving Jews. The town hall's ancient clock was said never to have stopped until Kalisz was shelled in 1914. Yakov also did a useful trade with the Russian cavalry division that was based next to the river. Laja would watch the cavalrymen ride into town, a band trumpeting their arrival. She sometimes went along when Yakov travelled overnight to the markets of neighbouring towns with his little convoy of nags, sleeping in his wagon until the sun rose if he arrived before dawn. She was exhilarated when he fretted about bandits on their way home, white-knuckle rides that she later transformed into bedtime stories for her children and grandchildren.

At home, Laja sliced cabbage and cleaned cucumbers, which her mother pickled, buried in the ground to marinate and eventually sold. She learned how to sew, a skill that would one day keep her London family alive. Sometimes she sold glasses of cold water to the Russians on the oaken Zlota Street bridge. But she spent much of her time hanging around outside Daum's pastry shop in Babina Street, or exploring the country-side and swimming in the Prosna with her sister. In the winter, when it froze, they slid along the river on improvised skates. She didn't get much schooling, which her family considered unnecessary or even deleterious for a simple girl and her marriage prospects.

So Laja never learned to read or write (like her father, according to her birth certificate, though Yakov may have read Hebrew, if not Cyrillic). English was her fourth spoken language, after Polish, Yiddish and Russian, but she couldn't read the decorous appointment letter Henry sent to her in August 1929. Nor was she able to read the excuses and promises that, before the First World War, had been sent back to her from Paris by the father of her children. In Kalisz her illiteracy was not unusual, but in London it became painful and shaming, and Leah hid it by enlisting her children, neighbours and landladies to decipher incoming letters and draft her responses. She prevailed on obliging souls to write out the price tickets for her various retail ventures; the addition she managed on her own. When Tauba, also illiterate, needed her sister's help in December 1930, she found someone in Kalisz who could set down her plea in English, to ensure that it could be read out to Leah in London.

That the Piechotas were, by the time Tauba sent that letter, surviving on remittances from their faraway relative, suggests how pinched their situation had become. The growth of the railways and the arrival in Kalisz of the Borak brothers, big-time horse-traders from the nearby town of Stawiszyn, would have squeezed the family horse business. So too would anti-Semitic boycotts, bad harvests and the coming of the automobile. By the time Miriam visited, the droshky drivers were fighting each other for fares from the railway station into town. Polish nationalists were beating up Jewish salesmen, and sometimes any gentile customers who patronised them.

But long before these misfortunes, the hardship of life under the Tsars had been driving Russian and Polish Jews across the border into Germany, and onward to Hamburg, Bremen, Rotterdam and Antwerp, where thousands of Jewish emigrants from across Eastern Europe embarked in steamships for better lives elsewhere. The exodus began in earnest in 1881, when Tsar Alexander II was assassinated in St Petersburg; a young Jewish seamstress was tenuously implicated; and thugs exacted their revenge in an outbreak of pogroms across the empire. The trouble started in Yelizavetgrad, spread to Yalta and Kiev, and had terrorised 160 towns by the end of the year. After the Jews of Kishinev in Bessarabia, south-west Russia, were accused of the ritual slaying of a Christian child in 1903, their neighbours observed Easter by murdering dozens of Jews, injuring hundreds more and making thousands homeless; some impatient Romanians crossed the border to join in the killing. New laws redoubling restrictions on where Jews could live in Russia, and how they could make their living, were followed in 1904 by the Russo-Japanese war. (For Jews, conscription to fight in the war meant forced conversion, as well as likely death. Prospective recruits starved themselves for weeks before their medical examinations in efforts to fail them; if they were called up, their parents would tear their clothes, a Jewish gesture of mourning.) Then came the revolution of 1905, and the worst pogrom of all, in Odessa. Altogether, more than two million Jews fled Russia, Austria and Romania in the three decades after 1881.

Laja Piechota's journey from Kalisz to her life as Leah Claret in Boot Street, Hoxton, constituted only one droplet in this emigrant wave. She used the same smugglers' trails to cross the Polish border, and sailed in one of the same crudely adapted cattle boats as thousands of others. But the reasons for her departure distinguished her from the bulk of the human traffic flowing across the North Sea and the Atlantic. Laja didn't leave Kalisz (as she tried to pretend to Henry) because of the alluring pageantry of the British monarchy. Nor was she fleeing the pogroms. Laja seems to have left because she had disgraced herself and her family.

She had been engaged to marry a devout glazier named Fishel. An old Kalisz acquaintance of the Piechotas who also arrived, much later, in London hazily recalled that my great-grandmother and the glazier had actually wed. But, as the Polish archives make clear, the marriage was never solemnised. With a stubborn independence that baffled her family, Leah demurred, as her son was to do on their cold return to Kalisz in 1930. This was the original sin that was to shape her life. In that place and time, breaking an engagement was as scandalous as divorce, and as expensive, since the Piechotas were obliged to buy Laja's way out of the marriage contract, and compensate the jilted glazier for his public humiliation. Laja would never live it down, and neither would the Piechota household as long as she was in it. She was dispatched to London to marry a distant cousin instead, who had already fled Poland to avoid the Tsar's draft. Her family hoped that she would make it to England ahead of the news of her delinquency. She was packed off to the port of Bremen with a token trousseau, the address of her intended in Spitalfields and just enough money for her fare.

Leaving the Russian empire officially required a passport, and procuring one meant bribing a variety of capricious functionaries and enduring months of bureaucratic procrastination.

Like many emigrants, Laja avoided this costly ordeal by borrowing the border pass of a peasant from one of the frontier villages not far from Kalisz. Many such accomplices turned out to be in cahoots with the border patrols: the guards would be tipped off about an impending crossing, and would share with the informant whatever valuables the intercepted emigrants were carrying. Laja was lucky, crossing unmolested into Germany and making her way by train to Bremen. She and her clothes were disinfected by the medical officers of the shipping company. She eluded the white slavers known to prey on naïve Polish girls at docks and railway stations, occasionally subjecting them to sham wedding ceremonies before consigning them to unwholesome lives in Buenos Aires or Constantinople. She spent nearly three days in steerage, sharing a straw mattress and eating the pickled herrings that were her mother's sole gesture of maternal care. She passed muster with the British health inspector who boarded each arriving boat to check for smallpox and other scourges. Then, some time in 1902, she blinked into the light at St Katharine's Docks, stared from the stern at the Tower of London, and stepped onto London's dry land.

Everything she saw on her way – the German trains; German towns; the port at Bremen – seemed to her to be the acme of modernity, until the next revelation superseded it. London topped it all. She made her way through the press of confused and dishevelled passengers, milling around in their long leather boots and astrakhan caps and the tell-tale beards of new arrivals. Some were holding up pathetic little placards inscribed with the names of their home towns, which they hoped would attract a friendly face. She negotiated the crew of bogus porters, front men for over-priced doss-houses and vendors of seats on non-existent trains, who swarmed around each shipload of newcomers, sometimes beguiling them in their native Yiddish. She was momentarily transfixed by the ragged Chinese sailors bustling around the docks. Then a

kindly man from a Jewish relief society escorted her on the short walk north to the address in Spitalfields at which she expected to meet her putative fiancé. There Leah (as she thenceforth became) discovered that news travelled as slowly from England to Poland as her family had hoped it would in the other direction. As she later told it, her cousin and only contact in London had already married someone else.

Exactly how my great-grandmother, friendless, penniless and illiterate, lived in London when her marriage prospects evaporated is now obscure. She probably scratched a living in the tailoring sweatshops that then hummed ceaselessly across east London, as she did again when she had two children to feed, alone. Before long, though, the thing most likely to happen to a headstrong, rebellious, lonely girl happened. Around the beginning of 1904, she met a man.

Almost everything about this man and their liaison – where he came from; where and how they met; why, after ten years, they parted; even his real name – is opaque. Leah usually maintained that he was French, and the Gallic inflections in the clumsily passionate letters he sent to her when he was away in France and she left behind in London, bear her out, as does the way he records the dates and places of their composition. Leah sometimes said that she had met him in Paris on her way to England. But only a bizarrely circuitous path would have taken her to France en route from Kalisz to the ports of northern Germany. She told Henry that his real name was Abraham Singer, a *bona fide* Jewish moniker that French anti-Semitism had obliged him to change. It was for this reason, according to her, that he had adopted the pseudonym Auguste Claret. She was sure that somewhere she had Mr Singer's passport, if only she could lay her hands on it.

Leah's claims about his name and his religion are less convincing than that of his Frenchness. He does seem to spell what Leah said was only a pseudonym in two different ways, oscillating between 'Cleret' and 'Claret', which endorses the idea that it was merely a *nom de plume*. His letters and postcards are sometimes addressed to a Madame Singer. On the other hand, if his name really was Singer, why bother to disguise himself as 'Claret' (or, sometimes, as 'AC') in the safety of a personal letter? He makes none of the invocations of God's providence, nor expresses any of the gratitude for His beneficence, that might be expected of a real, if disguised, Jewish Abraham Singer at the time he was writing. He makes no mention of any religious festivals or responsibilities. On balance, it seems most likely that his name was and always had been Claret, which his sloppy writing sometimes seems to mangle into Cleret. Still more disreputably, it seems unlikely that he and Leah were formally married, either in Paris, as she sometimes averred, or anywhere else. Though he refers to her as his wife in correspondence with other people, Monsieur Claret never does so in his letters to Leah herself, and he never alludes to a wedding anniversary. Henry's pan-European trawl could turn up no record of a ceremony. (The English marriage registers promisingly offer a likely-looking hybrid, one August Theodore Singer, a hosiery merchant who was wed in a Catholic Church in Islington in December 1906 – but to an Alice Swertz, not a Leah Piechota. An Abraham Singer was married in the East London Synagogue in Mile End in February 1903 – but to Sarah Shiner, a paperhanger.) 'Singer' may just have been a name that Leah sometimes lived under to bamboozle her creditors. Perhaps it was borrowed from the sewing-machine brand that she had learned to master, and which provided her livelihood more reliably than any spouse.

How, and how unreliably, Claret made his living are among the few particulars of his life that are clear. He mentions his occupation in a letter to Leah's landlord of 27 March 1912, a letter Leah must either never have passed on or been given back, probably in anger. He assures the landlord that 'My situation is coming better and I will be able to pay regularly', before hastening to his real point: 'Sir I come to ask to be good enough to wait til the 6th of April . . . I Hope you will favour us with your kindness.' That promise of regular payment seems not even to have satisfied its author, who felt obliged to add a more definitive postscript: 'Certain on the 6th April you will receive the amount of Rent Due. I am in Paris as a traveller in the furniture line.' In this capacity he appears to have scuttled back and forth across the Channel to and from Boulogne, selling or failing to sell his curtains, pillows and other wares in Paris and beyond, and visiting Leah when he could.

No other concrete information about my great-grandmother's lover has come down to his London descendants; the shortage of names, dates and addresses in the fragmentary clues available makes it impossible to resurrect him from official records. Among the leftovers of Leah's life there is an unmarked, fuzzy photo of a middle-aged gentleman, sporting a moustache and a bowler hat and standing in front of some

railings, which may be a likeness of my puzzling ancestor. But this stolid-looking character somehow seems hard to reconcile with the only two properly documented aspects of Monsieur Claret: his fecklessness, and his feelings for Leah, which in his letters crowd out mundane facts.

My grandfather Henry never saw these letters. Leah herself burned many of them, in fury or despair. The ones that survive are written on yellowed paper that looks as if it was torn from a business ledger or a child's exercise book. They wasted away in the corner of an attic for half a century; tight folding and packing has broken some of them into pieces. Still, beneath their jaundiced appearance, and behind the writer's careless hand and erratic English, can be deciphered a passion that Leah would have been unlikely to find with the glazier in Kalisz, or her other intended in Spitalfields, and that she never found again.

At first, when his continental forays separated them, Claret sent Leah jaunty postcards with views of the Eiffel Tower, Parisian street scenes, the Musée du Luxembourg and forbidding Normandy beaches. When he writes to his infant son Paul, born in June 1907, he prefers cards depicting cherubic little boys, odd little paper totems of the real thing he had left behind in London. On Paul's birthday his father wishes him

'Happy many returns'. To Leah he sends hurried asseverations of love, sometimes in the form of cryptic abbreviations, presumably in a private amorous code: 'DL' perhaps stands for 'dear love', 'YL' for 'your love'. On New Year's Day, 1908, he writes from Paris to tell his 'Dear Love' that he 'would be more Happy if you was with me but believe that my hart is with you and our Lovely boy'. He is forever vowing to 'come to Angland' and clear her debts, from time to time sending along a placatory postal order, goods for her to sell, or material for her to make up into clothes.

The favours he wants in return are postal rather than carnal. He makes only one allusion to the physical sort, telling Leah that 'I hope to have you in my arms very soon.' But he is continually entreating her for news and, unaware of her illiteracy, complaining about her silences, as Henry would later complain of Miriam's. In a later letter, written one New Year's Eve, he makes a trade-off between cash and information explicit: 'Love I cannot understand of your silence. I have send you a large parcel of goods that certainly you have receiveid last Saturday, you have not answer to me no letter from you, please writ to me at once what is the matter, Love please let me know . . . I will send to our two little Dears a present During the week, but I must have news from you. Certainly you made mony with the goods that you received. Kiss my two poor Love for me and writ at one.' Most of the time, though, Claret sent promises of money rather than the thing itself, and Leah had at least as much cause for complaint as he did.

During the early stages of their affair, when he was still intermittently in London, impecunious as she was Leah enjoyed a life of fantastical gentility: a life in which tradesmen made deliveries on credit, the days punctuated by strolls in Regent's Park, if also by moments of high anxiety. For several years she lived in St John's Wood, north London – not then uniformly the wealthy district that it is today, but not so far from it either. Perhaps she found it easier to gull prospective landlords in swanky parts of town than to dupe the hard-nosed rent-collectors of the East End, who were used to the sort of chicanery in which Leah came to specialise. In Hoxton, as she would discover, landlords would send in the dreaded 'broker's man' to seize assets and instil fear at the hint of a rent default. Wearing her one good dress, and maybe with Claret in tow to make her appear solvent, she could turn up in St John's Wood and be installed in a smart little flat by the end of the day. In the end, of course, the landlords of St John's Wood would not favour her with their kindness indefinitely. When it became clear that a creditor really and finally meant business, Leah would pack up her belongings and her children, and do a moonlight flit. She tended not to flit very far, moving from Calworth Street to Titchfield Street; from Titchfield Street to Titchwell Terrace (where, on or around 8 June 1910, Miriam was born: it is impossible to know precisely); and from there to St John's Wood Terrace, in brazen proximity to her creditors.

It couldn't last, and it didn't. In the autumn after Miriam's birth, Claret vanished; the remittances dried up; and Leah was obliged to quit St John's Wood altogether. She moved out of town to Edgware in Middlesex, then a satellite village that the tentacles of the Tube had not yet drawn into London's grimy embrace. She boarded with a Mrs Page, in a room above the Ideal Laundry on Edgware High Street. Five months after my grandmother was born, Claret wrote to explain himself. He has been 'very unlooky'. It was not his fault: 'I add to run away from London without a penny and I have loste every thing, it is really a new life that I have to beguine again.' Nevertheless, 'After a small time you will be happy and our two little loves.' He didn't dare show his face on her side of the Channel (unpaid debts, presumably), but 'I will never forgette you and the two little Dears.' Leah had evidently become sceptical about his failure to supply a personal address, rather than that of the poste restante in the Rue de La Bastille; but it was, he explains, because he was living peripatetically between friends: 'that is the raison . . . and not a storie as you thinks'.

After her move to Edgware, Leah became less and less impressed by Claret's garbled reassurances and exhortations of courage. She was lonely and struggling to feed her children, but her lover frequently proffers nothing more substantial than the promise of another, more encouraging letter. By 17 February 1911 his postal orders had evidently become irregular enough and her anxiety high enough for her to threaten drastic action. From Paris, Claret pleads with her not to act rashly: 'I dont believe you to send away our little Loves. I know it is and had be a terrible time for you.' At the top of the letter he scrawled an urgent postscript: 'believe me, better times is coming.' On 17 March he vows that he will 'manage to send you for the rent up to Date and every week from next week . . . excuse it is so little . . . I am going to do my best to find a one or two firm ou will give some goods on sale or return . . . I think that the worse is pass and you will be happy again and our dear little Paul . . . Tell him I love him and I think him very much.' He asks her not to worry about her insistent landlord: 'certain if he is a good man he will wait a few Days,' he writes of Mrs Page, with his perennial optimism about the generosity of creditors.

'I which you and our two lettles Dear a better new year and a good helf,' Claret writes at the end of the year; but 1912 brought Leah nothing but more promises and increasingly frantic cross-Channel requests for news. In 1913 Claret was a little more fortunate in business, and in July confides that 'I have a appointment this week. It will be a big business again. So Love by patience only a 2 or 3 weeks and you will be Happy again, I cannot tell you no more for the time only that things are coming good.' By 4 November 1913 Leah has been assailed by an unspecified ailment: 'My poor Love I am so sorry to hear that you are not well. I hope that will be alwright . . . Dear I have to finish some work and I will come in two weeks and I will stay a little time, I will come direct to you and will see a doctor with you and we will see as I dont believe in operations . . . Have courage and everything will come to good. Kiss my two little Dears for me and say that I will come with some chocolates from Paris.' Leah's condition was serious enough for him to be harping on about the dangers of surgery on 14 December, when he regaled her with a selection of anecdotes about French acquaintances who had recovered from similar afflictions, without submitting to the knife: 'I will do all I can to come before the end of the month.'

Perhaps Claret did descend on the Ideal Laundry at the end of 1913, bearing chocolates for the children and money for a doctor's visit. But by the spring of the following year – and despite the grave tendency of European events, which seem not to have intruded on the cocooned struggles and stratagems of Leah and AC – the new plan was for her and the children to join him in Paris. On 4 July 1914 – a week after Archduke Franz Ferdinand was assassinated in Sarajevo – he responds with bewilderment to another ultimatum: 'My poor Love, what as happen, you say That you are going to go a way from Edgware . . . I Dont Know What to think.' He promises to send the cash to pay for her move to France: 'I will arrange every thing to make you comfortable here and you will see that I love you . . . Come herè Dear – you will be happy, and out of troubles.' A beguiling offer; but three days later, on 7 July, as the armies of the great powers were mobilising, he explains that the move has been postponed, for financial rather than political reasons. Until it happens, 'I will send you every week as much mony that I will be able to do . . . Love, have Courage I will do all my possible for you to come.'

'All my possible' cannot have been enough, because when he writes from Paris on 18 July 1914 – two weeks before Germany declared war on France, and the lamps went out all over Europe – nothing has changed. 'Love I hope you have no troubles,' he writes, 'if you have some creditors are warning you tell them to writ to me so I make arrangement with them.' He will soon 'come to England' but still needs 'a little time to arrange your coming' to France. By this stage, either Leah or her latest amanuensis must almost have lost patience with the rigmarole of long-distance love, because AC makes an especially anguished complaint about her brusqueness. 'I have received your two lines. What is the matter that you say you cannot writ', he asks: she had, it seems, finally tried to tell him about her illiteracy, but he hadn't understood. 'Please writ me longer giving news of what you are doing. As even Paul and our dear little girl, you dont say a word of them . . . Love Herewith 10/- and please writ a letter long giving me more news.' Then he signs off, as usual, and as Miriam was to sign off her letter to Henry from Kalisz, as 'Your Love for ever'.

If Leah had gone to Paris in 1914, my grandmother would never have met Henry, and her life would have been very and dangerously different. But Leah didn't, and Claret seems never again to have visited her in England. After the letter in which he upbraids her about her measly 'two lines', no further correspondence from him to her survives.

Why their relationship ended is as obscure as how it began. Leah herself seems never to have known exactly what became of him. For all the disorganised devotion of his letters, perhaps Claret decided that she was more trouble than she was worth. Perhaps he had a pan-European harem of dependent women, each strung along with occasional remittances and endlessly postponed migration plans. Perhaps, not long after he signed off as her 'Love for ever' in that last letter, his forever was shortened on the western front. Among the Frenchmen who had registered as temporary residents with their consulate in London before the war, there is indeed an Auguste Claret who was subsequently killed during it; but he was much too young to have been the same AC who fought epistolary battles with the landlords of St John's Wood. In the vast lists of First World War casualties kept by the French army, there appear eighty-eight Clarets (and fifty-two Clerets), as well as twelve Singers; but none of them seems quite to correspond with the few extant details of my elusive great-grandfather. Maybe he met a less heroic death as an unrecorded civilian victim of bombardment or disease. The fact that Leah hoarded some of his correspondence for more than fifty years suggests that their parting was involuntary on her side at least.

But it is also possible that, obstinate and temperamental as she was, my great-grandmother pocketed the ten shillings (no mean sum) that he managed to send in July 1914, and, realising that he would never manage to 'arrange your coming' as his letters promised, decided that she and the children would be better off without him. She may have cut herself off in haste, and then, because of the disruption of war and her difficulty with writing, been unable to repair the breach, leaving AC to carry on sending his amorous malapropisms and sentimental birthday cards into a void. Perhaps he spent the rest of his days disconsolately selling furniture and checking for mail at the poste restante in the Rue de la Bastille, his affair with Leah a romantic cameo in an otherwise parochial life.

This version of events is lent some credence by the surviving fragment of a letter sent by Claret to Leah's landlady above the Edgware laundry, which she in turn must have passed on to her lodger. 'Dear Mrs Page,' he writes, 'I must ask you to be good enough in case Mrs Claret is not with you to writ to me to let me know where is Mrs Claret. Please writ so I have a letter Friday morning . . . Oh my poor dear I must know a bout herè and my boy and little girl – Yours Faithfully A Cleret.'

She was not to be better off without him. Monsieur Claret had been a crucial if flimsy bulwark against outright destitution. When he vanished, or was banished, poverty enveloped Leah, my grandmother Miriam and her brother Paul. They were obliged to leave Mrs Page and the Ideal Laundry. They couldn't go back to the broad streets and smart iron railings of the St John's Wood terraces; so Leah and her children wound up in Hoxton. They fled briefly again to the suburbs during the First World War London air raids, which, though mild by the standards of the Blitz and now virtually forgotten, seemed incredible and apocalyptic at the time. Policemen rode around on bicycles, blowing their whistles to signal the approach of a German Zeppelin and, later on, of the first bomber planes, which infamously destroyed a school in Cable Street in June 1917. 'We ran away from the bombs,' as Miriam put it, many years later. Otherwise, they remained in Hoxton until Miriam met Henry in 1929.

To survive, Leah fell back on two of the classic expedients of impoverished women. One of them was the needle. When Miriam was too young for school, Leah locked her on her own in the dank basement, to keep her away from the drunks and the fights on the streets of Hoxton. (If my grandmother sneaked out or otherwise misbehaved, Leah would sometimes hit her, hard, striking her with her fist and the bronze ring on one of her fingers. Afterwards, she would bring Miriam tiny tokens – a flower or a ha'penny-worth of sweets – to make up for what she knew she shouldn't have done but, in her exasperation, couldn't help.) Then she made her way to the tailoring factories and workshops that by then had spread north into Hackney, churning out cheap, ready-made clothes for the country's growing population of white-collar workers. A partial list of Leah's jobs is contained in a letter Henry drafted for her when, later in her life, she experienced a little trouble with the tax man. She had, he wrote, worked 'at Simpsons, Stoke Newington in a supervisory capacity for two years. Previous to that she was 5 years at the Co-op. Society's Clothing Factory at Tabernacle Street and afterwards at Leman Street as needle-hand and supervisor. She was three years at Glassfields, Wentworth Street, in a similar position. Previous to that she was 4 years at Polikoffs at Well Street, Hackney and she has also spent a number of years at the Army & Navy Stores factory at Golden Lane.' She also sewed in converted attics, cellars, front rooms and back rooms, where the bosses would claim that their employees were all daughters and nieces (and therefore beyond protection by the law) when government inspectors came round to check on their working conditions. In some, the workers had to hold umbrellas over their sewing machines when rain came through the roof. Leah often sewed through the night when an order was due, sustained by sweet tea and the knowledge that she might not find another job for months.

But even in the busy times, a lone needlehand's income couldn't pay the rent and support two children, especially when food prices spiralled during the war. The sweatshops were only managing to hold out against the factories, which had begun to dominate the clothing trade, through cut-throat cycles of underbidding for contracts, by paying their labour next to nothing and by working it to the bone. So, when she could get it, Leah took in extra jobs to do after she had trudged home in the evenings. She sewed the buttonholes of greatcoats and the eyelets of soldiers' kitbags: they lay about her cramped home in inviting piles that Miriam sometimes slept on, lullabyed by the whirr of the Singer sewing machine. When the khaki work dried up, she sewed the ends of trousers late into the night.

Even so, Leah's ends never quite met, and her family oscillated into and out of a kind of deprivation that was then as commonplace as it now seems incredible. Miriam and Paul would be sent to scrounge offcuts and shavings for the fire from the back-room Boot Street chair-makers and the Curtain Road cabinet-makers, or to scour the markets for discarded boxes after the traders had packed up. In very old age, Miriam once burst into tears when the submerged memory of these scavenging missions suddenly caught up with her. Her family went cold in winter and hungry more often. Yet Leah's idiosyncratic morality wouldn't permit her children to pickpocket or steal from the market stalls, two popular pastimes of their Hoxton peers.

On the other hand, she would not countenance them going barefoot, as other Boot Street urchins did. In 1921, when the needlework was thin and Leah was already desperate, Miriam wore out her boots. So Leah took her daughter to Gardiner's, a department store at the junction of Whitechapel High Street and Commercial Road, whose clock tower was an East End landmark until the store burned down. Gardiner's specialised in the odd combination of surplus military kit and children's clothes. Miriam took off her battered old boots and tried on the new shoes that her mother had asked for. She was admiring their buckles when the assistant turned her back, Leah grabbed Miriam's hand, and they bolted, leaving the old boots behind in apologetic part exchange. They plunged across Whitechapel High Street, almost getting run over by one of the hay carts that still collected supplies for local livestock from the market on Aldgate High Street. They panted up Commercial Street and Curtain Road, a tank of a woman in a long, shapeless black dress pulling along a wisp of a child in a pair of new shoes that were pinching her ankles. When they made it to Boot Street Miriam began to laugh, but stopped when she saw her mother sitting on the floor and sobbing from the shame. My grandmother once cried too, decades later, when she remembered the theft, and her old boots left behind, and her mother's desperation.

Paul and Miriam worked as soon as they were able to. At fourteen, Paul was apprenticed to a printer's, but the trade didn't suit him and he struck out on his own as the 'Celanese Kid' of the East End markets. (Celanese is a type of artificial fibre, which Paul's customers made up into clothes.) He doubled as a palmist on Sundays and at holiday fairs: life lines were always long, and the future always rosy. Although there were plenty of Jewish tradesmen in the Hoxton markets there were very few Jews among the local residents, and the neighbourhood would later prove hospitable to Mosley's blackshirts. Paul spent his evenings learning to box at an athletics club on City Road.

Miriam's schooling, though better than her mother's, wasn't good enough to land a clerical job that would have meant a steady income and advantageous white-collar introductions. Her education was administered in huge classes of fifty or more, in which the teachers' main concern was to maintain order or administer corporal punishment when they failed. Then, in 1924, it ended. Leah went to a commissioner for oaths to swear that Miriam was fourteen, the age required for her to leave St John's School in Hoxton. In her oath, Leah claimed that she had no birth certificate to prove Miriam's age, because the girl's father had 'refused to permit the birth of my said daughter to be registered in England, as he was under the impression that by so doing my said daughter would be prevented from becoming a French subject upon our contemplated return to France'. The document carries two versions of her signature: one, it appears, inscribed by the commissioner for oaths; beneath it is a shaky imitation in Leah's own, uncertain, embarrassed hand.

My grandmother couldn't be a secretary but she managed the next best thing, which was to find her way into millinery, considered a more ladylike craft than needlework. Everyone said how lucky she was, but she didn't always feel lucky, especially not when glue from the master hatters working above the apprentices dripped through the floorboards and into her hair. She spent half her evenings pouring jugs of cold water over her head in the yard at the back of the Boot Street basement to get it out. She caught a finger in a clamp, splitting one of the nails of her left hand in two. It stayed split, leaving a blackened clue to her working-class past long after the skin of her hands had softened and lost its calluses. She also helped out on her brother's stall, as she would later help her husband. This retail experience was to prove surprisingly useful when my grandmother evolved into a socialite twenty years later, wowing ladies with surnames such as Astor and Parker-Bowles at high-end charity fêtes.

Even with a little extra money coming in from the children, Leah was obliged to pursue another classic survival strategy, which was to consort with and occasionally marry men. Her many and sometimes pseudonymous surnames make it difficult to ascertain precisely how many marriages she made. After Claret, lovers and husbands were necessary but expendable commodities: she treated matrimony with a disdain that would have mortified Yakov Piechota. For a little while she was, in practice if not in law, a Mrs Wyatt. Mr Wyatt was a grocer who lived at Number Three, Boot Street (shared with a wood-turner and a chair-maker). He would obligingly lower baskets of provisions to Leah's basement on a rope, and ended up descending into it himself. For a few years she appears as 'Lena Wyatt' in the electoral register of the old borough of Shoreditch. There may also have been a short-lived union with a pauper, whose borrowed nationality at some point helped her to avoid repatriation to Poland. Just before the Second World War she was to find yet another husband, a thin, elderly Russian by the name of Levine, who also did not much suit Henry's aspiring tastes. Happily for Leah's testy relations with her son-in-law (if not for poor Mr Levine himself), he too survived only a few years of marital bliss with her.

Still more happily, when Henry was courting Miriam and poking his nose into her background, Leah was between husbands. The enigma of Miriam's paternity tormented him; but the truth of her parentage and of Leah's sad, eventful life might have frightened him away altogether. Henry never knew why Leah left Kalisz, or the whole story of 'AC', or about the moonlight flits in St John's Wood. After her religious credentials finally checked out, he concluded that all the shenanigans over Leah's identity had been a perverse attempt by her to frustrate him, and to keep Miriam as her own devoted vassal. The truth was better and worse, less selfish and more scandalous. Given who Leah really was, where she had been and with whom, keeping *shtum* was exactly the right thing to have done.

*

My 'good' great-grandmother Millie Freedman was born Malka Kanfer in the village of Nadworna, in May 1886, which may or may not have been the year of Leah's birth too. Nadworna sits on a bank of the Bistriza river, not far from the Carpathian mountains and the Bukowina forests. It was and is still a beautiful, alpine environment, but a volatile one. When the ice in the Bistriza burst, and the snow in the mountains melted, some of Nadworna would be submerged. Of its 7,500 residents, around half were Jews; the remainder were ethnic Poles and Ukrainians, and there were occasional transient Hutsuls, pastoral tribesmen from the mountains. Many of them, including many of Millie's relatives, fled from the Russian army that swept through the region soon after the First World War began, leaving famine in its wake. The Russians, and especially the Cossacks, were brutal when advancing and worse in retreat. They deported some Jews to Siberia and slaughtered others. There were more pogroms when, after the war, Poland became independent. Nadworna passed through Polish, German and Soviet hands before coming to a political rest in present-day Ukraine.

In 1886 Nadworna lay in Galicia, a province of Habsburg Austria created after the Polish partition of 1772. The Habsburg empire was complacently regarded by many of its subjects as the peak of civilisation, even by many of its Jews, who since the constitution of 1867 had (unlike their Russian co-religionists) enjoyed most civil rights. During their Sabbath services they prayed for the health of the Emperor Franz Josef. When Malka evolved into Millie and lived in Whitechapel among Polish and Lithuanian Jews, she always spoke of her Austrian origins with pride. (For their part, the Poles and Litvaks considered the Galician Jews coarse and backward, and their Austrian airs preposterous.) But while Galicia was technically Austrian, much of it was temperamentally closer to the violent rancour of Kishinev and Odessa than to the salons of Vienna, and geographically too close to the pogroms of Russia for comfort. Natural resources were scarce; levels of malnutrition and illness were gruesome; poverty and prejudice were rife. Many gentile peasants found some consolation in anti-Semitism, which local priests helped to foment: the Jews were blamed for every social ill, from alcoholism to illiteracy, and the blood libel was a favourite homiletic theme. Many Jews emigrated. Many of those who stayed embraced extreme forms of Hassidic mysticism, and an ardent faith in the imminent coming of the Messiah.

These beliefs shaped Malka's childhood. Among the members of his particular Hassidic sect, her father Nuhim Kanfer was reputed to be a *lamad vavnik*: one of thirty-six righteous men who walk the earth in each generation, averting God's just wrath towards the errant world through their modesty, piety and good deeds. His advice and blessing were solicited by the sect's adherents across the region. His reputation was bolstered by his long red beard and ascetic lifestyle. His shoes, it is said, always shone like a mirror, but beneath his black-and-white striped *talis*, or prayer shawl, his kaftan was patched and threadbare. Nuhim had once trained to be a *shochet*, or ritual slaughterer, but had proved too soft-hearted for the work: according to a memoir written by one of Henry's Galician cousins, Nuhim had fainted when he first tried to wield his *shochet*'s knife. His income, such as it was, came from the bible lessons he gave local children, and the alms that their parents disguised as fees. Chaje Kanfer, Malka's mother, tried to supplement this pittance by selling colourful ribbons and belts to the Ukrainian farmers who came to the market in Nadworna's main square.

Chaje died young. Malka, her sisters Menie and Rifka and her brother Herschel were brought up by their father in his barely furnished, two-room wooden house, with a combination of tenderness and an iron religious orthodoxy. He would

wake his children at dawn, wash their hands and feet, pour them a cup of black tea and then supervise their prayers. Despite the municipal fines that truancy incurred, they were kept away from school to stop them being contaminated by Christianity. They studied the Talmud, and played in the ruined castle on the grassy bluff above the village. Unlike Leah, Malka learned to read and write. But she grew up knowing more about the world of the Old Testament than about the contemporary one beyond the Carpathians. The boundary of her universe was Stanislau, the nearest sizeable town, where Nuhim's brother-in-law Moses Kaswin lived. Moses had made what was considered a fortune in the fur trade – local rabbit skins first, then astrakhan from Russia. He had four horses, his own coach, two cows, and a house that was said to have running water. But he had lost twelve of his thirteen children to an epidemic; to keep his surviving daughter company, he took in Malka's sister Rifka when she was a teenager.

Everything Malka did learn about the modern world beyond her province was gleaned from letters sent home by

Nadwornans who had already emigrated. These were passed around by the village youngsters as surreptitiously as the anarchist and socialist Yiddish tracts that were then circulating across Europe. The letters were enough to convince her that her penurious life in Nadworna was too small for her.

Fishel Friedman was to be her chance for something bigger. He was born twelve years before Malka and, with his sister Basse, grew up in Solotwina, a few miles to Nadworna's north-west. Solotwina was around half Nadworna's size, with a similar ethnic composition. Fishel was the son of a rabbi, Moses Friedman, and his wife Eidel, and a scion of an august rabbinical family, like the Kanfers part of the religious aristocracy of Jewish Galicia. A fraying Yiddish document, written by one of Fishel's relatives, purports to trace his genealogy as far back as 'Hillel the Babylonian from the Kingdom of David' and 'Ezra the Scribe'. It lists the many esoteric publications and accomplishments of his forebears, which, in parts of nineteenth-century Galicia, counted for as much as titles and estates: 'Rabbi Isaac of Koritz of blessed memory, may he live in the world to

come . . . Rabbi Abraham of Stanislau . . . Rabbi Abraham of Mikalav of blessed memory . . . ' Some of these distinguished ancestors, the founders of famous rabbinical dynasties, are buried in the Jewish cemetery of Nadworna in prominent, ornate graves, now neglected and overgrown.

Early pictures of Fishel make him look worldly, even tough, rather than rabbinical. But photographs from this period often bore deceptively little resemblance to the everyday versions of their subjects. The photographer would apply pomade, and lend canes and cigars to the gentlemen and parasols to the ladies, ensuring that the images dispatched to far-flung relatives portrayed the sitters at their best, and often better. The photos of Fishel disguise his piety: as a young man he trained to follow his father's calling, and throughout his life he devotedly observed his religion's innumerable requirements and rituals. They also exaggerate his affluence: after quitting his rabbinical training, he tried to make a living as a dealer in honey and cigarette papers. But he failed to prosper in this profane career. In 1893 a Catholic convention in Cracow had proclaimed an economic boycott against the Jews, and new, covertly anti-Semitic hurdles were established for Jewish traders. In 1894 Galicia suffered an epidemic of cholera. Fishel ignored his family's warnings about the godlessness of the lands to the west of Germany, where, it was said, Jews declined to grow beards and prayed fewer than the requisite three times per day. He ignored the adverts placed in the local Yiddish press, in which well-to-do English Jews, concerned that the bedraggled hordes disembarking in London were jeopardising their own hard-won emancipation, advised Galicians to stay put. He left Solotwina and travelled to Hamburg on the cheap overnight trains, then spent two nights in a barracks run by a shipping company, and another two in the belly of a German liner. In June 1897 he arrived in the Pool of London.

Most of the Jews who poured out of Eastern Europe in the decades before the First World War, as Fishel and later Leah did, wanted to go to America, the new land of milk and honey. Many of them travelled via London only because price wars between the steamship companies sometimes made it cheaper to do so than to cross the Atlantic directly from the Continent. Most of those who played the system and came to Britain only stayed as long as it took them to make their way to Liverpool, and there re-embark for New York. But there were some who couldn't afford the transatlantic fare; others who had paid it, but were landed by swindling captains at London or Grimsby and told they had reached Ellis Island; and a few who could bear the foetid on-board conditions no longer. In time, friends and family came to join them. New York was Fishel's original goal too; but the unofficial exit charge levied by the guards at the Austrian–German border had left him with little more than the eighteen shillings that would get him to London. To begin with he slept on the floor of a side-street synagogue, until he found lodgings with a fellow Galician at Number Four, Hope Street. Its four rooms also housed his landlord Joseph Reicher (whom the 1901 census describes as a 'pouch dealer'), Mrs Reicher and their nine children: May, Fanny, Isaac, Solomon, Pinkhas, Florence, Anne, Leah and Minnie. Soon afterwards, Friedman evolved into the anglicised Freedman. Fishel never made it to America.

Hope Street was a narrow turning off Old Montague Street, Whitechapel, a parish that in 1897 was really two places at once. In patches it was still the district whose squalor was exposed by the Ripper murders of 1888 and documented in *The People of the Abyss*, Jack London's 1903 account of life among the city's casualties. London writes about a 'new and different race of people, short of stature, and of wretched or beer-sodden appearance', whom he met in the East End's gin palaces, workhouses and slums. Fishel Friedman/Freedman encountered these people when he passed the brothels at the junctions of Old Montague Street with Brick Lane and Great Garden Street, and the nearby pubs from which children fetched beer for their incapacitated fathers. He was just as wary of the Christian philanthropists who endeavoured both to warm worn-out bodies and to save lost and Hebrew souls.

But while pockets of the old East End lingered and malingered, much of his new neighbourhood was more recognisable to Fishel than to native Londoners. Like other immigrant communities that have since encamped around London's airports and railway stations – as if, having arrived, they resolved to go no further – the Jews mostly settled in Whitechapel and Spitalfields, just to the north of the docks, and close to the smaller, older community formed at the east of the City after the Jews' readmission to England in the seventeenth century. This was the same part of London that had previously sheltered silk-weaving Huguenots and starving Irishmen: history is packed into the area as tightly as the Jews once were, and as their Bangladeshi successors are today. By the time Fishel arrived, the new foreign colony had subsumed the streets as far west as the Aldgate Pump, the symbolic threshold of the City of London. It had pushed south through Cable Street towards the docks, and north to the Great Eastern Railway tracks. It had a hazy eastern boundary somewhere along Mile End Road. Such was the pull of kinship and clannishness among the Jewish immigrants, and such the demand for space in Whitechapel and Spitalfields, that some of London's most verminous accommodation came to command its most extortionate rents.

Fishel quickly ascertained that there was no call for more cigarette-paper or honey merchants in London. He took a job with Solomon Landes, a fur merchant at 84 Whitechapel High Street – on the corner of Angel Alley, whose notorious inhabitants fought running battles with the police and rent-collectors. A hundred years ago, fur was neither an object of moral disapproval nor a pricey luxury. Like hats and waist-coats, it was still worn by ordinary people, and importing, treating and making up furs was a staple industry on the shabby eastern fringe of the City and in what was then the eastern borough of Stepney. Fishel's boss imported skins from Leipzig and the Continent's other fur hubs – mainly seal, but also cheap rabbit that could be disguised as something grander, and the odd batch of squirrel, opossum, skunk, marmot or fox. In descending order of skill, these had to be graded, counted and packed. If they hadn't been 'dressed' in Germany, they would then be passed on to another workshop to have the flesh scraped out, and be softened (by hand and sometimes foot), cleaned, beaten with canes, brushed, combed and dyed. Then the skins would be sent to the manufacturer, where they would be cut, sewn and finally nailed into shape as coats or trimmings. Fishel probably started as a packer.

After a few back-breaking years, the money was good enough for him to move into a room of his own in Turner Street, which runs between Commercial Road and Whitechapel Road, only a short walk from Angel Alley. Fishel lived in Number Thirty-six, above a tailoring shop, and just around the corner from the synagogue in Philpot Street that he prayed at. His cosy routine was disrupted in early 1904, when a letter from Solotwina informed him that he was engaged. A *shadchan* (matchmaker) had identified the daughter of the holy man of Nadworna as a suitable bride for the Solotwina rabbi's expatriate son.

Fishel and Malka seem to have first met just before their wedding. But they were not absolute strangers, having exchanged photos and letters in the long hiatus between their engagement and the ceremony. Only one of these letters, sent by Fishel on 28 July 1904 and brought back to London by Malka, survives. Like his other correspondence, it is written in the sloping Hebrew script used for Yiddish. In its way, the letter is surprisingly flirtatious, as if writer and recipient are archly trying to modernise an arrangement foisted on them by tradition. But it also suggests the perils of epistolary relationships. It begins formally: 'Much beloved and highly esteemed Malka, my life, for a hundred and twenty years, Amen!' After protracted niceties, Fishel addresses a complaint his fiancée has made about an impropriety in his last letter. She has accused him of being a *shmoozer*, a word connoting untrustworthy oleaginousness, and Fishel protests his innocence: 'What I wrote to you in my first letter is the truth as God, praised be He, knows.' He assures her that his compliments were well meant, and 'must tell you that I was very upset by what you wrote. I only hope that you will understand the mistake for yourself and,' he concludes a little presumptuously, 'I forgive you.' He thanks God that he is busy, and tries to soothe Malka's anxieties about moving to England. Like many later immigrants, her biggest worry was language, and in 1904 there were no state-sponsored induction courses available to help her. 'Next week, God willing, I will send you a Yiddish–English dictionary,' Fishel writes. 'You should write every day in Yiddish, German and English.' Perhaps repeating his earlier impertinence, he ends with 'I kiss you from afar.'

It wasn't a good time for him to be leaving England to meet and marry his bride. In 1904 the Jewish residents of Whitechapel and Spitalfields were more unpopular in Britain than they had been since the anti-Semitic eruptions of 1888, the year of the Ripper murders. The Ripper terror had indicated how the Jews could and would be blamed for the ills of their adopted city. Jack himself seems to have attributed his handiwork to 'the Juewes' in graffiti found scrawled on a wall near the scene of his fifth evisceration, and sensibly removed by the police lest it ignite a pogrom. By the end of the nineteenth century the Jews were also accused of depriving the natives of work, and at the same time (an impressive trick) of being a burden on the rates. The demolition of slums and construction of railways, combined with the old legend of streets paved with gold that still drew in England's rural poor, had created dreadful overcrowding in east London well before the Jews arrived. Even so, they were impugned for doing to the city what in reality the city had done to them. They were described in much the same dehumanising vocabulary as are today's importunate foreigners: they were flotsam, vermin, scroungers, parasites. They were said to be fomenting revolution with their seditious continental ideologies; the fact that such plots almost never came to light was yet more evidence of how secretive and insidious they were. It was well known that the Jews could subsist on a cup of tea and a piece of herring a day, enabling them to work for less than upright Englishmen could live on. Speakers at raucous public meetings in Mile End and in Parliament argued that the Jews' sufferings were imaginary, and that their admission to the country made Britain an international laughing stock.

In 1904 a Royal Commission set up by the government acquitted the newcomers of all the sociological charges against them. Nevertheless – and despite Winston Churchill's plea for Britain not to shut out foreigners 'merely because they are poor' – in the following year an act restricting immigration was passed by Parliament. It was mild by the standards of the later and current immigration laws of which it was the harbinger. But in the political frenzy before it was passed, it seemed that Britain's drawbridge was about to be pulled up, and that many of those who had already crossed it might be thrown back over the fortress walls.

To ensure that he would be able to get back in after complying with his summons to Galicia, Fishel decided to become a British subject. In April 1904 he found the money and four character witnesses needed to apply. According to the police report submitted to the Home Office with his application, now stored in the National Archives at Kew, his witnesses were all 'respectable, responsible persons, householders and British born subjects'. The applicant himself, the Whitechapel police judged, 'appears to be a respectable man'. His naturalisation certificate records that on 28 April 1904, at a commissioner for oaths in Spital Square, Fishel Freedman, 'a subject of Austria-Hungary, having been born at Solotwina in Bohorodczny on the 2nd day of February 1874', swore to 'be faithful and bear true allegiance to His Majesty King Edward, His Heirs and Successors, according to law. So help me GOD.' On paper, the son of the Solotwina rabbi was now an Englishman.

By the summer of 1905 Fishel had saved and borrowed enough to go back to Galicia. He had travelled to London with a passport issued in the name of Franz Josef; he returned under a British one, issued to naturalised aliens by His Majesty's Secretary of State for Foreign Affairs, a florid document whose calligraphy and antiquated rhetoric seem more suited to the seventeenth century than to the beginning of the twentieth. He sailed back to Germany and took the continental railway to Stanislau, riding backwards through his own life and in European history.

Fishel found Galicia convulsed by the murmurs of revolution from across the Russian border. He rode in a cart along the straight but hilly road from Solotwina to Nadworna, a route now as then flanked by patchwork fields and horse-drawn ploughs, headscarfed women hoeing by hand, walnut trees, swollen rivers, distinctively teat-shaped Carpathian haystacks, goats, storks' nests and low-slung bungalows with outhouses behind and perkily decorated wells at the front. When he met my great-grandmother, Fishel thought her shorter and prettier than her photograph had suggested. They were married in July 1905 in one of Nadworna's twenty-three synagogues – the one that had a concealed entrance to protect it from *pogromchiks*, which was close to Nuhim Kanfer's wooden house and to the town's *mikveh*, or ritual bath. There was a little party afterwards, the mood perhaps dampened by an unspoken understanding that the newlyweds would probably never meet most of the guests again.

Malka had never seen the sea before, and she had never seen anything like the metropolis to which Fishel conveyed her, or like the Whitechapel Road. They took a room at Number 234, an address they shared with one Bertie Wood (described in postal directories as a 'publican's broker'). The building was on the corner of Sidney Street, where a few years later a band of renegade anarchists infamously holed up after a botched robbery; Churchill, then the Home Secretary, personally directed the resulting siege. Malka transliterated her name, which in Hebrew means 'queen', into a variety of English approximations. She experimented with Amelia and with Amelie, as on the certificate from her second wedding to Fishel, which took place at the Mile End registry office on 31 January 1906. This English repeat was necessary for her to share her husband's new nationality, though perhaps the six months they had spent together in married courtship made the ceremony more than just a businesslike formality. On the birth certificate that records Henry Emmanuel Freedman's arrival at 234 Whitechapel Road on 10 August 1906, she appears as Emalia. (Eight days later, as religious law requires, Zvi Menachem ben [son of] Ephraim Fishel, as my grandfather was named in Hebrew, was screamingly circumcised in the same room, a ceremony attended by Fishel's employer and a small company of fellow Galicians, and performed by an off-duty butcher.) In the end, Malka settled on Millie.

Three more children followed in swift succession: Soloman (known as Sid), Ida and Marcus (known as Mick). To support them, Fishel broke from Solomon Landes and Angel Alley and started up his own fur interest, importing skins with the help of Millie's Uncle Kaswin in Stanislau, and with an initial workforce of himself and his wife. Acquiring boss status in the Jewish East End was easy, but losing it was even easier: of the many who reached for it by converting bedrooms into workshops in which they laboured longer, harder and often for less money than the workers they employed, most sank back into the ranks of the proletariat. By the standards of these punctured

dreams, Fishel's skin trade did nicely. He took a workshop at 30b Commercial Road, above Joseph Liggins's coffee rooms and close to the Aldgate. He was better placed than Leah to answer the begging letters that arrived from Galicia, hedged about with the same assurances of heavenly rewards for his anticipated generosity. Before Henry's brother Mick was born in 1911, Fishel had moved his family to what was then St Peter's Road and is now Cephas Avenue, a little to the east of their old address, and just off the Mile End Road.

St Peter's Road was flanked to the north, east and south by neighbourhoods of 'chronic want' and ill repute, notorious (so contemporaneous police records attest) for their thieves and prostitutes and Sunday gambling. It was encircled by pubs that the Freedmans would rigorously avoid, especially on pay day. But the road itself, with its neat three-storey houses, was respectable and placid in comparison to the carnivalesque

Whitechapel Road. Henry and his siblings attended Essex Street School, a little way to the north and close to an asylum known locally as 'Barmy Park'. It had a playground on the roof, on which the boys played football and the girls played hopscotch. The school gave Henry a prize for good conduct, industry and attendance; he kept the certificate of his award for the rest of his life. The Jewish pupils were allowed to skip morning prayers and be given scripture lessons instead. In the Freedmans' case these were supplemented by thrice-weekly Hebrew classes at a synagogue in Great Garden Street, where the teacher would bash their ears or rap their knuckles if their minds wandered or their Hebrew pronunciation faltered. These mortifying sessions left Henry with a faith that waxed and waned, but a love of books and respect for learning that were constant. On *Rosh Hashanah*, the Jewish New Year, Fishel took the children to Wapping Docks to perform the traditional *tashlich* ceremony, beneath the gaze of amused stevedores: the casting of breadcrumbs into moving water – in this case, the murky waters of the Thames – to symbolise the renunciation of sin. For the harvest festival of *Sukkot*, Fishel marched to synagogue with his children and his *lulav* (a long, symbolic palm branch) propped against his shoulder, looking like a sort of agricultural fusilier.

Nuhim Kanfer, Millie's father and the *lamad vavnik* of Nadworna, died in 1913. Fishel had done well enough at the big fur sales in January and March for Millie to fulfil a promise and take her children back to Galicia, to meet what was left of her family. She went in July, with a caravan of four small children and all the presents necessary to create an impression of prosperity, but without her husband, who could not afford to leave his business. The journey must have been scarcely less daunting for her than her honeymoon migration to London eight years earlier. But, despite the bereavement, her return seems to have been much better humoured than Leah's to Kalisz. The

Freedmans and Millie's siblings went for a couple of days to Dorna, a spa town in the Carpathians. Then they went to Stanislau to immortalise their reunion in the Rembrandt Picture Studio. They emerged with a set of fairyland images posed against an alpine background, the artifice of the scene betrayed by the rumples in the rug beneath the sitters' feet. One image depicts two Kanfer women wearing traditional dress and leaning on a staff; another, the four Freedman children in front of a romantic chasm. What most impressed the six-year-old Henry about Galicia, so he would later tell his own children, was the religious discipline of his relatives, one of whom threw a knife at him across the dinner table after a minor and unconscious breach of decorum. He befriended a cousin several years older than himself, but they fell out after a one-sided and acrimonious wrestling match, broken up by Millie's brother Herschel, who was by then working for Uncle Kaswin the furrier. Her sister Rifka had married an innkeeper's son; Menie had been widowed. Fishel's sister Basse had been matched with a rabbi and moved to Romania. She

came up by train with her children to meet the Freedmans for tea, at a railway station near the border.

In 1915 Millie had a fifth child, a daughter, officially named Miriam but always known as Babs. Fishel was by then doing sufficiently well to be contemplating another move, this time to the calm and clean air of Stamford Hill, a neighbourhood known locally in Yiddish as the *hoich fensters* (literally, 'high windows'). Unfortunately, my great-grandfather's health was deteriorating as steadily as his finances were improving. In the summer of 1915 he did what he might have done in the circumstances had he still been in Galicia: he retired to a spa, though instead of taking the waters in the Carpathians he went up to Harrogate, in Yorkshire.

Fishel boarded at a bed-and-breakfast called The Hollies, and wrote to his wife every day on headed paper from the writing rooms of Harrogate's Royal Baths. She is always, still in Yiddish, 'much beloved Malka, my life' and he is always, at the end, 'your faithful husband'. These letters reveal how devout

84

Fishel and his family still were after (in his case) eighteen years in England. In contrast to those of Auguste Claret, Fishel's letters are studded with supplications to God and heaven. He asks several times after the *shabbos goy*, the term for a gentile who would visit Jewish homes on the Sabbath and, for a few pennies, light fires and perform other tasks prohibited by religious law, thus enabling the residents to adhere to its letter while remaining warm. Fishel asks Millie to make sure the children say their prayers every day, and to take Henry and Sid to synagogue, but to be careful on their way across Whitechapel. Such regular navigations of rough neighbourhoods from a tender age gave the boys an intuitive understanding of which situations were liable to turn nasty, when to cross the street and when to run. Like Claret, in none of his letters does Fishel mention the larger danger that had engulfed much of Europe, laying waste the homeland that his wife had revisited with her children two years earlier.

At the same time, the letters portray him as an embryonic version of the Englishman his son would become. He dates them according to the Gregorian calendar rather than the Hebrew one, which numbers the years from the creation of the

ROYAL BATHS
HARROGATE
· WRITING ROOMS ·

C. J. C. BROOME
AL MANAGER OF WELLS & BATHS
J. LEIST ASSISTANT MANAGER

Telephones CENTRAL 184 & 200.
Telegraphic Address "CURE" HARROGATE

July 28th 15

world, and which his Galician correspondents still used. He writes a great deal about the weather. And he is not so unwell that he neglects his trade. On 28 July he asks Millie to tell a colleague 'to write to me every day about the business. He should not give anything to anybody who hasn't paid, except for Mr Weiss.' On the back of one of his letters Millie has written a shopping list, using Hebrew lettering to spell out the English words for bread, butter, milk and grapes – a typographical metaphor for the family's dual identity.

This burst of correspondence also reveals how, despite its involuntary origins, my great-grandparents' marriage had evolved its own kind of tenderness. In one letter Fishel devises an elegant acrostic to express his affection: the first letters of each line spell (in Hebrew) 'Long live Malka!' He inquires compulsively after his children and never neglects to send them kisses. On 28 July he is anxious that Henry should write something to his lonely father; on 1 August he is delighted that his son has complied. He reminds his wife to remember Henry's impending birthday. Perhaps genuinely, perhaps to reassure her, he seems optimistic that drinking and bathing in the Yorkshire waters have cured his chest ailment. By 6 August he has gained two ounces, though the therapeutic repetitions seem to have been a little boring, and only enlivened during his ten-day sojourn by a trip to York. A request for Millie to send up a hundred cigars, from a tobacco merchant in Aldgate, suggests that Fishel's understanding of respiratory complaints may have been shaky.

Soon after he returned to London, his optimism was crushingly discredited. On a Saturday morning at the beginning of September, Fishel walked home from synagogue in the rain. Carrying an umbrella (or anything else) on the Sabbath was forbidden, and his weak lungs contracted pneumonia. On 13 September 1915, at the age of forty-one, he died in his bed in St Peter's Road; the death certificate records the cause as a combination of heart failure and asthma. Henry, Ida and Sid came home from school to find strangers in their house, and at first thought that their mother was throwing a party. When she explained what had happened, Henry worried that he had killed his father by talking roughly to him that morning. Everybody told him that he was now the man of the house, so germinating a determination and self-reliance that would one day power his family up into solvent comfort.

Immediately after Fishel's death, however, the Freedmans sank downwards towards 'the abyss'. On 14 September 1915 Fishel was buried in the Jewish cemetery at Edmonton. His widow followed the customs of the *shiva*, the intense seven days of ritual mourning that Judaism prescribes. She covered all the mirrors in the house (a renunciation of vanity), tore her clothes and sat at home on a low stool as visitors filed awkwardly past. After the *shiva*, she contemplated her situation. Her marriage had brought her a passage to England and five children, and in its way it had worked. Widowed, her prospects were grim. The First World War had made life uncomfortable for anyone with a German or Austrian background. Placards declaring allegiance to the Crown were affixed to foreign-owned shops and businesses across the East End, to deflect xenophobic vandals. Dachshunds were being assassinated. Millie was not threatened with internment, as her unnaturalised neighbours were, but it was a bad time to be heard speaking with an accent, to look different, and to be alone. Fishel died intestate, but after his business was wound down Millie seems to have inherited a fair sum of money. Guided by ruinous advice – 'all over by Christmas, and then they'll be worth a fortune' – she invested the cash in French government bonds, which almost instantly became worthless. If her husband's death made life difficult, this misstep made it desperate.

Millie might, like Leah, have found another breadwinner among the exiles of the East End. Photos from her early widowhood depict a still-attractive woman, with a slender waist and luxuriantly thick hair, and an expression of serene bafflement at where her life had taken her. But Millie wouldn't consider it. Unlike Leah, she knew no trade and hadn't been raised to ply one. Local welfare officers advised her to give some of her children away to an orphanage. She was summoned by a Home Office immigration panel, at which government officials tried to persuade her that, notwithstanding the agonies of war on the Continent, she would be happier back in Galicia. My nine-year-old grandfather, who accompanied her, was old enough to sense the menace, and would always remember the way his mother quailed and shook in the face of gentile authority, and how she grasped his hand and ran away when the interview was over, and what could happen to you and how people could speak to you if you were poor and an outsider.

By the end of 1916 they were subsisting on handouts of food and coal. The following spring, Millie turned to one of the few

openings available to the unqualified. A small charitable loan enabled her to buy some stock, and some fellow Galicians helped her to stake out a pitch in Wentworth Street. So this holy man's daughter, thirty years old and with five children to provide for, found herself selling underwear in one of the craziest commercial thoroughfares in the biggest city in the world. She rubbed shoulders with escapologists, tooth-cleaners, weight-guessers, fortune-tellers, crockery-jugglers, strongmen, a growing army of mendicant war veterans and the three kings of Spitalfields: the Corn Cure King; the Eel King; and Harry the Banana King. Among the mêlée of howling costermongers and ancient bearded hawkers who wailed their patter like a liturgy, she tried to turn a penny from London's most practised hagglers.

In 1902 Jack London hailed a horse-drawn cab and flustered its driver by asking to be taken to 'the East End'. The driver's uncertainty, the American writer thought, was yet more evidence of the ignorance and indifference of well-fed Londoners to the life and premature deaths of the city's poor. But the cabby's confusion is telling in another way. It reflects the East End's existence more as a vague, mythic region of poverty, resilience and lawlessness than as an identifiable place – a sort of cramped, urban version of the American West. After they left, the Jewish immigrants created their own myth of the East End. It came in retrospect to be regarded as a prelapsarian region of innocence, camaraderie and opportunity, where everything was familiar but at the same time anything was possible.

Like many myths, this one was not without foundation. All the same, few former residents truly wanted to return to their lives in Spitalfields and Whitechapel, any more than they and their parents really wanted to go back to Cracow, Vilna or Łódź, however much they cooked the old recipes and sang the old songs. Many forsook the East End well before the Luftwaffe drove out most of those who hadn't, decamping as soon as they could afford it to the calm of Hackney, Dalston, Stoke Newington, Clapton and the *hoich fensters*, the gentility of Cricklewood and the greenery of London's north-western suburbs. Life in Whitechapel and Spitalfields may have been colourful and intimate, but it was also suffocating and hard.

In 1917 Millie Freedman moved her brood into the two rooms at Number Seventeen, New Castle Street, an address that bombs and city planners later conspired to erase altogether from the modern map of London. A few doors away, at Number Twenty-seven, was the Three Crowns pub, frequented mainly and noisily by patrons of the infamous doss-houses in nearby Thrawl Street and Flower and Dean Street. But most of the other residents were immigrants: the exotic names on the inter-war electoral rolls for New Castle Street include Michaelowskys, Huvskovitches and a squad of Streletskys.

Among the many problems that arose when six Freedmans were squeezed into a pair of rooms and beds, two were especially pressing. The first was the problem of privacy, for which there was no solution. The second was the problem of hygiene, for which the solution was perpetual scrubbing, washing, delousing, whitening, blackening and boiling. Until they were too big, Millie bathed the children in a zinc tub, which also saw service as a cot. After that she packed them off with tuppence each to the Goulston Street baths, though sometimes the boys, and especially Sid, wet their hair under the public pump at Aldgate and spent the tuppence intended for the baths on sweets. Millie herself bathed in one of the *mikvehs* overseen by the local synagogues. Clothes were boiled in a copper basin. The children took turns to whiten the front step, blacken the fireplace fender, scrub the outside toilet and clean the candlesticks, which Millie had brought with her from Galicia. She pawned them every Monday at the back of Hohn's the jewellers on Whitechapel Road – where she and the other indigent Jewish matrons would pretend not to recognise each other in the queue – and redeemed them every Friday. However humble the menu, the candlesticks and a pristine white tablecloth always adorned the table for that evening's Sabbath meal.

There was no money to buy food in large quantities, and no way to keep it cold if there had been. Every evening, Millie bought knock-down leftovers from her fellow traders, and little bunches of 'soup greens' for a penny. The children fetched milk every other day from a dairy in Black Lion Yard (a court off Whitechapel Road, since supplanted by an office block). Smelling incongruously of wet straw and manure, the dairy kept company with a cluster of jewellers – Shlosberg, Segalov, Brilliantstone and others – which Henry would also utilise when the time came. The dairy was run by two Welsh brothers, one of whom was known as 'old 'alf and 'alf' for his habit of watering down his merchandise. As a boy, Henry would creep in when the Welshmen weren't looking to pat the cows. At home, the milk was kept submerged in a bucket of cold water until it soured. At lunchtime, the children convened around Millie's stall in Wentworth Street, where they would receive a piece of herring and a greasy pinch on the cheek from Mrs Marks from the deli, and a bagel from the man who lived in New Castle Street and had a cake stall outside Number Forty-four. On very special occasions Millie haggled for a chicken from the poultry stalls in Leyden Street or Cobb Street, saving the nutritious fat to smear on hunks of bread. She made honeycake and cheesecake on birthdays and festivals, and, when she could get the ingredients, a *cholant* for lunch on Saturdays.

*Cholant* is a kind of all-in stew – it was best not to inquire too closely – that would be taken to a baker in the Lane on Friday for him to heat up on Saturday morning, when cooking was prohibited: like the *shabbos goy*, a time-honoured religious dodge. Henry would queue up, with the other hungry couriers, after the morning service at the synagogue the boys then went to in Old Castle Street, to retrieve the *cholant* and rush it home before it cooled. (It was in Old Castle Street that, in 1919, Henry recited a portion of the Hebrew law at his extremely humble *barmitzvah*, celebrated with a family lunch rather than today's weekend of festivities.) He and Sid supplemented their diet by pinching the cat food that a grizzly old man with a barrow delivered to their neighbours in brown paper bags. After swiping the bags from the cat-owners' doorsteps, the two boys roasted the fatty nuggets of meat over surreptitious alleyway fires. They stopped when they found out that they were eating horse, just like the ones that brought the coal and drew the buses, or like the giant drays that distributed the beer from Truman's brewery in Brick Lane, Charrington's on Mile End Road and the Albion brewery on Whitechapel Road. Had Millie found out about these equine feasts she would have been dismayed, both because of the implied criticism of her maternal care, and because her sons were eating a forbidden animal. But she never caught them.

Aside from the thrum of sewing machines, and, on Sundays, the din from the Baptist church on Commercial Street, the soundtrack of New Castle Street was the racket of children. Now and then the Freedman boys patronised one of the local youth clubs designed to make modern English gentlemen out of medieval Russian immigrants, at which they learned to play cricket and dance. But they mostly lived in the streets. When they were young they would watch for the arrival of an old man who came to New Castle Street with a little horse-drawn roundabout; he could be paid for rides in scrap metal and old clothes as well as cash. There was an itinerant barrel organist who played requests for a penny: when he came by, the drunks and floosies would stream out of the Three Crowns pub and dance with the children. Henry found a busted violin in the Lane, which he and the others took turns to screech on, accompanied (after Henry brought him back from Club Row) by Teddy. They procured a wind-up gramophone that Millie

considered faintly immoral. On the more jovial of the religious festivals – *Purim* around Easter time and *Chanukah* at Christmas time – the boys and girls improvised fancy dress by swapping clothes, the schools were closed and the synagogues packed. On the eve of *Pesach*, in her husband's absence Millie prowled the two paltry rooms bearing a candle and a feather as Fishel had always done, symbolically hunting for *chametz*, the leavened foods forbidden during the eight days of Passover.

When they were bigger, Henry, Sid and Mick salvaged fish heads from among the cats that congregated in Goulston Street when the fish market closed, for use in territorial struggles with other neighbourhoods or battles against the boys from the Catholic school. They played in street football games, for which the itinerant glaziers were grateful, but which killjoy policemen broke up. They hung out with the tramps in 'Itchy Park', the colloquial name for the dishevelled gardens of Hawksmoor's Christ Church, Spitalfields. They also took turns as runners for their mother in Wentworth Street, sprinting up to Mary Lipshik's stall to fulfil an order if Millie didn't have the right goods, while she kept the customers talking. They sneaked in to the first FA Cup Final at Wembley Stadium in 1923, famous for the grainy film images of a policeman on a white horse, struggling to keep back the crowds swollen by ticketless gatecrashers.

After they moved to New Castle Street, the Freedmans were educated at the Jews' Free School in Bell Lane, reputed to be the largest school in Europe, which disseminated free boots and clothes as well as learning. They were taught to speak English with better grammar than their parents and without so much gesticulating. It was in Bell Lane that Henry acquired his lifelong reverence for royalty, and for a textbook version of Britishness that meant decorum, Magna Carta, the mother of all parliaments and the empire on which the sun never set. On Empire Day in Bell Lane, Jewish mothers from Latvia and Romania sent their British daughters to school with red, white and blue ribbons tied in their hair, and the children assembled in the courtyard to sing 'Rule Britannia' and 'Land of Hope and Glory'. There was an annual pageant in which each of the King's dominions was embodied by a pupil. Henry's youngest sister Babs once represented England: swathed in white muslin and carrying a foil-wrapped silver trident, she earned a compliment on her appearance from Lord Rothschild, the school's patron, which she never forgot.

Millie's exile and her loneliness and her toil were to her a sort of collateral: she was determined that her children should redeem it by becoming more than she was. She abetted their education by insisting they speak English in New Castle Street, even when that meant she couldn't understand them. She herself never grew out of the trouble with prepositions widespread among her peers ('How is it by you?'; 'you smell from herring'), or their characteristic inversions ('a suit he wore'). But her children's English had to be the King's version. If she heard them talking in Yiddish, into which they sometimes slipped amphibiously at home and in the markets, she would chastise them out of it. On no account would they be 'Peruvians', the inexplicable term for newcomers who retained their foreign ways and accents long after they had arrived in London.

Had she not been so poor, my grandfather might have requited Millie's grander hopes while she was still alive. He was a talented pupil, and at twelve, along with one other boy in his class, he won a junior county scholarship, which was supposed to mean five years of free schooling at the Davenant Foundation on Whitechapel Road, an opportunity then afforded to only a tiny minority of working-class children, and one that might even have conveyed him to university. 'Hearty congratulations on their success,' says the school magazine, now stored in the London Metropolitan Archive in Clerkenwell. (The same magazine also published a running tally of the school's war dead, proudly informing readers that 'these boys, sons of aliens for the most part, were not one jot behind the general youth of the country in the readiness to risk life and limb when the call came'.)

But even though staying on would have been free, Henry knew he couldn't afford it. In the pinched post-war economy, trade on the stall was thin, and his mother needed an extra income. (When she had to, Millie took in lodgers to keep the family going, pale young men who slept on the floor next to the gas range, in the same downstairs room as Henry, Sid and Mick. They spent their days looking for work at the unofficial labour exchange on the pavement outside Black Lion Yard, moving on, as Fishel had done, when they found it.) According to the Jews' Free School's attendance records, Henry left for good in June 1920, ostensibly because he was sick. Aged thirteen, he entered the full-time labour force, his education being thereafter confined to the stash of encyclopaedias under his bed and the odd visit to the Whitechapel library. He never told his mother about the scholarship.

Most Jews' Free School graduates were initiated into the mysteries of boot-making, cabinet-making or tailoring by their fathers; the less fortunate wound up in blind-alley jobs as under-pressers or *shleppers*, which they often lost on the day they qualified for adult rates. Fatherless, Henry might easily have succumbed to one of the three sirens of hard-up Whitechapel youths: politics, crime and gambling. Various exotic ideologies, expounded in smoky side-street clubs, competed for the allegiance of disaffected Jewish youngsters. There had been a famous battle in Brick Lane one *Yom Kippur* (Day of Atonement), when the local Jewish anarchists riled the devout by eating ham sandwiches at the synagogue gate, and inviting the local rabbis to their party. By the end of the First World War, during which both the Russian secret police and British Special Branch kept the East End under close observation, communism had ousted anarchism as the radical creed of choice. It gained more ground through the wage struggles and rent battles of the twenties and thirties, and when the communists organised the resistance to the London blackshirts. Its recruits included Henry's brother Mick.

The dual axes of the Whitechapel criminal scene had once been two fearsome gangs, the Odessians and the Bessarabian Tigers. Later on the dominant bosses were Darkie the Coon and Alf the *Gunef* (crook), two local toughs who, like most gangsters, were said to look after their own and give money to charity. There were pickpockets of Henry's age who were reputed to swipe watches from wrists at the Aldgate end of the Lane, then sell them back to their owners at the Bishopsgate end. Some of them graduated to become razor-wielding hoodlums who ran protection rackets and racetrack scams. Then there were the illegal gambling dens, such as the one overseen by Oscar the Great in Philpot Street, a couple of doors along from Fishel's synagogue. The Derby was popular enough in the East End for the railway company to print the timetable for summer trains to

Epsom in Yiddish; less mobile gamblers handed over their wages to bookies' runners, who slipped illegally into the sweatshops to take bets during tea breaks. A favourite in the boxing ring was Ted 'Kid' Lewis, born Gershen Mendeloff, also known as 'The Aldgate Sphinx'; all the *yiddishe* fighters were heavily backed when they fought at the Wonderland hall in Whitechapel Road. (The Wonderland's ring was sometimes occupied by visiting Jewish cantors rather than pugilists: when an especially renowned performer came to town for a concert from Russia or Romania, bemused English police officers had to be drafted in to regulate the pious crowds straining for admission.)

But Henry went straight, and straight into the markets, to which he had effectively been apprenticed since he started helping out in the Lane when he was ten.

Petticoat Lane acquired its name when the old-clothes men who once stalked the City were thrown out and migrated to what had once been known, because of the livestock farms it bordered, as Hog Lane. Petticoat Lane is a name old enough to have been mentioned by Ben Jonson in *The Devil is an Ass* in 1616, and has survived the official changes designed to make the area seem more respectable. For hundreds of years it has magnetised immigrant paupers with the promise of a ready living, just as the medieval monasteries that once stood nearby had earlier attracted indigenous ones with their alms. Like Hatton Garden and its diamonds and the meat of Smithfields, the Lane and its old clothes are an ancient landmark of London's economic geography.

But the living it offered was a precarious one. George Orwell, driven by the same indignant curiosity as Jack London to linger incognito among the East End's down-and-outs, calculated that a costermonger was twice as likely to lose his mind as a soldier, and five times as likely as a farmer. Orwell attributed this vulnerability to the strain of knowing that a few days of poor takings could mean ruin.

Avoiding insolvency and insanity required two talents, as Henry swiftly discovered. One of these was the art of selling: landing customers with a repertoire of bluff, braggadocio, astonishment, special prices and once-in-a-lifetime offers. Equally important was the art of buying: the right stock, at the right price and in the right quantities from the wholesalers on the edge of the City, to whose depots Henry always walked to save the fare money. In 1920, when he left school, survival in the Lane also required brute force. Every morning, a policeman would blow a whistle, and a war of all against all would ensue as the stallholders catapulted themselves onto the coveted pitches. Scallywags with nothing to sell would occupy and then auction the best spots. Before Christmas and at other busy times the traders would camp out all night to stake their claims. Until her son relieved them, Millie's more robust neighbours helped her to overcome these daily ordeals. When Henry took over, if he didn't secure a place he would have to push their barrow through the streets all day, delivering his *spiel* on the hoof and stopping only to close sales, lest the police finger him for illegal trading.

So it was a relief when, in 1927, Stepney Borough Council began to issue licences governing who could sell what, where and when. The minutes of the council licensing committee record that, alongside the pitch Millie Freedman had secured in Wentworth Street, there traded Sam Cohen, who sold linoleum and mattings, and Myer Palkowski (herrings, and carp that he would execute by walloping their heads on the side of the barrel). Nearby were the grocery shop belonging to Lazarus Skylinsky, Sarah Landspeigel's china emporium, the Perlmuttas' stall and the Marks deli. The market operated from eight till eight, Monday to Friday (setting and packing up added an hour to either end of the working day), but the busiest day was Sunday. Then, Petticoat Lane market colonised the offshoots of Goulston Street, Cobb Street, Strype Street,

New Goulston Street, Leyden Street, Bell Lane and Old Castle Street, transforming them all into a sprawling maelstrom of touting and haggling over new and old clothes.

The privilege to trade on Sundays that the Jewish stallholders in the Lane enjoyed had to be defended against the resolute efforts of Christian sabbatarians to have it withdrawn. As a compromise, business in Wentworth Street was prohibited on the Jewish Sabbath instead of the Christian one. But Henry came to consider any kind of Sabbath an unaffordable luxury, and when he was old enough, in spite of his mother's protests, he ran a stall selling shirts, drapery and underwear in the separate market on Whitechapel Road, where Saturday trading was permitted from nine until nine. Henry's pitch was outside Number 237, near the Royal London Hospital, and just over the road from the room at Number 234 in which he had been born, surrounded by bigger ambitions and greenhorn optimism. His neighbours on Whitechapel Road were Sam Ackerman (handbags) and Max Spitzer (glassware, chinaware, toys, gramophones, and ice creams in summer).

He worked in every weather, on every day of every week, except for Christmas and *Yom Kippur*. When he wasn't manning the family's two pitches, he perambulated with Teddy and his barrow from Hackney to the docks. When the council had made his mother's livelihood a little more secure, he looked further afield for the main chance. In the early thirties, when Henry was urgently raising the money he needed to marry Miriam, he and his brother Sid sometimes hired a primitive van. Then they sallied forth, like knights to tourneys, to the country fairs that, half-entertainment and half-serious business, were still part of the calendars of provincial English towns.

In London, Henry, Sid and the rest of the family earned their crusts through a more or less honest trade. On the road, they were less scrupulous. They sold whatever came into their hands, and perpetrated assorted, audacious hoodwinks. 'The chocolate run-out' was a speciality. The 'run-out' involved auctioning boxes of chocolates, in a way that somehow persuaded the gullible to buy back the money they had parted with as a down payment, but at a mark-up. The customers would later discover that the boxes contained fewer than the advertised number of layers, and that the chocolates ('Vinadoora cream liquors') were more ornamental than edible. The Freedman brothers sold reject stockings with holes in them ('holes as big as your fist', Henry later told his children, awed by his own youthful *chutzpah*). The price kept falling, because the last pair of stockings had to be sold before the first one was unwrapped. They sold volatile hair-colouring and unscientific medicine: dressed in matching frock coats and wielding a forceps, the traditional garb of the 'crocus' or quack doctor, and assuming suitably outlandish pseudonyms, they promoted their remedies by finding out the names of all the local doctors and systematically slandering them:

'Dr Brown? I know another one of his patients. Or should I say knew. Very moving ceremony it was.'
   'Dr Jones? He was a vet until the animals complained. Now this tonic, on the other hand: complete restoration of your health, or your money back.'

Via one of Sid's Whitechapel connections, they had a sideline as stooges in a boxing scam. A fairground champion would take on all-comers, and one of the diminutive Freedmans would raise his hand, take off his shirt and step into the ring, to the derision but delight of the bloodthirsty crowd. Then the champ would suffer an improbable thrashing, the bookies would make a killing, and Henry and Sid would make a swift exit. They hustled, Henry always said, from Land's End to John o'Groats, long journeys into unfamiliar territory with uncertain returns. They arrived late at the Goose Fair in Nottingham and found that all the pitches had been taken; so they hired a stretch of tramline for the afternoon, scuttling out of the way whenever a tram interrupted business. They were once so flat broke, on their way to the Town Moor fair in Newcastle, that they had to pawn the overcoats their mother had made for them to pay the penny-a-wheel toll on the Tyne Bridge. They sold socks outside the dockyard gates on Tyneside, where Henry encountered men with no shoes on their feet who were even worse off than he was. They learned how to spend money when they had it and survive when they didn't. They became good sprinters and agile getaway drivers. Their family had degenerated from revered rabbis to small-time swindlers, from *lamad vavnik* to the chocolate run-out, in a generation. So much for the new world.

When he got home after a few nights in the van, my grandfather's younger siblings would take off his shoes and put him to bed. If, after paying his share of the rent and his creditors, he had a shilling left over at the end of the week, he considered himself a rich man. Such was Henry Freedman's estate when he married Miriam Claret, a milliner's apprentice, in 1932.

# THREE:
# 'I am in a whirl'

77 Jerningham Road

SE 14

Sunday 9 pm
10/9/39

Miriam Dear,
I Love you so much, I cannot even tell you. My Life is only
Life if I have you with me. As I sit here and think of you
alone, I am in a whirl. I do not know what to do for the
best. Everything is empty without you. I can feel that you
are thinking the same, at this moment. I know you Love
me as much as I Love you, and that is the greatest consolation, at this moment.

Our children are wonderful both in looks and character, and the full credit goes to you, my Dear, for all their
goodness and health. Please write to me every day, and I
will do the same, too. Please look after yourself, and do
not worry. All will come right again. Do not think yet
about the moving. Try as much as possible to have a rest,
and treat it like a holiday. All in London is quiet, and it
does not seem possible that something is wrong. I am on
duty tonight and I shall be thinking of you all the time.

I could keep on writing to you all night but you must
already know what I want to say, and how much you

*mean to me. Give my children my Love and take as much*
*as you want for yourself.*
   *I am Your Ever Loving Husband*


Replying to the plea for cash that Henry was obliged to dispatch from his honeymoon in Canvey Island in 1932, Mick Freedman wrote to his brother exultantly: 'Dear Henry, Thank God I have good news for you. Babs and Morris [Feltz] are getting engaged', which would shortly mean a little more breathing space in New Castle Street for the newlyweds. Peace had broken out – or so Mick wanted Henry to believe, at least for a few days – between Leah and Millie. 'Thank God they at last understand each other,' Mick adds, 'their lives are so parallel that there is a mutual bond.' And: 'More good news. Sid has found himself at last. We had a good talk last night. He's decided to give up his "pals" and he wants to go out with Miss Goldsweig. Mum and Mr Goldsweig spoke this morning and they are both happy' – though their children may have been less pleased with the durability of the chaperone system. 'We received your rather late telegram and are glad that everything is ok. I'll do my very best to send on money tomorrow . . . '

After she married my grandfather, in January 1932, my grandmother threw in the millinery, which had in any case been hurt by the beret fad inspired by Marlene Dietrich. Instead, she stood on the Wentworth Street stall with Millie during the week, and at the Saturday pitch on the Whitechapel Road; Henry continued his rounds of east London's other markets, and made seasonal forays beyond the capital. (Sid was now only an occasional accomplice: he served a short apprenticeship as a furrier, then worked sporadically as an acrobat in a circus.) Miriam found the Lane hard going. There were more thieves than in the Hoxton markets, and more policemen who had to be persuaded with tactful disbursements that the road was not, after all, being obstructed. As the Depression ground on, the Lane became swollen with unemployed men trying their luck with army surplus, a couple of old gramophone records, or whatever bric-à-brac they could lay their hands on. Legions of sandwich-board men cluttered the roads and pavements. Almost everyone in the Lane was a 'busker', reeling in passers-by with wit and flattery, whereas Miriam had always been more of a 'grafter', hoping that a pretty arrangement of goods and an all-weather smile would do the trick. She spent almost every day under the supervision of her mother-in-law, a fixture in the Lane where Miriam was a novice. Then she spent every evening under Millie's roof, distressing her with her fuzzy appreciation of Jewish ritual – though things improved when Miriam learned by heart the short Hebrew prayer with which Jewish women welcome the Sabbath on a Friday evening, and when she figured out the right moments to chime in with strategic 'Amens', as Henry recited grace after meals. Miriam taught Millie to make the Polish beetroot borscht she had learned from her mother; Millie inducted Miriam into the mysteries of Austrian apple pie, an art she then refined to perfection over the following sixty years.

Miriam was still grafting in the Lane in the winter of 1932, selling longjohns by the blue glow of the naphtha lamps that some of the stallholders still used for illumination when the nights drew in, when she found out that she was pregnant. On the morning that she told Henry, he went round to the synagogue in Old Castle Street and banged on the door until Rabbi Gutnick let him in. As he was later to tell his children, Henry asked God, in English and then in Yiddish, to show him a way out of the markets before he became a father. Help me to get out, he prayed, so my child will not have to watch me packing up in a hurry when the market inspectors pay a visit. Or see me come home, exhausted, after three days sleeping in the van. Let me not live hand-to-mouth for the rest of my days. Let me not be ashamed.

Soon afterwards Henry took the bus to Stoke Newington and told his brother-in-law Solly that the two of them, plus Sid when they could lay their hands on him, were forming a garment-making partnership. Just as most lives are bent by happenstance and coincidence, by overlooked details that turn out to be crucial, the weather on a particular afternoon, chance meetings and missed trains, so it was with my grandfather's trade. It was determined partly by his market contacts, partly by the size of the kitchen table in New Castle Street, on which he and his partners ran up their first samples. It was too small for them to make anything bigger than underwear.

Next morning, Henry put on his suit and watch chain and the bowler hat that he had worn to ask for Miriam's hand, and marched down to the National Provincial Bank in Liverpool Street, where he asked to see the manager. They took a look at Henry and told him the manager was busy. He sat there in his hat for two hours, ignoring the cashiers' smirks. Finally, without inviting him to sit down, and as he stood holding his bowler with both hands in the middle of the back office, the manager told Henry that no, he wouldn't lend him the £50 he wanted to borrow to start his business, 'for your own good'. My grandfather would thank him one day, the bank manager said. He stopped talking, and Henry realised that he was supposed to leave.

So he and Solly went round to see Solly's brother-in-law Alf Green. Alf was older than the Freedman brothers, and had already established himself, in a modest way, making up dresses in the Commercial Road. He had also won an undisclosed sum of money on the Irish sweepstakes, some of which he was happy to loan to still-stretched relatives. Alf asked Henry to wait outside; then he told Solly that he would indeed let them have some cash, but only if they traded under Solly's name (by now anglicised from Nemenchinsky to Newman). My grandfather, Alf considered, had too colourful a reputation in the markets to have his own name above the door. Solly agreed; Henry decided it was for the best, since it might anyway be tricky if, while he still ran the stalls, his suppliers discovered that he was making his own merchandise as well as selling theirs. 'S. Newman Ltd' it was, and would remain. Next Henry went to see a man he knew from the Jews' Free School who worked at Courtaulds, the chemicals and fabrics behemoth founded in the nineteenth century by descendants of Huguenot refugees. The man agreed to slip them the tail-end of a roll of rayon locknit fabric at the side entrance of the Courtaulds warehouse in St Martin-Le-Grand, so long as they came round first thing next morning before the foreman arrived. Then Henry went up to sign on for evening classes at a cutting school in Clapton, where he met Daisy Ritherford from Bethnal Green. After that, they were in business.

My grandfather's recruitment record was patchy, to say the least. He was dangerously susceptible to a hangdog look and a hard-luck story, and to the notion that anybody could be anything, if only they were given a break. But Daisy Ritherford, Henry's first ever employee, was a godsend. A skilled cutter, she marked out and divided up the Courtaulds fabric into pieces on the New Castle Street table. Henry and his brothers then delivered the pieces to half a dozen outdoor tailors in White's Row, Green Dragon Yard and Fournier Street, and sometimes, when she absolutely couldn't do without the work – and when charity overcame Henry's resentments – to Leah Claret too. Accuracy in measurement and precision in cutting could determine whether a small manufacturer stayed afloat or went under. Daisy was so accurate and precise that the tailors were left with virtually no 'cabbage' after they had made up the order. ('Cabbage' was the ancient term for the scraps left over after a subcontracted tailor stitched the items ordered by the manufacturer, using the fabric he provided. For centuries – until superior mechanisation and all-under-one-roof factories put a stop to it – cabbage was an unofficial perquisite of the trade, which the tailor could convert into his own patch-work garments to bring in some extra money.)

Daisy was also a knockout blonde – people said she was the dead spit of Betty Grable – who could be deployed against wholesalers when they were wavering over orders. Later on she earned some cash on the side by modelling, especially of her hands and feet, which were even more beautiful than the rest of her. In the early thirties she was mixed up with a shaggy tough known as Curly, and before turning on the charm she would sometimes have to powder away the bruises she had earned by smiling at another feller in a pub or speaking out of turn. Daisy was both a perfect lady and an utter cockney. She starting wielding her cutting knives and shears in New Castle Street in 1933, and she stayed with my grandfather for the rest of her working life. She ended up as his company's lace buyer, and Henry gave her an honorary seat on the board.

They were a useful team. Daisy was the cutter and *shmoozer*. Solly was a self-taught sewing-machine engineer, who could work miracles with string, wire and glue, transforming dis-carded junk into a means of production, at least temporarily. Henry was a natural deal-maker, making unkeepable promis-es that Solly and Daisy somehow kept. Known variously as 'Jolly Sid' and 'Dapper Sid' in the Lane and across the other markets, Sid had a wide and varied network of acquaintances, and heard about it early when somebody needed to shift some fabric in a hurry, or when a local manufacturer went *mehulah* (bust) and was ready to part with his stock for a song. In a reversal of the hierarchy of fortunes in better-off families, Mick, as the youngest son, had privileges that his older siblings did not. When he too passed the scholarship exam, he was able to stay on in education. In 1931 he went on to the London School of Economics, helping on his mother's stall by day and studying at night. It was at the LSE that Mick caught communism; but his political views didn't prevent him from joining the new family firm when he graduated in 1934.

As he confided to his children in his old age, if he could have chosen my grandfather would have been a doctor. He always admired medical men for what seemed to him to be their inordinate learning and the honour of their calling. During the thirties Henry added leather-bound volumes of Rabelais, Carlyle's *History of the French Revolution*, Rousseau's *Confessions*, complete sets of Balzac and Disraeli and an illustrated *Rubaiyat of Omar Khayyam* to his library. But however many books he piled up under his bed, they never filled the gap that he felt had been left when he gave up school for the markets. Still, while he was denied the opportunities for learning and the concomitant chances and choices that his grandchildren were to enjoy, Henry found and nurtured something else. Henry had a craft, a little part in keeping the world turning that he made his own, and that, perhaps in spite of himself, he came to love. He loved it not so much for what he made, but for the expertise and perseverance that went into the making of it. When he ran his hand down a seam or checked a colour in the light, what he saw was not a Princess slip or a pair of French knickers, but a challenge overcome.

After he left the Jews' Free School, the closest Henry ever came to anything resembling academic prestige was when, in the late fifties, he was asked to deliver a series of lectures on the lingerie business, to a class of aspiring industrialists at a vocational school in Shoreditch, reprising them, by popular demand, at several similar institutions in the Midlands. In the carbon-paper pads he used to make his notes, Henry worked and reworked the lectures until they sounded right. He talked about every aspect of his trade: fabrics, design, cutting, sizing, colours, and stitching; machines and gizmos, pressing, packing, packaging and advertising. In his opening lecture – after

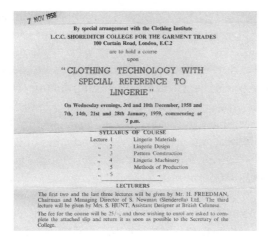

an overture in which he traced the etymology of the word 'pants' back to Pantaleone, an early Christian saint, and speculated on the underwear arrangements in the Garden of Eden – Henry described the great revolution in the philosophy of underwear that took place just before he had entered the business. Until the First World War, he explained, 'these garments were worn mainly for decency or warmth . . . any exposure of the female form was [considered] either unhealthy or indecent'.

Two related developments changed everything. One of them was the mass production of rayon, a class of artificial fibres that was generally half the price of the silks, satin and lawn that had hitherto been used to manufacture the undergarments of well-to-do ladies. Rayons were cheap enough even to replace the rough longcloth that was until then used to make functional shifts for the poor (in the winter, the poor wore cambric wool). With the advent of rayon, as Henry put it in his opening talk, 'the most beautiful creations can be made at prices that every working girl can pay'.

Second, the styles were as new as the fabrics. Like the wider sexual upheaval that it echoed, the transformation of ladies' underwear was partly a consequence of the war itself, and the exigencies of wearing mannish uniforms, as many women had been obliged to do between 1914 and 1918. Partly the change was necessitated by the clinging fashions of the twenties, through which pre-war undergarments showed up improperly; partly it was brought on by the energetic new dances, which needed a bit of give. These and other factors demanded that underwear slim down, and in a hurry. A respectable woman would still baulk at leaving home unless she were properly encased in some combination of vest, brassiere, girdle, camiknickers (a camisole and knicker hybrid) and slip. But 'spencers' and other such vindictive contraptions, and the bulkier petticoats, were finished, just as they themselves had usurped the baggy pantaloons endured by women until the early nineteenth century. French knickers were shrinking into panties, tracked as they ascended the thigh by stockings and suspenders.

In the twenties the fashionable quest for perfect androgyny, which drove women to pluck their eyebrows and chop off their hair, also obliged them to flatten their curves wherever possible. Whale-boned corsets were eschewed, but only in favour of less painful elastic and roll-on replacements. So for all the shrinkages, it wasn't until just as Henry and his partners were starting out that 'frillies' or 'pretties', as they were then called, began to be designed to showcase the anatomy, rather than suppressing it. Largely through the offices of Mae West, Greta Garbo and the other Hollywood glamour queens, breasts were back. Lurid peaches, champagnes, corals and cyclamens muscled out virginal whites and funereal blacks. My grandfather would take this tide at the flood. By the late forties he was manufacturing pyjamas, housecoats, petticoats, nightdresses, slips, camisoles and negligées, as well as every imaginable species of knicker, out of satin, crêpe de Chine and drip-dry winceyette. These fabrics would themselves soon be ousted by brushed nylon. As Henry recounted in his Shoreditch lectures, just as rayon had eclipsed its competitors after the First World War, so nylon, specimens of which had been bartered into many British homes by GIs during the Second, conquered the underwear world after it.

All that was to come, and soon. But in 1933, at the very beginning, Henry, Sid, Solly and Daisy catered exclusively to the big-knicker market: to the cadre of die-hard matrons who were still clinging to their corsets and their chemises. The knicker of choice for these ladies – ladies such as Millie Freedman, who would have been unlikely to countenance her sons and their alarmingly pretty gentile acquaintance cutting out anything racier on her kitchen table – was the DK, or directoire knicker, popularly known as the 'passion-killer'. DKs looked like breeches, with elastic around the knees that had first been introduced to safeguard the wearer's dignity as hemlines rose to the knee in the twenties, but which was appreciated by the modest even when full-length skirts came back. Refined versions of these garments, made of satin and crêpe de Chine, were decorated with flounces, bows and embroidery imported from St Gallen in Switzerland and from Austria and Germany. The ones devised in New Castle Street were made of plain locknit, and coloured with a batch of khaki dye left over from the First World War (a superfluity that also explained the glut of flesh-coloured stockings). When there was no locknit to be had, the Freedmans reverted to cheap gingham and itchy wool. There were three sizes and no refunds.

Why, despite his truncated education and his fatherless adolescence, his claustrophobic household and his obvious candidacy for criminality, did my grandfather prosper? Partly because he was in the right place at the right time. More working girls than ever before were able to afford the 'beautiful creations' that, after their early 'passion-killer' phase, the Freedmans churned out, cheap and ready to wear. George Orwell described this generation in *The Road to Wigan Pier*:

'for two pounds ten on the hire-purchase,' Orwell wrote of the prospectless but style-conscious young man of the thirties, 'he can buy himself a suit, which, for a little while and at a little distance, looks as though it had been tailored in Savile Row. The girl can look like a fashion plate at an even lower price.' Chain stores were opening all over the country to give these young people what they wanted. The biggest market, as well as the biggest pool of cheap and ready labour, was in London. The Lane helped Henry too: it was a tough school of customer relations, and after it there would never be a task too menial for his attention, and he would always be up at dawn.

Then, although his family was intermittently as poor as anyone in London outside the workhouses, it was wealthy after its own fashion. Aside from a thimbleful of Sabbath wine, Millie Freedman never drank. She brought her children up to believe that here, in London, if only they emulated her industry and had a little more luck than God had given her, they could make it in ways that would never have been possible for their ancestors. Potential thwarted for centuries by discrimination and insularity, or able to express itself only rabbinically, could in my grandfather's life finally explode, like compressed oil deposits from a suddenly tapped well. His father's death contributed: I *have* to do it, Henry had learned when he was nine; nobody will do it for me, nor for my mother and siblings. Perhaps he didn't see the obstacles ranged against his progress quite so clearly as did the indigenous poor. Or perhaps he saw them more clearly, and saw that they were less Himalayan than they appeared to those unable to see around the edges of their English lives.

All of these influences contributed to my grandfather's powerful sense of 'why not?' Why shouldn't I have as much as other people? Why shouldn't I be a boss or a big-shot if I want to be? Who says I shouldn't? And, Henry asked himself, why shouldn't I wear a gentleman's Homburg hat – the sort popularised by Anthony Eden, then the most fashionable politician in the land – when I go to see potential customers, even if my old acquaintances wolf-whistle and hoot at me when I pass them with my samples? And, of course, why shouldn't he plant enthusiastic buyers – 'jees', in market parlance – to get the ball rolling when Millie and Miriam laid out his earliest DKs for sale on the stalls in the Lane and on Whitechapel Road? When the first genuine customer picked a pair up and tested the elastic, Millie and Miriam held their breath, and in their thrill managed only a perfunctory haggle.

'You are one of us – and we are glad,' the other Freedmans wrote to Miriam on her birthday in June 1933. 'There will soon be another one – we are still gladder. This is our fervent wish: that you will be as good a mother as you have been good a wife.' Written in Mick's hand, and in his forthright intellectual style, the letter was also signed by 'Mother', Ida, Solly, Sid, Babs and Morris. Eighteen-year-old Babs and Morris Feltz had married earlier that year (another photo from Boris, and another unaffordable Philpot Street shindig). So there was more space in New Castle Street, at least after Daisy packed up in the evenings. On 19 July 1933 Miriam had laid out the fish for frying and was whitening the front step. She had to: it was her turn, and to leave a step unwhitened meant that the world was beating you. She was on her knees when her contractions started. Millie took her up to a nursing home in Hackney.

Henry arrived from Chatsworth Road market to find that he had a son, my uncle, whom he and Miriam named Philip in English, and Fishel, after Henry's father, in Hebrew.

My grandparents weren't quite clear of the markets, but they were on their way. After a couple of years of relying on outside tailors, Henry and his partners decided to take all the work in-house. Solly reconditioned six foot-treadle Singers; Sid found a spare fourteen-pound gas-heated iron and an electric cutting knife for Daisy; and Henry hired half a dozen machinists, a finisher to sew on buttons and insert the elastic straps by hand, and a presser-cum-*shlepper*. Then he rented a floor in a warehouse, soon strewn with cotton and locknit and as hot and noisy as an engine room. The minutes of Stepney's market-trading committee record that, early in 1935, because he was no longer using it, Henry was stripped of his licence for the stall outside 237 Whitechapel Road (by then flanked by Sam Beresofsky, a perfume-seller, and on the other side by a seller of belts and braces). His first mini-factory was on the corner of Strype Street and the Lane, the old axis around which his life still revolved.

Until August 1936 Henry never had a holiday more exotic than his honeymoon. In 1934 he, Miriam, their baby and Millie Freedman went back to Canvey Island. In the following year, they went again with Leah, who sat in deckchairs on the beach in long sombre skirts and unjovial shawls, looking like an actor on the wrong set or an ambassador from another age among the sun-worshippers and day-trippers. Then, in 1936, Henry was invited to celebrate the fortieth wedding anniversary of a distant relative in Scheveningen, Holland.

He sailed from the same Harwich quay whence Miriam had left for Germany and Poland in 1930. Because he knew how much she'd like it, before he got on the ferry to come home on the evening of Sunday, 30 August Henry wrote to his wife,

even though he would see her again before she saw his letter. 'The boat was waiting and with our British passports we got through very quickly,' Henry reports with pride. 'There was no trouble at all about sleeping berths as we had already booked them at Liverpool Street. Naturally as it was 2nd class the noise and vibration of the engine was rather loud, but after talking to you a while I was soon fast asleep until 4.30, when I got up and after washing and dressing went on deck to see the boat dock. It was still rather dark and I noticed many lighthouses shining on both sides of the river.' Then he tells her all about the grand welcome he had received, and the food at the party, and how he had been prevailed upon to recite the Hebrew blessings for wine and bread before the meal, and after it to stand on a chair and sing 'My Yiddishe Mama', a tear-jerker sung variously in Yiddish, English or both, and adored across the Jewish diaspora in the thirties and after:

*My Yiddishe mama – I miss her more than ever now*
*My Yiddishe mama – I long to kiss her wrinkled brow*

*I long to hold her hand once more as in days gone by*
*And ask her to forgive me for things I did that made*
*her cry . . .*
*. . . Oy vey gliklakh un raykh iz der mentsh vos hot*
*Az a sheyner matone geshenkt fun Got*
*Az an altichke yiddishe mame*
*Mamenyu mayn.*

'To tell you I miss you and the baby,' Henry goes on, 'would be putting it very mildly, as it is only now when I can't see you and talk to you face to face that I realise how much you both mean to me . . . Give my love to my darling baby and tell him I will not be away long. Also to you my Darling wife I send my whole love and spirit and,' he concludes, exhibiting a religiosity not yet eroded further, as it soon would be, by the grind of war and the allure of upmarket secular pleasures, 'may the almighty spare us together for 40 years of happily married life, to bring up our children in a fine Jewish way. With all my life, I am, Your Henry.'

For most of the thirties the newspaper headlines were only the backdrop of my grandparents' lives. Apart from his weekend in Scheveningen and the odd country fair, London was Henry's world. He read about the League of Nations and Abyssinia and rearmament in the papers, but the struggles that most preoccupied him were with rival underwear manufacturers in Stoke Newington and Mile End.

Except that, in the East End, the news was hard to avoid entirely, because so much of it was happening there. Just as in earlier decades east London had nurtured trade unionism, the temperance campaign and the women's movement, in the thirties the streets of Stepney offered Britain's closest approximation to the political turmoil on the Continent. There were dramatic rent strikes in the tenement buildings around the

Lane. 'Hunger marches' from the depressed industrial north plodded through Whitechapel, where they received a warmer welcome than they did at Westminster. Then there were the fascists: both the ones in Spain, whom many East End radicals bicycled and hitchhiked across France to fight, and the ones closer to home.

In retrospect, Oswald Mosley and his motley British Union of Fascists look like risible, fancy-dress villains, who had somehow failed to notice that Britain just wasn't that kind of place. But, at the time, Mosley and his blackshirts seemed much less harmless to the Jews of the East End. They held public meetings in Hoxton and Bow, mouthing the same propaganda of parasites and swindlers as had their anti-immigrant predecessors thirty years earlier, and roughing up anyone who objected. On 14 July 1936 my grandfather had watched from the corner of Strype Street as the fascists made their most violent incursion into Jewish territory, smashing up the stalls in the Lane, coshing their proprietors and chanting their rhythmic battle-cry: 'The Yids! The Yids! We gotta get rid of the Yids!' The main event, Mosley had announced, was to be a march of his toy army through the heart of Jewish London: up Royal Mint Street and Leman Street, past the Aldgate and up Cambridge Heath Road to a rally in Victory Park Square. 'They Shall not Pass', the anti-fascist slogan imported from Spain, jostled on the graffitied walls around the Lane with the blackshirts' quasi-biblical 'Perish Judah'.

Everybody would like to have a hero in the family. It would be nice to be able to recount my grandfather's exploits at the subsequent showdown misleadingly known to posterity as the Battle of Cable Street (misleadingly, because the decisive encounter between the blackshirts and their police escorts on the one side, and the anti-fascist dockers of Wapping and Jewish tailors of Whitechapel on the other, actually took place in front of Gardiner's department store on Whitechapel High

Street). It would be gratifying to recall Henry's place in the vanguard of the resistance, to see him tearing up the cobbles from the streets to use as ammunition, or scattering marbles and ball bearings under the horses' hooves, as the mounted police charged baton-first into the throng, to clear the way for the blackshirted marchers. Or to remember how he fell back behind the barricades in Cable Street, as women hurled bottles and bricks from the upper windows of the houses. His brothers Mick and Sid were certainly there in the pulsating crowd; and although he was a less political animal than either of those two, Henry may indeed have been there too.

But if he *was* there on 4 October 1936 Henry never told his children about it. Nor does he mention it in any of his surviving letters, even when he described Mosley's puny post-war resurgence to an anxious correspondent in America. ('There is not a great deal of anti-Semitism in England on the surface,' he wrote, 'and it is possible that newspapers make a greater play of it abroad. So far as Mosley is concerned, his party is very much like the Communist party, in as much as it is practically non-existent.') In its own, local way, the 'battle' has become one of those iconic events, whose familiarity can seduce many more people into believing that they were present at them than actually were. For all the crowds that massed at Gardiner's Corner and at the mouth of Cable Street that day, most people in London were getting on with their banal, dramatic everyday lives, just as Leah and Auguste Claret were, in Edgware and Paris, as the world fell apart in 1914.

So it is just as plausible that Millie Freedman would have prevailed upon her eldest son not to risk his neck with the other excitable *meshuganas* (crazy people) who were out on the East End streets. Like the other older immigrants who had lived through the pogroms, my great-grandmother thought that the thing to do when the Cossacks or the nationalists came looking for trouble, or when the peasants got drunk after the market, was to lock up the synagogue, hide in the basement of your house, and pray that neither of them got burned down. It is easy to imagine my grandfather acquiescing to the wishes of his mother, to whom he never refused anything. In which case he would have missed the small, symbolic triumph as the fascists were turned back, and Mosley skulked away westwards along the river, and missed the dancing in the streets of Spitalfields that followed it. Henry was a fighter, but of another kind.

Politics and its risks may have been behind a strange and telling quarrel between Henry and his more politicised brother Mick. It was resolved only after Mick wrote two extraordinary letters to his brother – letters that encapsulate the honesty and intensity of their relationship, and the psychological legacy of their childhood. 'If only my heart could speak,' Mick begins his first letter after an unspecified disagreement, 'my pen now would not seem to me to be so inarticulate. I have often tried to analyse my thoughts regarding you and us, and each time I have seen how wonderful is our relationship. If you only knew how much I think of you, and how I think of you. Atheist as I am, and sceptic of the world, you are my God; and when suddenly you descend from the heights to the level of a normal person, my whole world collapses. It is as if an infallible ideal has burst.' Anticipating the charge of hyperbole, Mick explains that Henry 'may think that I place you on too high a pedestal, but no: your whole life, conduct and feeling towards us all – and me in particular – has been such that, if you were to say to me, in all sincerity – cut off your arm to save me pain – I would do so. My one ambition', Mick writes, 'has been and is to be worthy of your respect and confidence. I have let you down, and myself . . .'

The letter ends abruptly, trailing off without a signature, though Mick must have posted his confession in its unfinished form. But the next day, he tried again to distil his feelings of gratitude and deference, and the resentments that can accompany them, and which complicated Henry's relationships with all his siblings. 'My heart is so full that I hardly know how to start,' Mick writes. 'I love you so much that I would do anything to save you pain and worry. I value your opinion so highly that I brood when you "pick me up", and although outwardly I may seem surly and impatient of advice, inwardly I resolve and try to do just what you would like and want. I have never doubted or questioned your superior experience or knowledge. You have always been and always will be my "Guv'nor",' he pledges, 'and throughout I have always known of and felt that deep bond of love that really ties us together and reflects itself in our every act and deed . . . No brother could have a better brother, and no pupil a better teacher. I have no pretensions,' Mick winds up, 'no great vices and no outstanding qualities except faith, love and loyalty and these have ever been yours. You are more than brother, better than father, and to think of not seeing you and having your respect and confidence and love is more than I can bear. Your letter' – which, unfortunately, has not survived – 'is our bond for life.'

In the autumn of 1936 Henry achieved what his father Fishel had never managed, moving his new family out of the East End and across the river to a flat in Jerningham Road, New Cross, a broad, tree-lined, residential avenue sloping down to the New Cross Road. It was only a few miles away from New Castle Street, but it felt like another world. On the fresh socio-economic maps of London prepared by Booth's heirs, thirty years after his great turn-of-the-century survey of London poverty, Jerningham Road shows up as sturdily middle class, though there were evidently some very rough types just on the other side of the main road, up towards the docks. In the thirties the road was mainly populated by shopkeepers and the better class of artisan. The house my grandparents shared was

and is a handsome Victorian villa, with ornate bay windows on the ground floor. They now had their own bath, albeit shared with the family who lived above them. (According to the electoral records of the old borough of Deptford, in which New Cross then lay, they cohabited at first with a family called Mussett, later with another called Myhill.) They had a patch of garden, albeit backing onto the tracks on which commuter trains rumbled to and from London Bridge. They finally had electricity, even if, as with the gas in New Castle Street, they had to put money into a slot to make it work. There was a household up the road that was reputed to have its own telephone. There was a little park with a bandstand at the top of the road, and there was sometimes open-air dancing on a Sunday afternoon. Henry could get across the Thames and back to the Lane in no time at all on the East London Railway from New Cross Gate to Aldgate East. Later he borrowed some more money to splash out on a second-hand Cubitt car, which he and his brother Sid had to push home from the dealership because it wouldn't start. 'What do you expect for twelve quid?', the salesman asked them.

In the same year, 1936, Leah Claret finally left the Boot Street basement, moving in with her now-married son Paul in Walthamstow, north-east London, not far from the dog-racing track. Millie Freedman went to live with Ida, Solly and Sid, who had also migrated south of the river to a bigger place in Canadian Avenue, Catford. So in Jerningham Road it was just Henry, Miriam and the baby, and after he was born in a Jewish nursing home on Bromley Road in May, 1938, their second son, my other uncle, Michael.

As a certificate issued by the clerk of the borough records, Henry went down to the local town hall and signed up to be an air-raid warden on 8 June 1938. He was an early recruit, motivated, perhaps, by the memory of all the suspicion towards Jews during the last war, and a wish to pre-empt it this time. The manuals that he was given to study and the training he received were dominated by one horror in particular: gas. Along with his blue warden's uniform, his beret with its ARP badge, his whistle and the black helmet with a white 'W' stencilled onto the front, he was issued with yellow anti-gas oilskins and galoshes, and a gas mask that smelled perpetually of disinfectant. He and his fellow wardens would rustle sweatily up and down the streets in this extra-terrestrial get-up, cheered ironically as they passed the crowds outside the New Cross pubs. ARP stood for 'Air Raid Precautions', though 'Angling Round Pubs' was a more popular rendering in the days before the Munich crisis, when most people thought the wardens were just uniformed peeping Toms or coppers' 'narks', and their chaotic exercises all seemed a bit of a lark.

My grandfather spent hours sitting in his mask in a training van filled with tear gas. He learned to distinguish the odours of the various substances expected to engulf London in the event of war: the garlicky smell of mustard gas; the rotten-vegetable whiff of phosgene; and the tell-tale geranium tang of lewisite. He knew which ointments to apply to the burns and sores and ocular ailments that each gas would inflict. He practised putting out an incendiary bomb: first cover it with sand using a long-handled shovel, then put it in a bucket and take it to a patch of barren land. He mastered the operation of a stirrup hand-pump: one man pumps with his foot, a second refills the bucket, while the one who drew the shortest straw crawls up to the fire with the hose, sheltering behind a dustbin lid he has commandeered, and staying close to the ground where the air is cleaner. In a burning building, Henry discovered, he would have to skirt a room or a flight of stairs to minimise the risk of collapse. He was taught how to rescue an unconscious casualty, and how to fix a splint for a broken bone and a tourniquet for a gushing wound. He must not, under any circumstances and however much they asked, give the casualty a stiff drink. Hours of catechistic reiteration had drilled into him the routine to follow if a bomb fell in his patch: report any injuries; check for signs of poisons; warn people downwind of fires; rope off the crater; ascertain whether the water or sewage or gas pipes had been ruptured, and whether any buildings were likely to fall down.

But even to Henry, who as a boy had seen the Gothas fly over London in the First World War, it all seemed surreal: gas – bombs – in London? Perhaps in Spain, as the Pathé clips he and Miriam saw before the main feature at the Lewisham Hippodrome revealed; but in London? When he first helped to hand out gas masks in the high street, in September 1938, there weren't many takers. When the wardens ran a big drill to test their anti-gas procedures, complete with volunteer casualties wearing bathing suits under their clothes, there were more lewd than sensible observations. Then the rumours began to spread of lime pits being dug in London's parks in preparation for mass burials, and of the factory secretly churning out thousands of cardboard coffins, and about how there were hardly any proper deep shelters in the city. In May 1939 the Deptford ARP team had a recruitment drive: 134 volunteers signed up in a week, and the borough's head warden wrote to Henry, by then the head of his post, to thank him. 'This result could never have been achieved,' the letter said, 'without your loyal co-operation and support. To know that such a fine team spirit prevails is the greatest encouragement one can have in carrying out the many difficult tasks we have to face.' In July the Town Clerk wrote with 'pleasure in informing you that as a result of the recent course you have qualified as a Local Anti-Gas Instructor', enclosing another certificate to that effect. Henry later signed on to be a billeting officer, and was issued with another card that authorised him 'to require the occupier of any premises (a) to furnish true information with respect to the accommodation contained in the premises and to the persons living therein, and (b) to provide accommodation in the premises for all persons whom he may assign to the premises'. But my grandfather seems not to have exercised these powers extensively or even at all, perhaps because, as the joke did the rounds about how, under the billeting system, the rich got richer and the poor got children, it was not a post that was conducive to popularity.

His other personal anti-Nazi measure was to help bring a young cousin on his mother's side, a girl named Erna, over to Britain. He kept a copy of the form he submitted to the Inter-Aid Committee for Children from Germany, one of the bodies that organised the rescue of some European Jews, clipping to it a photo of the child in question. It shows a cherubic adolescent, with her hair in a bun and a serious expression on her face, staring into the middle distance. The form required Henry to specify where (should she be admitted) the child was to live; where educated; and how she was to be trained, so that under no circumstances would she become a burden on the state. Her hygiene had to be vouched for, and she would have to be registered as an alien with the local police. The committee itself, the form makes clear, can offer no guarantee that the application will be successful: it wants to bring as many children over as possible, but 'many factors, financial and sociological, must be taken into consideration'. In January 1939 my grandfather prevailed upon his bank manager to write a reference in support of the application; since the business was named after Solly, he was to be the official guardian. 'With reference to the guarantee under which we understand Mr Solomon Newman undertakes to become responsible for the maintenance of Ema of Heinestrasse 9/9, Wien II, a refugee child from Germany,' the bank manager wrote, getting her name wrong, 'I can confirm that Mr Newman is regarded as a respectable man and from our knowledge of him we should consider him as a suitable and trustworthy person to undertake an obligation of this nature.' Lest there be any confusion or unpleasantness later, the writer makes clear that 'this information is for your private use and is of course given without any responsibility attaching to the Bank or the Manager'.

Erna was just too old for the *kindertransport*, the convoys of unaccompanied children from Nazi Germany and its territories admitted to Britain in 1938-9. But she seems to have made it to London. She would have been given one of the little booklets prepared by London's anxious Jewish authorities, which advised refugees not to speak German loudly in public, and in general to be as inconspicuous as possible. 'The Englishman attaches very great importance to modesty, understatement in speech rather than overstatement, and quietness of dress and manner,' it instructed. 'He values good manners far more than he values the evidence of wealth.' What happened to Erna thereafter is unclear. She is said to have been unhappy in her new country, and she drifted away from the Freedman family and then lost touch with them altogether. No clues about her fate can be gleaned from the records of the Central British Fund for Jewish Relief and Rehabilitation, into which the Inter-Aid Committee was later subsumed. The records specify only that Erna had been born on 20 February 1922; that she described herself as a typist (though that may have been a profession invented to smooth her passage to Britain), and that she was, technically, 'stateless', having lost her Austrian nationality after the *anschluss* because of her religion. Her name does not appear in the lists of refugees whom the British government rounded up and interned on the Isle of Man, alongside a few stranded Nazis. Nor is it among the names of untrustworthy aliens whom the authorities shipped off to Canada and Australia, some of whom died when their convoys were torpedoed en route. Had she stayed in London, Erna would probably have made more of an impression in the aid committee's files; so it is likely that she moved on to Leeds or Manchester, or to Israel or America, as several of the refugees whom Henry hired to work in his factory in the late thirties also did after the war. (One desperate exile stopped him as he was walking down the Lane to beg him for a job, any job.) My grandfather continued to donate money to the Central British Fund well into the fifties, but that may have been out of general beneficence, and not given for the upkeep of a specific individual; the accounts for such donations and their purposes have not been retained. Erna is untraceable: a little, tragic, wartime mystery.

'I feel I cannot let this auspicious day go by,' Henry wrote to Mick on V.E. Day, 1945, 'without recording the great thankfulness in my heart, that our family has in so large a measure been spared so much that the vicissitudes of this war have doled out to others.' Had he then been sure of the fates of his relatives in what had been Galicia and was by then part of the Soviet Union, and of Miriam's family in Poland, he might have been less sanguine. But the only direct fatality of the conflict among his extended British clan had been Mick's brother-in-law, killed in Royal Air Force action in September 1943. Babs's husband Morris spent much of the war skirmishing with Rommel in the Middle East, but he came back in one piece. Neither Henry nor any of his close relations had been maimed by a bomb, or imprisoned in a POW camp, or come home to children whom they didn't recognise. When war broke out, my grandfather had been earning £5 a week: more than he could have dreamed of taking home when he met my grandmother a decade earlier, but hardly riches. Between the two 'V' days, he would open a new factory on Tyneside. He and Miriam had moved to the green belt, and he had taken up fox-hunting. As the Allies took Europe back from Hitler, my grandfather was embarking on his own conquest of the City and the West End, learning their codes and rituals as surely as he had come to navigate the side streets and synagogues of Stepney.

So the Freedmans had a lucky war. All the same, they experienced the pain of separation and the terror of bombardment, and faced the attritional daily struggles and moral quandaries that the war brought to almost everyone. By the end of 1940 they had also suffered two private, unrecorded calamities, which, to my grandparents, were as pivotal as the fall of Paris or the flight from Dunkirk.

Henry didn't want to subject his family to the caprices of the government evacuation system. He ignored the taunts about queue-jumping to which the self-evacuated were subjected, and the racial embellishments that sometimes accompanied them. On the day war was declared in 1939, in between what Churchill described as the 'banshee howlings' of the experimenting air-raid sirens, he drove Miriam and their two sons, plus his mother Millie, south into Sussex. He deposited them in Camber Sands, the seaside hamlet near Rye on England's south coast, finding them digs in a boarding house in Pelwood Road, whose pre-war buildings have long since been knocked down to make way for a housing estate and a maze of holiday chalets. In September 1939 Camber seemed continents away from London, where the war was expected to arrive from the skies at any moment. There were even a few oblivious holidaymakers sheltering behind windbreaks on the beach, even though only the broad eponymous sand dunes and the few miles of the Channel separated Camber from France. An Italian ice-cream vendor, in his straw boater and white jacket, still peddled his wares on a bicycle ('Stop Me and Buy One!'), his livelihood not yet compromised by Mussolini's entry into the war.

On 10 September 1939, a week after Neville Chamberlain's famous radio broadcast, Henry wrote to Miriam from London, finishing his letter by the light of the kerosene lamp in his sand-bagged air-raid wardens' pillbox, just off New Cross Road. 'I Love you so much, I cannot even tell you,' he begins. 'My Life is only Life if I have you with me. As I sit here and think of you alone, I am in a whirl.' Henry was half petrified by the prospect of annihilation, half mortified with boredom from watching the two other wardens at his post playing gin rummy and cribbage. According to the stamps on his Deptford warden's card, in the autumn of 1939 he was on duty for two or three evenings a week. On his turns around the neighbourhood to enforce the blackout regulations, he averted his eyes from the opportunistic couples clinging together in shop doorways. He was terrorised by all the local comedians who thought the best joke in the world was to make him fetch a policeman, and only then agree to turn their lights out or to fix their blackout curtains. 'Everything is empty without you,' Henry tells Miriam. 'I can feel that you are thinking the same, at this moment. I know you Love me as much as I Love you, and that is the greatest consolation, at this moment.' With only a little hindsight, the south coast of England had already come to seem an inadvisable getaway, and much of it would soon be off-limits to civilians altogether. They would have to find a better refuge from the Luftwaffe, but Henry asks Miriam 'not [to] think yet about the moving. Try as much as possible to have a rest, and treat it like a holiday. All in London is quiet,' he assures her, 'and it does not seem possible that something is wrong.' In the Lane, near Henry's workshop, the eternal Prince Monolulu was selling gas-mask boxes in a range of brassy colours, instead of his enveloped racing tips. London's cinemas and theatres were closed, and the streets had been emptied of half their children and filled with sandbags and barbed wire. Yet without any bombs it felt as much like a charade as the real thing. 'I am on duty tonight and I shall be thinking of you all the time . . . I could keep on writing to you all night,' Henry closes, 'but you must already know what I want to say, and how much you mean to me.'

Perhaps, despite her old anxiety about expressing herself on paper, Miriam did write to Henry every day from the seaside as his letter requested; if she did, her mail has not survived. For his part, true to his word, on the day after he told her about the odd quietness of London, Henry wrote again. 'I will be down on Saturday in the car to bring you and the children home,' he tells her, 'and later I will find you a place nearer to me, so that I can be with you more often.' A week apart was already too much; anyway, other mothers and children were already beginning to creep back to London. 'I have been to business today,' he goes on, 'and I think it will be very busy.' He had been exempted from the call-up to run his firm, which was now producing silk parachutes for the government as well as the regular underwear lines. 'I am managing fairly well here but look forward to having you back home again. My love to mother. To you my darling, myself, and to my children, my life.' On Saturday, Miriam and the children were back in Jerningham Road.

In November Henry's brother Sid married Nita Nemenchinsky, a niece of Solly, in Philpot Street; in keeping with the mood, Nita wore an ordinary dress instead of a festive white one. It was during the blackout that Mick, Henry's only still-single sibling, proposed to flame-haired Freda Caplan. When Mick dropped Freda home after a blackout date – the chaperone system had finally been killed off – he left what she thought was his handkerchief in her hand when he said good night. When she got inside and around the blackout curtain, she saw that she was holding a crumpled pair of DKs. They were married in Philpot Street on 18 February 1940, along with a dozen other couples: the East End synagogues, like London's

registry offices, were clogged up with a rush of giddy, last-dance weddings. Henry and Millie chipped in to help Freda's parents with the party, and the newlyweds had a short but sunny weekend in Torquay. 'When we think of all you have done for us,' Mick wrote to Henry on 20 February, 'fixing our home up and setting us an example; giving us the benefit of your advice and experience, more as a father than as an elder brother – we really are overcome. Sentiment is a part of every-body's make up; but we feel now, not sentiment, but a com-plete awareness of the love we have for you – which normally is more dormant – and the respect in which we hold you.'

The following month, after Miriam told her husband that she was expecting another baby, she and Henry moved again, a little further south-east, to Crantock Road in Catford, close by the rest of the tight Freedman family. Crantock Road was a bit less posh than Jerningham Road, but now they had a whole semi-detached house to themselves and, after Henry scraped together a deposit, they had bought it. That part of London was becoming one of the favoured destinations for East End Jewish families making good. The little synagogue that now stands in Crantock Road, which Mick and Freda helped to found (and to which Henry would later dedicate a pair of stained-glass windows in memory of his parents), had not yet

been built. But Newquay Road, a parallel street a little further up towards Lewisham High Street, was already known locally as 'Jewquay' Road. My grandparents' house had a grand, oriental-style chandelier in the front room. There was a useful hollow under the stairs that, as an alternative to a back-garden Anderson bomb shelter, Henry insulated from gas attack with a piece of damp felt, and furnished with a precautionary bucket of sand, plus some candles and bandages. He transferred his warden's registration to the borough of Lewisham, and was assigned to the same post as his brother-in-law Solly, also a local warden, on the corner of Bromley Road and Canadian Avenue.

Apart from the move and the humdrum warden's duties, my grandparents' life in the first few months of 1940 was oddly normal. There were no fireworks at the Crystal Palace on bank holidays as there used to be; but the live acts between the features at the Gaumont cinema in Lewisham still commanded more attention than the newsreels about the 'bore war'. Henry and Miriam won a 'spot waltz' competition at a *palais de danse* in Bromley (the first time she had won anything, Miriam said): a single spotlight would illuminate the floor, tracking each of the couples in turn before settling on the best performers at the end of the number. Then, as the war became dauntingly real, my grandparents suffered the first of their private calamities.

In April 1940, worn down by the markets as surely as the fur trade had done for her husband, my great-grandmother Millie

Freedman had a heart attack. She was living with Henry's sister Ida, but was moved into a nursing home on the corner of Crantock Road. Only then did she quit the Lane altogether. She had lost her licence for weekday trading in Wentworth Street in 1936, but she ran a small Sunday stall outside Number Forty-five until the end: retirement wasn't something she expected from life. On 13 May 1940 – as Belgium and Holland fell to the Nazis, and Chamberlain's government fell in the House of Commons – she got up from her bed to make a cup of tea in the nursing home's communal kitchen. While the kettle was boiling, she heard a radio report about Hitler's conquests, and died, aged fifty-three. On the following day, in beautiful sunshine, twenty-four years and eight months after her husband had been interred, she was laid to rest next to Fishel in Edmonton cemetery. (Henry's receipt from the Federation of Synagogues Burial Society records that he paid a substantial £41 and ten shillings for the removal and burial.)

Millie's children sat for a week on low chairs underneath the oriental chandelier in Crantock Road, the men not shaving and the mirrors covered up, as are the customs of the seven-day *shiva*. They had idolised their mother, and they took it badly. 'You say that Mother is always with you,' Babs wrote to Henry when she was back in her evacuation billet in Buckinghamshire; 'its different with me, because I am away from the family so I hardly ever talk about her and then not the way you do. When I think of her I always seem to think of the way she suffered all her life and especially at the end, it always makes me cry. I often cry myself to sleep when I think about her.' Millie had been born in an empire that no longer existed, then moved to a strange, industrial land with a man she barely knew. She had raised five children in poverty, and from a distance seen her old Galician world overrun by the First World War, then threatened by an undreamed-of new barbarism. Yet those who remember her recall a sweet, imperturbable, unimposing figure; nobody would guess from looking at her that half a century of European turmoil was embodied in her slight frame. 'A year has gone by,' Mick would write to Henry in 1941, 'and she has never been out of my mind. Part of me has gone never to return, for she was the best of all that is in me.' In his V.E. Day letter to his brother, Henry tried to rationalise their loss. 'It is almost five years since our beloved mother departed this world, and on looking back, I feel it was for the best that she was not able to have those awful fears that mothers have had, and the pain at the terrible gaps that have been torn in people's hearts. As I said on that never to be forgotten night, our mother is still with us, wherever we are, only we cannot stretch out our hand to feel her. But we have the advantage that we carry her with us for the rest of our days, as the most beautiful and wonderful woman this world could ever produce.' Henry said the *yahrzeit* prayers – which a child recites for a deceased parent – every year on the anniversary of Millie's death, and on the anniversary of his father's, until his own. His life's greatest regret, he would tell his children, was not to have done more for her.

Their grief was interrupted by the Blitz. Because of south-east London's proximity to the airfields at Croydon and Biggin Hill, the bombs started falling there before the famous armada of German bombers swept up the Thames estuary and began the Blitz proper on 7 September 1940. On 6 September dog-fights were visible in the skies to the south of London, looking, to Henry, at once close enough to touch and entirely fantasti-cal. That evening, up the road at the Lewisham Hippodrome, the star turn sang fifty-eight popular numbers to drown out the rumble of the planes and the thump of the bombs. For all his anti-gas certificates and theoretical proficiency, like the other wardens Henry hadn't been sure that he would be able to take it. They found out in Engleheart Road, where five houses and six people were wiped out by high explosives. On the 7th, the fires in the timber yards at the Surrey Docks illumi-nated the carnage caused by the bombs that fell on the big jam factory on Bromley Road. The fire at St Katharine's Docks three nights later looked like the end of the world.

In the first month of the Blitz, Henry was on duty for three nights a week, for twelve hours at a stretch. He did the rounds of the local shelters, cluttered with picnics, mattresses, suit-cases, children, children in suitcases. In the network of covered trenches that had been dug into the local sports ground, and in the basement of the jam factory, he tried to keep the peace between the people who wanted to sleep or pray or cry in silence, and the ones who wanted a mouth-organist or accor-dionist to play 'Bye-Bye Blackshirt', 'They Can't Black Out the Moon', and the already obsolescent 'We're Gonna Hang Out the Washing on the Siegfried Line'. He was supposed to know where everyone on his patch was sleeping, but the daily exodus at teatime from Lewisham to the Chislehurst Caves in Kent (soon equipped with their own cinema and chapel), and the smaller posses that trekked out to sleep in Epping Forest while the fine weather lasted, made the task impossible. From the door of their pillbox, the wardens watched for the descent of the flares that lit the way for the bombs. Then they raced over to assess the damage. They covered the bodies, dressed the odd wound and told survivors and distraught relatives what they knew, which usually wasn't much. They listened for voices in the debris, and directed the stretcher-bearers and ambulance-men around the tangles of telegraph poles and over the serpentine coils of the firemen's hoses, and after them the heavy rescue teams and the gas repair men and the women who came to make the tea. They tried to stop the little fires caused by the incendiaries from joining up into larger conflagrations, sometimes throwing upholstery out through the front windows of houses to keep a blaze from spreading. They restrained the residents who wanted to go back in to rescue a budgerigar or a photograph album or the savings hidden under the floorboards. They held back the sightseers who, in the early days, turned up to see what was happening, the looters who came to pinch the hurricane lamps and the lead from the roofs, and the dogs who came to sniff optimistically at the rubble and piles of broken glass. They reasoned with the people who tried to keep the firemen away from their burning homes, because they couldn't afford to replace the furniture about to be soaked by the hoses.

After a couple of weeks, Henry could discriminate between the booms and bangs of the various anti-aircraft guns, and between the vapour trails of the bombers and the fighter planes that darted around and in between them. He recognised the tin-can clatter of an incendiary bomb landing, and could tell the orange glow of the high explosives, licking up into the night as if from the surface of a little local sun, from the angry reds thrown up by an oil bomb. He had got used to that strange sensation that came over people after they heard the whistle of a bomb, and threw themselves to the floor, and felt like they were still falling for several seconds after they and the bomb had landed. He got used to the sting of brick dust in his eye, and the weird quietness of the bombsites, often broken only by the trickle of water somewhere in the entrails of a ruined house. He learned that the ones who cried were generally in a better way than the silent ones, and that anyone caught in a direct hit was a goner, like the poor souls lost in the shelter on Albion Way on the same day that the King and Queen had come to south-east London to raise its inhabitants' spirits. On 15 September, the night after the famous daylight air battles over London, five members of the same family perished in a house on his turf. The gas never came, but when the water mains burst another, unexpected version of the apocalypse did, as basements were flooded and people who had sheltered in them swam for their lives.

When the raids ended, Henry went back to the shelters to give the all-clear, and put his head round the door of the pubs whose customers had refused to budge. He went home to my grandmother and his children for an hour or two's sleep, feeling that he was at the epicentre of a cosmic injustice, and also that he was as lucky as any man alive, because he was still alive. Then he got up and dragged himself to the Lane, where he tried to prevail on the machinists to sew in straight lines, even though the jerry-built Stepney houses in which many of them lived had fallen down at the first hint of bomb blast, and many of them had spent half the night resting their heads on a stranger's shoulder: some alongside the sarcophagi in the crypt of Hawksmoor's Christ Church; others in the massive subterranean Tilbury warehouse, a cathedral of fear between Commercial Road and Cable Street that had been seized in a popular *coup de main* when the bombing began, and in which 10,000 people and a few horses now bedded down among

bales of newspaper and crates of margarine. On some mornings Henry's workshop had no electricity, and on very few of them did the telephone work. Some of his team had heard Lord Haw-Haw, the Irish-American Nazi propagandist, say on the radio that Stepney was getting so much more than its fair share because Hitler wanted to make an early start on its Jewish inhabitants. They mistook the sound of a bus changing gear for the siren, and bolted for the door and the shelter of Aldgate Tube.

My grandfather was not a designated hero of the Blitz. He cannot be traced in any of the official Home Front archives. The daily damage reports prepared for the central government describe only the premier air-raid targets – St Paul's, the Tower of London, mainline railway stations and the larger factories. The fire brigade's incident reports for his neighbourhood record only the baldest of details, and not the identities of the wardens who attended. His name does not appear among those who, according to the minutes of its meetings, Lewisham's civil-defence committee commended for their gallantry. He was not as distinguished as his brother-in-law Solly, who on the night of 17 September dragged an unconscious man from the burning wreck of the clubhouse of Catford Cricket Club. Five people died, including one of the teenaged messengers who hung around the wardens' posts trying to make themselves useful. Perhaps Henry was at that fire with Solly, but if he was he never told his children about it. There are no members of the cricket club old enough these days to remember what happened.

That night, 17 September, the Germans unleashed a new weapon: enormous mines that floated silently down to earth in pairs beneath green parachutes, landing just when the noise of the planes had died away and people in shelters and cellars thought it was safe to come out. Three sets of them landed in spitting distance from Henry and Miriam's place in Crantock Road. Next day, as the borough engineer's damage reports detail, a pair that landed even closer smashed the windows of my grandparents' house, and caved in part of its roof. After that, my grandmother decided she could spend no more nights sheltering in the hollow under the stairs, with the children crying, and the new baby kicking inside her, and the ground shaking as if the bombs were falling in the front room; with the guns booming and the engines of the bombers whining as they climbed out of range; the siren wailing and the bells of the fire engines ringing; with terrible, acrid smells wafting down from the docks; and Henry out God only knew where in the night.

The day after the mines blew in their windows, Henry drove Miriam, their two boys, plus their old friend Mrs Marks, the *yiddishe* godmother from the Lane, out of London once again, weaving through the labyrinth of diversions created by unexploded bombs, and the chaos left by mines in Lewisham High Street. This time they went north, to Hertfordshire. Miriam's brother Paul had already re-evacuated his own family and Miriam's mother Leah, first winding up in a cold caravan in a field, then negotiating for a room with the barman of the George Hotel in Harpenden, a small market town that was becoming a commuter dormitory. Leah already had her commercial eye on an empty little shop just off Harpenden High Street. So Henry headed for Harpenden too, and found a room for Miriam, the two boys and Mrs Marks in a crescent off Luton Road, just outside the town.

Then he went back, again, to London. After they were bombed out, on his off-duty nights my grandfather went up West to sleep in the Strand Palace Hotel. Perhaps he shared the conviction, common among those who lived east of the City, that the shamanic power of money must somehow preserve the West End. The Palace was owned by the company that ran the Corner Houses in which he had courted Miriam, and boasted a billiard room with an inlaid ceiling, an art deco lobby and fancy friezes and murals. But it wasn't as posh as it is today, or as the Dorchester, Claridge's, the Ritz and the Savoy, the adopted homes of those rich Londoners who hadn't sold up altogether and moved to America, and of half the displaced monarchs of Europe. The champagne was still flowing in these refuges, and the menus were holding up well. The hospitality at the Strand Palace was rather humbler. A wartime menu from the hotel proffers a '*ballotine de jambon Valentinase*' and an '*assiette froid et salade*': in plain English, hot spam, and cold spam with salad. Dinner, as the bills of that era retained by the hotel show, cost three shillings and breakfast was one-and-six. There were nearly 1,000 rooms, but Henry, like everyone else, slept on a cot in the hotel's vaults, in the company of French, Dutch, Belgian and Polish soldiers who had washed up in London after their countries were conquered.

On the evening of 2 October, a little over a month before my grandparents' third child was due, they suffered their second wartime catastrophe. The all-clear sounded unusually early that day, and Henry decided to take a stroll across the West End from the Strand Palace. Nelson was still perched on his column in Trafalgar Square, but the occupants of the other plinths had been evacuated. Outside the Empire cinema in Leicester Square there was a queue for the last show of *Gone with the Wind*, whose appeal no quantity of bombs could lessen. The lights were out at Piccadilly Circus, and Eros had been removed and replaced by an unsightly wooden box, now plastered with a variety of government slogans. Along Piccadilly, Henry had to squint through peepholes in the boarded-up shopfronts to make out the merchandise; the elegant arcades between Piccadilly and Jermyn Street had all been wrecked. There was a graveyard of baths salvaged from bombsites in Hyde Park, and horses were tethered to the backs of their carts to stop them bolting. As Henry was making his way up Park Lane, the sirens sounded again.

By 2 October the Luftwaffe had murdered sleep in London. A couple of days earlier, the government had distributed free earplugs to help Londoners function, but Henry was one of many who preferred daytime exhaustion to nocturnal oblivion. So perhaps it was wooziness that kept him on the streets that evening when the raid commenced. Or perhaps, like many others, he already regarded rushing into the shelters as poor form. As he later told it, he had been engrossed by a battle taking place above him: by the fandango of the searchlights, the tracer fire screaming into the sky, and the flashes of the guns reflecting off the clouds and off the silvery barrage balloons. It was the night when a solitary raider tried to evade the anti-aircraft defences by cutting off his engines and gliding into central London, then had to start them up again when he lost height, and was chased away by the guns. That may have been the spectacle that detained Henry when he reached Marble Arch, and was crossing Park Lane in the direction of Oxford Street. He was standing in the middle of the road, when one of the few London taxis not to have been converted into an ambulance bore down on him. As the regulations required, the taxi's solitary headlight was dimmed and masked. After road-accident statistics soared in the early months of the blackout, the government had advised pedestrians to wear white clothes or hat bands if they were out at night, to complement the white-painted kerbs and tree trunks ('Billy Brown's own high-way code/For blackouts is, stay off the road'). But my grand-father was on the road and invisible. He didn't see or hear the taxi in the hubbub of the raid. The driver didn't see him until it was too late. As Henry lay bleeding and unconscious in the road, the driver bolted into the Cumberland Hotel. The staff had already retreated underground, but the driver eventually managed to rouse them and an ambulance.

After Henry came round, as soon as he could he wrote to his brother Sid from St George's Hospital at Hyde Park Corner. 'The X-rays show my skull is fractured,' he explains in an unsteady hand, 'and I must lie flat on my back, and not move my head. The doctor says it will be many weeks before I shall be able to get up or sit up again, and I shall have to get it out of my mind to be present when the new arrival comes along. Meanwhile, the only way of setting my mind at rest will be to see you as often as possible, and to hear from you of any progress and news of business.' He asks after his other brother and sisters and their children, and repeatedly about Miriam.

'There is very little I need here,' he assures Sid, 'except for two pairs of pyjamas; also my handkerchiefs, a bit of smoked salmon now and then, some grapes and a few short story books to pass away the time, something like the *Strand* magazine.' Beneath his signature, there is a short, plaintive postscript that undermines the letter's upbeat mood: 'Let me see you somehow, three times a week.' As the doctor explained to Miriam when she came down to Hyde Park Corner, the truth was that the extent of the damage to Henry's brain was unknown, and he might yet relapse and die.

Sid went round to St George's immediately, but arrived after visiting hours and had to smuggle in Henry's contraband smoked salmon via a window and with the help of a co-operative orderly. Their sister Babs came with a cooked chicken. Henry's brother-in-law Solly wrote as soon as he heard the news, which 'has made my inside turn with fright at your fractured skull. All I can say from my heart is that you must get well and be patient about it. Do not worry about business we shall all do our best and run it in the best way for which you have brought us out. Henry there is one thing I miss in business is your shouting to us, so please get well and make up for all the shouting for which we have missed. Do not worry about the family we promise you we shall treat them like our own as our motto is your worries are ours our worries are yours ...' On the 9th Mick wrote to say that 'we had a fairly quiet night and everybody is feeling the benefit of it ... We are all right and feeling fine – though we miss your rollickings quite a bit.' Solly wrote again on the 10th: '*Thursday 7.30pm in the shelter all alone.* Just when I need you most you are in hospital but never mind so long as you are making progress. I hope you will forgive me for not making an attempt to see you as much as I love to see you.' Then he tells my grandfather about some early signs of trouble with his family's landlady at their Buckinghamshire billet: 'Ida phoned up she is very unhappy in Bletchly with the

143

people she is staying with there. Mrs Corby has turned from good to bad and is very jealous. Her eyes fall out if we eat fowl or buy cakes.'

In the middle of October Henry was moved to a sanatorium in suburban Harefield, where he shared a ward with other Londoners who had been bombed, burned or temporarily buried alive. He wrote to Miriam from North Ward 7 on 21 October at 5pm. 'My Darling Miriam,' he begins, on a note of mild reproach, 'I did look forward to seeing you on Sunday but of course, it was too much to expect.' Still, 'the photographs of the children are wonderful, and I could hardly go to sleep the night I received them. I could not take my eyes off them, and you can imagine my pride when people look at them too.' Then he turns to her: 'And you sweetheart, How are you? Still holding out, I hear. I hope you are keeping well, but I hear you are very nervous. You really must not be' – though it was understandable that she was. When she visited him she hardly knew what to say to his bandaged head, and she cried when she tried to think about life without him. Her baby was coming, and she had two other children to look after in one room, which they were still sharing with Mrs Marks. She was living in conditions as miserable as those in Boot Street (albeit with fresher air), had reverted to an outside toilet appointed with cut-up newspaper, and was bathing her sons in a basin on somebody else's kitchen table. She was not a favourite customer of any Harpenden shopkeeper; no one put a piece of fish or chicken aside for her as they might have done in Lewisham, and certainly would have in the Lane. It was whispered that she and Mrs Marks hadn't been to church since they arrived. When it came out that they were Jewish, they were allowed to overhear mutterings about how the Jews had started the war, and were now known to be taking all the best places in the London shelters. Other boys inspected her sons' foreheads for horns, and told them they had killed Christ.

Not knowing the half of it, Henry tells her that 'There is nothing to be afraid of in such an isolated spot and besides, the Lord is watching over us all. Therefore take it easy and don't worry . . . Please God, you will have a little Girl, with Lovely Hair and beautiful eyes, just like yourself. Eh Darling?' Finally, he says a little about himself: 'I am getting much better, and doctor says I may get up on Monday 28th. I suppose, however, that I will be here about another two weeks after I leave my bed. I have tried to stand up, but I am afraid I cannot, just yet.' Nevertheless, Miriam is not alone: 'Ida is your sister, and you can rely on her to look after the children while you are away.' Moreover, absent and invalid though he is, 'My thoughts are always with you, and I will instinctively know when you will need me most, and Darling, I shall be with you, even though you can't see me. With all my Love, I am Ever', he signed off, with his trademark combination of affection and epistolary propriety, 'Your Henry.'

Looking at the handwriting of my grandfather's letter, so much more jagged and erratic than normal, my grandmother cannot have been entirely reassured. Her Henry, the doctors at the sanatorium said, was lucky to be alive, and not yet out of danger. When, as Henry had wanted, she gave birth to a daughter in a nursing home on the Luton Road, just outside Harpenden, on 21 November, her husband was still at Harefield. They named my mother Amelia, after Millie Freedman (and, in Hebrew, Malka). It was a difficult birth, and Miriam had to stay in the home for several weeks, sending the new baby and her two boys to be cared for by Henry's sister Ida, and then by her mother Leah. 'We are so glad that you got what we all wanted – a little girl,' Miriam's sister-in-law Freda wrote to her, 'and I have the sweetest little pattern to knit for her.' 'Get well quickly,' Henry's brother Mick added to his wife's letter, 'so we can all be together again. You know how much we all love you, and we are praying that you should be up again soon

. . . Keep your chin up – God bless you.' 'I cannot express how happy I felt,' his other brother Sid wrote to Henry in the sanatorium, 'when I heard the news that you now have a daughter. Honestly I could not have been more anxious if it was my own child being born . . . It is funny I have been thinking of Mum quite a lot this week, and now she is back again.'

Miriam recovered. And as it turned out, instead of killing him the crack in Henry's skull came to mark a fracture in his life. While he was recuperating he met Walter Sherman – the third seismic event of my grandfather's war.

# FOUR

# 'Your friend, Walter'

*Villa Lambart*
*Cannes*

*Friday*

*Dear Henry,*
*I forget if you have been here or not. This is my second visit*
*& the present experience is simply wonderful. The villa*
*is perfect, large, lofty, beautifully furnished and the comfort*
*generally is superlative. Owned by a South American*
*millionaire who spends 6 months here & 6 months in BA.*
*The food is perfect & the chef knows his job (late second*
*chef of the Carlton). Just finished lunch: melon, salade*
*& jambon, baby lamb (not from Ciro's), pastries, cream*
*& peaches etc. The only drawback is that too many visitors*
*come to cocktail parties & meals. I spend a lot of time*
*in the garden, full of tall palm trees & shady spots.*

*Enough of all my enjoyment etc. How are you & yours*
*& business? I'm often thinking of you & helping you out of*
*your difficulties which I hope are few. Leaving here on the*
*26th & I shall be telephoning you on the Wednesday.*

*The shops are full of fine & exclusive goods, all the*
*renowned names are represented. Cartier, Charvet, etc*
*etc. No coupons & considering rate of exchange moderately*

*cheap. I have not been to the Casino, but I'm told the*
*gambling is very heavy & hundreds of millions (francs)*
*won & lost nightly by such people as the Aga Khan,*
*Prince Ali Khan, big industrialists & many others.*

*Cissie sends her love to Miriam & considers a weekend*
*with you is a happier time than the continual rush here.*
*Please do not trouble to reply as there is a strike and letters*
*seldom arrive.*

*Yours affectionately,*
*Walter*

After he was discharged from the sanatorium, in the deep snows of January 1941, Henry moved his family to a grand Victorian home on Lower Luton Road, just outside Wheathampstead and close to Harpenden. It was and is still a red-brick house with an elegant porch, a disused stable at the back, a below-stairs kitchen and a large lawn. To the front there was a picturesque view of the River Lea, and a wooden footbridge across it; when the full 'bomber's moon' was shining and the raids were heavy, the fires in London lit up the horizon. Except for the odd incendiary, jettisoned as the German planes flew back from their sorties to the tank factory at Luton, Wheathampstead was safe from the bombs. The rent was steep and, with the new baby and her two boys, Miriam struggled to keep it all clean: she seemed to spend half her time on her hands and knees in her white pinafore, making up the fire, blackleading the fireplace and scrubbing the front doorstep. But these seemed trifling details when hordes of Nazi paratroopers were expected to descend from the clouds at any moment, disguised, so rumour had it, as nuns. Later in 1941 Henry took over a defunct cinema on the corner of Amenbury Lane in Harpenden, converting it into a factory as a hedge against the destruction of his London operation, and turning the upstairs projection room into an office.

The Marble Arch accident had left him with a vertiginous condition that for the rest of his life induced occasional dizzy spells, in which he maintained consciousness but was unable to stand. Nevertheless, to prove something to someone, Henry signed up with what were then still known as the Local Defence Volunteers, later immortalised as the Home Guard. As his LDV registration card attests, he was assigned to the 20th platoon of the 26th company of the 5th Hertfordshire Battalion. This was one of the units responsible for maintaining the so-called Outer London Stop Line, itself one of the concentric defensive rings intended to protect the capital from invaders. By the time my grandfather joined, to deter enemy landings his platoon had already littered the fields around Harpenden with old cars, benches and cricket rollers. Henry went to a 'bottle party', at which he and other commuters and shop-keepers merrily filled milk bottles with tar, paraffin and petrol, ready for use against passing Panzer divisions. He listened to deadpan talks about how to knife a sentry; how to stretch a wire across the road to decapitate a motorcyclist; and how to disable a tank with a 'sticky bomb'. He went once or twice to the rifle range set up in the basement of Jarvis's store in Harpenden High Street, and was patronised by local veterans of the last war, and one even of the Afghan wars, some of whom possessed actual firearms. But he struggled with the long night watches at rural roadblocks. He had a nasty fall in the driveway of the Wheathampstead house; he lay on his back unable to move, until a bearded stranger, whom he never saw before or afterwards, picked him up and carried him inside. Eventually, the medical board at St Albans adjudged him unfit for all war duties.

Another attachment Henry formed when he came out of hospital lasted longer. The records of the Hercules Lodge of Ancient Free and Accepted Masons specify that Henry Emmanuel Freedman was initiated into the Lodge on 23

NATIONAL SERVICE (ARMED FORCES) ACTS.
GRADE CARD

Registration No. *L.HK. 17050*

Mr *FREEDMAN* *Henry Emanuel* whose address on his registration
card is *Lea House, Lower Luton Rd. Wheathamstead*

was medically examined at

on 13 OCT 1941 ST. ALBANS and placed
in GRADE IV (FOUR). MEDICAL BOARD

(Medical Board stamp.)

Chairman of Board

Man's Signature

N.S. 54.

January 1941, 'passed' on 27 March and 'raised' (the last of the
admission rites) on 28 August. Beneath the Masonic vestments,
it didn't matter, or it seemed not to matter, that Henry was the
son of Galician immigrants and his Masonic brothers were
something else. The abstruse rituals provided him with a sort
of substitute faith for the one that, by 1941, had been diluted by
work, war and ambition, and the move to the gentile countryside, even more than it had been compromised by life in the
markets. Later he was initiated into the Samson and Goliath
lodges, before the Titan Lodge became his long-term home. He
obeyed all the elaborate summonses to the Titan's meetings in
private rooms at West End restaurants and hotels, and accepted
the symbolic offices bestowed on him with alacrity. Then, some
time in the spring of 1941, he went down to a kerbside second-
hand car dealership in Warren Street, run by a relative of one of
his employees in the Lane, and bought himself a venerable old
Daimler. Thirsty motors were going for a pittance while petrol
rationing was on, and even cheaper if the buyer was prepared to
overlook the absence of a log book.

The big house; the Daimler; the Masons: because of his own
father's early death, so he later told his children, my grandfather
always half-expected to die young too. His accident convinced
him that there was absolutely no time to waste if he wanted to
be somebody. This was his frame of mind when his life collided
with Walter Sherman's in Jermyn Street, in the summer of 1941.

Henry had gone up West in search of a decent shirt. He was swapping complaints about the shortage of fabric in London with the salesman in what had been a grand, double-fronted Jermyn Street outfitter, whose windows had been blown in by a bomb and whose stock was sadly depleted. The showroom's owner interrupted, introducing himself as Walter Sherman. Walter and Henry saw things the same way: the shortage disastrous for the trade; the government inept; the Hun ultimately to blame. Henry was impressed by Walter's sangfroid amid the debris and the three-quarters empty shelves. But he would have thought no more about it had they not run into each other again in Torquay, in Devon, in May of 1942. Henry's doctor had ordered him to go away and keep as still as possible for two weeks. He had a miserable time, aching for Miriam and their children and failing to reach them on the telephone. 'I haven't forgotten what you look like,' he wrote to his wife, each of them marooned on their own while Britain's eastern empire fell ignominiously to the Japanese, and the country was enveloped in gloom, 'nor the children, as you are all ever in front of my eyes. I should be very proud to have you all here ... With all my love, I am ever Your Henry.' On the day before he was due to go home, he spotted Walter's familiar face in the dining room.

When Henry Freedman first met Walter Sherman, Henry was thirty-four and Walter was sixty-five. Walter had been born, as his birth certificate records, the son of another Walter, at the family home in Clapham in 1875. He and my grandfather made a comical pair. Henry was short, stocky and still hunched and slowed from his run-in with the taxi. Walter was tall, slim and (it seemed to Henry) impossibly elegant. He was never seen, in any of the various gentlemen's clubs and City livery halls that he frequented, without a tie pin, regulating a tie that signified his membership of some or other august London institution. Photos of Walter from around that time reveal his fondness for double-breasted suits, of which he had a pre-war stock large enough to see him through the 1941 injunction against double-breasting, a rationing measure that persisted for several years after the war. He wore only double-cuff shirts, and either round-rimmed spectacles or an Edwardian pince-nez. He and his wife Cissie – a plainish woman with glasses that matched her husband's – had a house under construction in the country and a pad in town.

Walter breathed golf: the trench shelters, allotments and anti-invasion obstacles that cluttered and scarred the nation's fairways were almost as galling to him as the privations inflicted by rationing on his gourmand's palate. He had three children: two sons (one of whom was an amateur racing driver), and a daughter whom he had educated at a Swiss finishing school, and had repaid him by marrying a King's Counsellor. He loved fine wines and holidays in the South of France. He had a private income, plus a large stake in a shirt-making concern, which had workrooms scattered across the city as well as the Jermyn Street showroom. The firm's headed paper lists its other directors: a duke, a pair of lords, a major, and Walter's brother, who saw to most of the management so that Walter needed only occasionally to drop in on his way between West End clubs. Relatives who still remember him describe an affable, mildly dilettantish gentleman of the old school. He occupied a niche in the class spectrum somewhere around the fluid boundary between the upper-middle and the truly upper class-es – a distinction invisible to almost everyone in the country except those at the very top, who would perhaps have divined in Walter's bought furniture, as well as in his friendship with Henry, something just a little *de trop*.

What did Walter Sherman – as English as Ascot and the Henley regatta, both of which he attended religiously – and my grandfather – a former (but only just) barrow boy with few gentile and no genteel acquaintances – see in each other? In part, when Henry looked at Walter's style, his poise, his discreetly advertised Society connections, he saw the incarnation of something that he had always obscurely wanted. The lavish patriotism of the Jews' Free School, he now saw, was a pastiche of Englishness; this was the real thing, effortless and at the same time governed by countless exacting if invisible regulations. Maybe as importantly, Walter gave Henry permission to admit his weaknesses and uncertainties – relieved him of the loneliness of being the boss, as Henry had always been in successive homes and in his business. Walter was almost exactly the same age as Fishel Freedman would have been had he not worked himself into an early grave, bequeathing the responsibilities of fatherhood to his nine-year-old son. When they met, being the *paterfamilias* had become more exacting for Henry than it had been since his siblings had moved out of New Castle Street. Evacuation and the call-up separated his sisters from their husbands; billets proved inhospitable; and Henry was supposed to fix it. 'I just hate to write this letter,' his youngest sister Babs nevertheless wrote to him at her lowest point, in the middle of the war, with her husband away and her two small children poorly and the money running out; 'but I feel as though I must tell you how I feel . . . Sometimes I really wonder whether I have an eldest brother named Henry, who had professed, and rightly, to have been a father to me.' Then she touches him where it hurt most: 'I am afraid you have sadly neglected your duty and the duty you owe to our dear mother . . . I know your argument against this, surely I should realise how ill you are, under what strain and hardship and worry you are living – true, Henry, all true, but all I ask is that you should get in touch with me from time to time. Being the youngest I feel as though you owe me at least this bit of fatherly thought.' Yes, she had three other siblings to call on, but '*you* are my eldest brother, my real companion and confessor of our happy days gone by'. (Her husband Morris weighed in from North Africa: 'Even if you can't find time to write to me, I did at least expect you would keep in touch with Babs, still I suppose that is the way big business men go.' Then he summarises his own situation: 'Plenty of fruit, sunbathing in the Mediterranean, yes, life could indeed be worse! I think I am doing a useful job of work, but my Colonel is not interested in any new designs for underwear!')

In Walter, Henry saw a chance for a little overdue fathering of his own. What did Walter Sherman see in my grandfather? First, perhaps, a younger man who, despite his post-accident infirmity, had the élan and alacrity that were seeping out of Walter's own life. Then, maybe, he saw an exotic. Walter had no more met anyone like Henry than Henry had met anyone like Walter. When Walter was growing up, in the last Victorian decade, to families like the Shermans the East End was a locale of serial killers, white slavery and foreign anarchists, to be visited only on the day excursions then organised for respectable Britons to gawk at the depravity of their compatriots. Here was the East End in the flesh. In this exotic, Walter saw a project, at once a sort of social experiment and a grand charitable gesture: to make Henry over as a West End patrician. If he pulled it off, perhaps his protégé would achieve the honours and distinctions that Walter had always vaguely assumed would one day come his own way, but had somehow failed to materialise.

Loneliness; curiosity; ambition; ambition thwarted: this was the chemistry of what very quickly became a beautiful friendship, and evolved into Henry's third great love, after his mother Millie and my grandmother Miriam. It was a friendship that

ECCENTRIC CLUB,
RYDER STREET,
ST JAMES'S, S.W. I.

defined the second half of Henry's war, and transformed the second half of my grandparents' lives.

In 1942 conversation between British strangers on buses and trains, and in the restaurants of provincial hotels – if only comprising the exchange of bomb stories – flowed with unwonted spontaneity. Along with a licence to extroversion, the war gave Henry and Walter their first and most enduring topic of conversation: food. Boarding school had left Walter with the same keen appetite that a boyhood spent pilfering his neighbours' cat food had inculcated in my grandfather. To begin with Walter's tastes may have been more refined; but, as rationing tightened, quantity became a more pressing concern than quality. He and his wife Cissie spent much of the war circulating between the grander English holiday resorts not embargoed by invasion scares (the Côte d'Azur being altogether inaccessible). They favoured the Cavendish in Eastbourne, which, with its views of the pier and grandstand, was then much smarter than it is today, and remote spots in Cornwall. If guests stayed for no more than three nights, they didn't have to surrender their ration cards, which meant they could still claim their rations and either store them up or eat them between hotel meals.

My grandfather introduced Walter to a new universe of illicit food. You could find anything in London if you knew whom to ask and where to look, and Henry did. There was an invaluable barber in Commercial Road from whom whisky, fruit, chocolate, razor blades, toys, lipstick, teats for bottle-feeding and other impossible luxuries could be obtained by tactful and trusted customers. The Lane was an entrepôt for black-market pilchards, smoked salmon and chickens ('for breeding'), which changed hands under-the-counter and round-the-back, with few questions asked and fewer ration coupons asked for. Supplies were reliable even when the shelves of the Harpenden butchers – Dunkley's, Baxter's and the Empire Meat Company – were as bare as the queues outside them were long, and when model bananas were hanging in the grocers' windows in place of real ones.

Henry's connections in this world were as valuable to Walter as, to Henry, were the entrées Walter would provide in Society and the City. Walter's gratitude for my grandfather's little favours is a leitmotif of their early correspondence. 'My dear Henry', Walter wrote from a hotel in Dorking, Surrey, not long after they met in Torquay, 'many thanks indeed for your parcel – contents just what I fancied.' 'Thanks for Salmon, it was delicious,' he wrote from the Cavendish in Eastbourne, when such delicacies had become virtually unobtainable. 'We are enjoying wonderful weather & either have a sun bath on our balcony or walk to Beachy Head or the shops (Cissie).' 'The food question is difficult,' he complained from Dorset; 'only basic rations for everyone. Can you find me a tin of tongue or something similar?' Henry also helped Walter out with what in their correspondence they refer to, not very euphemistically, as 'juice'. It may have been the sort that had been poured through a gas-mask filter, which, as someone somewhere had profitably discovered, removed the dye used to identify fuel designated for commercial use. Henry himself had wangled a businessman's petrol allowance, and he motored between Wheathampstead and London on roads emptied by fuel rationing, sometimes ferrying textile supplies between the Lane and the new Harpenden factory.

In return, Walter introduced Henry to the Hungaria restaurant in the Haymarket, Quaglino's in Bury Street and the dining rooms of the grander West End hotels. The five-shilling maximum prices imposed by the government – to fend off allegations that the rich were living it up while the poor went hungry – had made even the fanciest restaurants affordable. Some tried to keep the riff-raff out with inflated cover charges and bogus dancing supplements, but even these could not deter the Americans who flooded into London after Pearl Harbor, over-running the West End with the girls they picked up at Rainbow Corner and the other GI bars around Piccadilly Circus. (One of the Americans, a Jewish airman, became a regular weekend guest in Harpenden.) Tables and desserts seemed always to be available for Walter, however thronged the restaurant or curtailed the official menu.

Walter also thrilled my grandfather by inviting him to his clubs. Like all self-respecting London clubmen, Walter patronised several different members-only establishments in Mayfair and St James's. A clubman's various affiliations were designed to express the several aspects of his personality. In Walter's case his slightly raffish bent was manifest in his membership of the Eccentric Club in Ryder Street, which was associated with the worlds of sport and entertainment. The Eccentric had a grand dining room, and a bar known as the 'Owl's Roost' in which the clocks went eccentrically backwards. He was also well known at the Albany Club in Savile Row, and the Royal Automobile Club (RAC) in Pall Mall, with its Louis Quatorze façade, art deco bar, ornate library and famous Turkish baths, which were also utilised during the war by Generals de Gaulle and Sikorski, heroes respectively of the Free French and Poles. Walter always maintained that the ultra-exclusive clubs – Brook's, Boodle's, the Carlton – were unconscionably stuffy.

When he introduced Henry to clubland, in the summer of 1942, it was in poor shape. Half the waiters and doormen had been called up, and replaced by a rash of unsuitable foreigners. The grand frontages on Pall Mall and St James's Street were blacked-out in the evenings, and the wood-panelled interiors were sepulchral and dusty. The finer portraits had been stored in bomb-proof vaults or evacuated to the countryside. The chefs had been reduced to procuring their supplies from the same illicit, pre-dawn deliveries to Covent Garden (fruit) and Smithfields (meat) as the wide boys from the Lane. The Eccentric had been damaged by blast; the RAC was to be hit in February 1944.

Still, even in this diminished state, clubland was a revelation to Henry. The antique furniture; the unforced sociability; the injunction against talking shop; the IOUs unquestioningly accepted around the bridge and *chemin de fer* tables; the favourite waiters, and the favourite chairs in which members dozed and occasionally died; the impervious serenity, disturbed only by the rare drama of a blackballing: in its discretion and permanence, all this seemed to Henry to be the antithesis and antidote of his early life. Today, these clubs make the news only when a debate erupts over whether women should be admitted to some second dining room or upstairs bar. But in 1942 they were the respite and watering holes of great men, places known by name to thousands who would never be able actually to visit them. Like much that passes as quintessentially British, they are in fact of mongrel descent: White's, the oldest and the grandest club of all, is thought to have taken its name from its Italian émigré founder, Francesco Bianco. But, to Henry, to recline in the hard leather armchairs as if he belonged in them was an ecstasy of Englishness.

There was an awkward moment on his first visit to the RAC, at the end of August 1942, when, having ordered tea in the library, Henry was confronted with some bafflingly unfamiliar straining equipment. His parents had drunk their tea black, with the leaves dancing at the bottom of the glass and a piece of sugar clenched between their teeth (which meant one lump could serve for several cups). Walter saw his friend's discomfort, and without breaking off from his discourse on the tragic death of the Duke of Kent, leant over and poured. Late that evening, as he walked back to his car, ignoring the solicitations of the Piccadilly Commandos stationed in the doorways of the boarded-up shops, importuning potential tricks by flashing torches into their faces, my grandfather thought: look at me now. After Walter found 'seconders' for him at the Eccentric and the Albany, he went to both at least once a week, as the bills he never got around to throwing away record. To make up with his sister Babs, he took her to lunch at the Albany. They ordered asparagus in the panelled dining room, which came with finger bowls of water. Guessing, Babs dipped her asparagus in the water; Henry, having already learned that the proper way to respond to such a faux pas was to repeat it, did the same. ('I am sure you know that you have my love and respect,' Babs wrote to him, 'and even though at times it may have wavered, underneath it all it has always been there and always will.')

Henry loved the Honourable Society of the Knights of the Round Table even more than he came to cherish his clubs. One of the strange, semi-secret, slightly puerile associations that occupied and occupy well-connected London men with a distaste for modernity and a nostalgia for their public schools, it was formed in 1720 to cultivate the ancient virtue of chivalry and promote peace on earth. By the time Walter introduced Henry to the society in 1943, it mainly did so by entertaining ambassadors and other foreign dignitaries at white-tie banquets in West End hotels. During the war the banquets were less lavish than they had been before and would be later; the foreign dignitaries, on the other hand, were available in abundance. In March 1943 King Peter of Yugoslavia attended a dinner, along with the Egyptian ambassador. This was the occasion on which Walter was formally admitted to the society, having previously attended as the guest of friends, and he invited Henry along to witness his quasi-Masonic investiture. Among the ceremonial officers there were a Knight Remembrancer; a Knight Sword-Bearer; a Keeper of the Munitions and Chattels; a King Arthur's Champion, who offered a toast to 'The Immortal Name and Fame of Arthur, King of Britain'; and a Portcullis Pursuivant of Arms. The Knight President, who was a viscount, said good evening to Henry when he arrived, and, as the table plan that Henry kept enumerates, the place was stuffed with lords, earls, generals and admirals. It was not long after the Bethnal Green Tube disaster, in which 173 people had been crushed to death on the steep station stairs during an air raid, and the word on the streets and on the buses and trams was that the East End Jews had been to blame. At the Honourable Society, no such prejudices seemed to Henry to rupture the courtly atmosphere. He watched and copied his neighbours' cutlery selection as each cardboard course was delivered, and tried to say nothing that would embarrass Walter, and to straighten out his vowels when he said anything at all.

He was converted for life, eventually receiving his own 'knighthood' in 1951. That evening in 1943, Henry drove back to Wheathampstead in the blackout, running over the evening's highlights in his mind: handshakes; *bon mots*; devout toasts to the royal family; Walter introducing him to genuine aristocrats as 'my very good friend Mr Henry Freedman'; the illusion of equality with impossibly accomplished men, who listened to his opinions and nodded as if they mattered. The next day, he received a telegram from Walter. It said, 'My knighthood justified by your presence among the guests.'

Leah Claret moved from the billet she shared with her son Paul and his family into a small flat, like a little doll's house, just off Harpenden High Street and above a discount store called The Cut. She had a tiny bedroom and a kitchen-cum-sitting room, dominated by a set of oak chairs that she had spotted in a clearing sale. She had also acquired a pair of Georgian silver candlesticks, which adorned the flat along with the chandelier from Boot Street and an incongruously grand four-poster bed. She rented the small shop that she had spotted just over the road, where she sold handbags that Paul brought up for her from a London wholesaler. She sometimes thought that she had seen Auguste Claret passing by the shop window, and would rush out to catch up with whichever bemused Englishman had activated her memories. Occasionally, when Henry was driving her and Miriam into London, she would make him pull in abruptly so that she could scrutinise a pedestrian with a familiar build or a suit cut similarly to her supposedly dead lover's. Leah's last husband Mr Levine, whom she married, this time officially, just before the war, drifted out of her life. Remembered chiefly by Leah's grandchildren for his prodigious nose-blowing, Mr Levine died alone in Stepney, and Henry had to track down the details of his death (and his will) via a bank, a lawyer and the Mile End Hospital.

In April 1943 my grandparents also moved, from the rented house in Wheathampstead to one Henry had bought not far away in Milton Road, Harpenden. The road was known locally as 'Millionaire's Row', and the house was a substantial Edwardian affair, with a large garden, six bedrooms and a conservatory, in which, after the war, Henry installed several tanks of tropical fish, an aviary containing budgerigars and canaries, and two African Grey parrots, one of which had lived in a pub and would ambush visitors with shrieks of 'rotten old sod'. Henry and Miriam accumulated pets as if an ever-larger and more colourful menagerie could somehow compensate for the drabness of their own childhoods. Henry bought two horses from a local dealer: a white mare named Silver for himself, and a chestnut brown cob named Rufus for Miriam. 'Dear Mr Friedman [*sic*],' wrote the horse dealer, 'I sincerely hope Mrs Friedman gets on well with "Rufus" . . . If he does not suit your wife, I will willingly exchange him for another . . . I will see to a saddle as soon as possible.' Rufus had a funny gait, and Miriam kept falling off, usually painlessly and by sliding down his neck, which made her laugh too much to be scared. Henry soon began to ride to hounds with the South Hertfordshire hunt, which was based on the edge of Harpenden. He extolled the virtues of hunting in a wartime letter to his brother-in-law Morris, who was soldiering in the Middle East. 'I had a full day's fox hunting last Wednesday,' Henry writes. 'After 6.5 hours strenuous riding, I am glad to say I was not in the least stiff. I now ride every morning at 7.30am. Believe me it is grand.' It may have been Morris, or it may have been Sid or Mick – nobody can now remember – who first referred to Henry, perhaps not altogether respectfully, as the 'Earl of Hertfordshire'.

Miriam kept chickens in the Harpenden garden, which also contained a small but (in wartime) precious orchard: the tomatoes and plums she bottled, the runner beans she salted in big crocks to keep them fresh for the winter, her jams, and the eggs she preserved in isinglass kept the family fed as much as did Henry's London connections. The garden abutted the

Harpenden Bowling Club, and, by a quirk of land tenure, the members had to cross my grandparents' property to get to their clubhouse. When he and Miriam first moved in, to help keep him on side, the club's captain invited Henry to join. Then it came out that he was Jewish, and several of the members made their feelings known. The honorary secretary wrote to Henry on 20 April 1943 to put him off. 'Your name has been sent in to me by the captain as a prospective member of the club,' he begins. 'I enclose a copy of the rules, in which you will see by Rule 3, the club requires nomination by two members and for the moment, no seconder has emerged' – a technicality used in clubs and societies up and down the land to keep out Jews and other undesirable interlopers. 'When the matter has been completed I will post your name in the pavilion according to the rules and will notify you if your election goes through.' This is the special prejudice of the British middle classes: let them in if we must, these newcomers, and let them see the life that they can aspire to, if only they take off the skull cap or shave off the beard and wait a few generations. ('There is not a great deal of anti-Semitism in England *on the surface*,' Henry wrote in his letter about Mosley to America.) This enticingly, infuriatingly half-open door is also Britain's special favour to its immigrants. More than the blackshirts' goose-stepping and skull-cracking, such backhanded condescension was my grandfather's spur. If a man told him to go back to Poland, Henry knew he was a fool. But the idea that he might be not *quite* a proper Englishman because of where his parents were born, or because he sometimes prayed in a synagogue rather than a church, enraged him. He never was elected to the bowling club, but he never made a fuss. Britain in 1943 was not a place for Jews to make fusses in. But, in his own way, Henry had his revenge.

In June 1943, when Walter and Cissie first came to stay for the weekend, the house in Milton Road did not yet boast the ornate rockeries that Henry would later have installed by a landscape gardener. The back garden was cluttered by the chicken run, and the whine of the air-raid siren mounted on the water tower that overlooked the road interrupted the neighbourhood's sleep. The dining room was not yet decorated with the unusual stippling – a bronze overlay squidged onto a yellow base – that would impress subsequent guests. Nor had Henry and Miriam yet fully compassed all the niceties and etiquettes of house parties and upmarket entertaining: when to talk to your guests, and when to leave them to read *The Times* in peace; what the proper drinks were to serve before dinner (cocktails) and after it (whisky, brandy and liqueurs; ladies to retire while the gentlemen drink, even if there are only two of them); the proper place of children and the protocol of tea-pouring (always the hostess, and never the milk first). But they had found a high-church Anglican service for their guests to attend on Sunday morning, and Henry had asked Leah not to make any surprise appearances. Walter brought Henry a bottle of port from his cellar, unprocurable in 1943. Henry and Miriam sang duets after dinner, which comprised a chicken from the garden and a cake home-made from suspiciously appetising ingredients. My grandmother was mystified by Cissie's frequent changes of clothes, and her failure to offer any help with the cooking or the clearing up: to Cissie, offering would have been bad form. After church on Sunday, the four of them sat in the garden, the sun came out, and they chatted as if there were no war, and as if entertaining house guests and weekending with upwardly mobile Jews were the most natural things in the world. Walter remarked on the hydrangeas, and looking at him sitting in the garden, with his trousers pressed and his cup and saucer consummately balanced, Henry was even more smitten than he had been before: with Walter, and the idea of Walter, and the idea of himself that Walter allowed him to believe in.

How, a handful of years after he left the markets, did my grandfather afford the house, the horses, the car and the hospitality? Not to mention the various lesser appurtenances of breeding and taste that he soon acquired. There were hand-made shoes from Henry Maxwell, 'Makers of Boots, Spurs, Whips and Leather Goods' in Dover Street, suits from Savile Row, and hats from Lock's in St James's Street: all unostentatious but, as his new West End confrères would silently appreciate, all decidedly expensive. Later there were accounts with an exclusive turf bookmaker and a City wine merchant.

Part of the answer is that he couldn't really afford them. Just as, when he had almost nothing, Henry had spent it on going to the pictures or on taking my grandmother to a tea dance, when he had a little more he blew it just as improvidently. For my grandfather, excess funds had only two uses: to enjoy, and to be given away to charity or to impoverished distant relatives. He generally spent more than he had, on the assumption that naturally he, Henry Freedman, would somehow be able to make up the difference, if only he applied himself. Sometimes he did. But he never earned as much as his lifestyle suggested, or as was assumed by the post-war friends who accepted his reflexive generosity. Henry had a rich life, but he was never a truly wealthy man.

On the other hand, neither was he ever again a poor one. Wars are always the making of someone, and after it broke and nearly killed him at Marble Arch, the Second World War helped to make my grandfather.

At the beginning, as many of his countrywomen put on their uniforms, and most of the rest decided that it would be improper to dress too gaudily in the circumstances, underwear became a popular secret extravagance, a totem of embattled femininity. 'In lingerie at least,' advised the *Queen* magazine, a posh style bible, 'you can indulge your longing for silks and satins and lovely unpractical colours, all the shamelessly frivolous things that are now sternly forbidden in your other clothes. For those lucky ones who can and *do* go to bed at night there are gloriously foolish nighties; for the day time slinky silken things.' After June 1941, when clothes rationing came in, the life of the lingerie manufacturer became much tougher. As the Board of Trade's inaugural 'Clothing Coupons Quiz' sets out, every British adult had sixty-six coupons to spend on clothes each year (a number that was eventually trimmed to thirty-six). Two coupons had to be surrendered for an ordinary pair of knickers, three for a pair of passion-killing DKs. Not surprisingly, sales of clothing plummeted. Production was disrupted by conscription, and as machinists were drafted into the munitions factories. Fabric was even harder to come by than labour, and elastic almost impossible after the Japanese overran the South-east Asian rubber industry. Strict quotas for cloth consumption were imposed on all manufacturers. In 1942 the utility scheme was introduced, under which, to save materials, the government dictated the design, prices and profit margins of most garments. For underwear, the severe regulations insisted that there were to be no frills or embroidery or any unnecessary elaborations whatever: less controversial rules than the banning of turn-ups on men's trousers, but keenly felt nonetheless. Utility fabric was distributed only to selected manufacturers; the non-utility stuff vanished.

Worse still, on the night of 28 December 1942, an accidental fire had gutted Henry's workshop on the corner of the Lane, which had by then expanded to occupy three floors. According to the London Fire Brigade logs, now stored in the London Metropolitan Archive, the damage was concentrated on the first floor, which housed Henry's stockroom. The other levels were affected by smoke and water, and by the firemen who smashed windows and broke down doors to get at the flames. Lefkowitch, Bloom and Cohen, the tailors on the top floor, got off lightly, as did Goldwater and Halpern, the second-hand clothes dealers who occupied the ground floor and basement. But my grandfather's stockroom was ruined. His machine section on the second floor was reparable, and so was the packing room on the third, stacked floor-to-ceiling with boxes of finished goods. But, as his correspondence with the insurance company spells out, his stocks of locknit, crêpe, satin, winceyette, lace and striped flannelette were incinerated. The ginger workshop cat – who defended the premises from the rat population that flourished in the London rubble – suffocated in the filing cabinet that he slept in. When Henry arrived the following morning, he thought that he had been ruined by one of the lightning raids that the Germans were conducting over the city, their planes darting in and out to remind Londoners that they were still out there, even if the full-scale Blitz had ended in May 1941. He had to send the machinists, pressers and packers home, and drove back to Harpenden, found Miriam feeding the chickens, and told her that they were finished.

He wasn't finished, because shortly after the fire he made an acquaintance almost as lucky as running into Daisy Ritherford in Clapton. At a meeting of a trade association for clothing manufacturers, which in vain deplored the government's bank-rupting strictures during and after the war, Henry met a sharp woman named Nan Jones. Nan Jones worked for a man named Alfred Soob. Mr Soob had an allocation of utility cloth from the Board of Trade. But he had lost half his staff to the call-up, and of his two factories, the one in Golden Lane, Shoreditch, had been bombed, while the other, in Enfield, had been requisitioned by the Ministry of Aircraft Production. Henry's machinery had mostly survived the fire, and his workforce had been reinforced by eleventh-hour Jewish refugees from the Continent. He and Mr Soob came to an understanding; Nan Jones came to work for my grandfather.

In the end, for all the bureaucratic hurdles and material hardships, it was possible to make a good living honestly during the war. But you could do even better if you interpreted the rules creatively. The ruses available to clothing manufacturers were manifold and enticing. They could produce more than their prescribed quota of skirts or trousers or underwear, and pass on the excess to be sold, coupon-free, in street markets or out of suitcases on Oxford Street or by unofficial sales reps in the canteens of factories. They could produce less than they were supposed to and sell on the remaining fabric. Or they could use some of it to make up illegally attractive merchandise, with the odd frill on a pair of knickers or pleat on a pair of trousers, for which many drab, hungry Londoners would cheerfully pay over the odds. Allocations of cloth could be transferred; coupons could be sold or 'lost'.

To be an underwear manufacturer was to face particular temptations. There was a stocking famine: women were painting seams up the backs of their legs using eyebrow pencil, sometimes also daubing them with gravy to disguise their nakedness. Such was the popular craving for silk that, seeing a parachute mine descending silently and lethally in the middle distance, women would hurry towards the point of impact in the hope of picking up a few silk scraps for home-made 'pretties'. Anyone with a contract to make silk parachutes for

the government would also find themselves in possession of leftover silk 'cabbage', and thus of a moral dilemma.

It was said by some among his acquaintances that my grandfather, like many others, succumbed to these temptations. In June 1943 he wrote bitterly to the master of the Hercules Lodge, after some of his Masonic brethren had teased him about his alleged wide practices and high-rolling lifestyle, with an admixture of racial calumnies. 'My business is carried out with a policy of strict principles,' he protests in fury, 'not only in the letter of the law, but in the spirit, and in strict conformity to every moral obligation.' What's more, 'I am glad to say that 99% of my dealings are with non-Jews, by whom my business methods and my personal self are held in high esteem. Ostentation is one of the characteristics which have always appalled me, but it seems that my actions have been badly construed and misrepresented as to make me the butt of a certain section of the Lodge.' After this contretemps he joined the Trades Advisory Council, an anodyne-sounding organisation set up to arbitrate in disputes involving Jewish businessmen, and in general to defend the community against charges of racketeering.

I don't believe that my grandfather did anything truly shameful to make his money. Along the moral spectrum of wartime, between ascetic self-abnegation and outright criminal opportunism, like most people in Britain he placed himself somewhere in the middle. As the war wore on, and came to seem unloseable but at the same time interminable, everybody, more or less, reconciled their consciences to a little innocuous black-marketeering, if only in the form of an extra, under-the-counter slither of butter or special-occasion string of sausages. Any peccadilloes of Henry's would have been a long way from the big-time rackets and organised larceny that actually undermined the war effort. But it is possible that he did some things in his efforts to get ahead of which he was not always proud.

When, after Walter's weekend in Harpenden, he and Henry graduated from the friendly little notes and telegrams of their early acquaintance, they began to write to each other compulsively, sometimes at length, sometimes on scraps of paper dispatched at opportune moments during the working day, or left in discreet envelopes with the concierges of their mutual haunts. Walter favoured headed paper from the Royal Automobile Club. He wrote in a graceful, aristocratic hand, of a kind that was inculcated in prep schools during the Victorian era, but is now virtually extinct: long elegant double stems on p and h; billowing, calligraphic Ds and Bs; lavish curlicues on fs. Perhaps because, with his ordinary, unadorned handwriting, Henry felt intimidated, or perhaps because he preferred dictating to his slim, bespectacled secretary Pat, my grandfather's letters were often typed on carbon paper, which is why copies of many of them, especially those from the last years of their friendship, were left alongside Walter's in the boxes of correspondence that Henry amassed. Before long, their letters begin to reflect a longing to be together that is reminiscent of Henry's letters to Miriam a decade earlier. Sometimes there are echoes of those earlier exchanges in the rhetoric and phrasing: the same impatience, the same frustration that Henry's words would not quite compass his feelings. To our more knowing age, this correspondence sometimes reads almost like a chronicle of infidelity, and, in a way, it is one. Not in a literal sense, and it wasn't exactly a betrayal of my grandmother. But in these letters there is a creeping repudiation, through his fondness for Walter, of Henry's past.

In the hungry summer of 1943, and the dismal winter that followed, with its freezing fogs and whisky drought that even Henry could not relieve, the ostensible subject of their letters was the grim slog of the middle years of the war. A secondary concern, on Walter's side, is Henry's health. 'My Dear Henry,' Walter wrote on RAC headed paper on 6 July 1943, 'I thoroughly enjoyed your welcome & amusing letter. Delighted to hear that you are both having the rest you deserve.' Henry and Miriam were staying at Ruthin Castle in north Wales, now a country hotel, then a sanatorium to which Henry intermittently returned for therapies of varying credibility for a decade after his road accident, sometimes taking my grandmother along to keep him company. 'I'm afraid the arrangements as you describe them are not ideal & the food perhaps not up to your standard, but you are together and having a holiday which is everything. I've just been talking to a friend who returned from Llandudno last Friday. He found the place terribly crowded & the Welch [*sic*] people only out after money & not the convenience or happiness of their visitors. Of course this week being Wake week things cannot have improved but I know you will make the best of it & enjoy thoroughly the good weather you are having . . . Looking forward to seeing you. Cissie joins me in love to you both. Your friend, Walter.'

Soon after Henry returned from Wales, Walter retreated to Dorset. 'I'm thinking of you and wish I were in Town today,' he wrote. 'This is a really lovely place & quite unspoiled,' though 'there is practically nothing to buy except cigarettes and tobacco.' Like all visitors to wartime hotels, to save on the fuel that heated the water he and Cissie were only permitted to fill their baths up to a shallow line that had been stencilled, at regulation height, in every commercial tub in the land. Walter ends with a straightforward affection that was perhaps even more unusual among grown men then than it would be today: 'Henry, I miss you very much & shall want to see a lot of you when I return. Hope everything is going well in business & that health, happiness & prosperity will stay with you for another 60 years. I'm trying to write on my knee with three people jawing! With Love, Walter.' In September he sent my grandfather a postcard with a view of the West Bay at Bridport: 'Been constantly thinking of you during a quiet week,' Walter scribbled, '& hope you have not been overworked. Will expect to see you on Wednesday.' At the end of the year, Walter was confined by flu to his bed in a hotel in Dorking. 'My Dear Henry,' he wrote, 'My Doctor was very angry with me last week for coming to town & today tells me I must not leave my room for some days. Please do not trouble to come down. It can do no good & I know you have quite enough on hand to occupy all your time . . . Doctor has been all over me 3 times & tells me there is nothing wrong with me organically, in fact I am A1 . . . He's got me all right now & being a Scotchman will hang on to me until I'm fit. Love to Miriam. Yours, Walter.'

At the beginning of 1944 the Luftwaffe returned to London, dispelling the tedium of war with a fresh bout of acute terror. On the night of 23 February, as the fire brigade's logs attest, the London Library in St James's Square was hit, losing most of its theology section. King Street, Ryder Street, Bury Street, Duke of York Street, Appletree Yard and Mason's Yard were all wrecked. The offices of the American Red Cross in Jermyn Street were crushed. Down the road, Walter's shop was damaged by the blast and the smoke, and came out even worse than it had done in 1941.

People took this 'Little Blitz' badly. They were sleepless and cranky and resentful, and the reinforced anti-aircraft guns were unbearable. But when, on 7 March, Walter wrote to Henry, then back at Ruthin in Wales, his manners and his poise were unruffled: 'I'm so pleased you are having such a complete rest & hope you will come back full of beans . . . Of course I miss you very much & today although Murray's [a fashionable West End cabaret club] was fairly full to me it was particularly empty.' Only at the end of his letter does Walter allude to the inconvenience of being bombed: 'We are getting a bit straight but it is very heart-breaking after nearly 50 years with the old firm.' Then he stiffens his upper lip: 'I'm trying to pull my weight, and one day let's hope in the near future everything will be normal.' (During this Little Blitz, Babs wrote from a nursing home in Harrow, where she had just had her third child, to thank Henry for the duck and the tongue he had sent up. 'We have to trot down to the Morrison shelter here when we get the raids,' she tells him, 'the babies sleep in them all night – what a life.' Could he possibly rustle up a little more tongue, and perhaps a baby's bath? And why not come to see her? 'Bring your horse.')

In April 1944 Henry took Walter home again. Not to Harpenden this time, but to see *The King of Lampedusa* at the Grand Palais theatre on Commercial Road.

By 1944 the Jewish East End was disintegrating. Everywhere tarpaulins were stretched across shattered houses, many of whose former inhabitants would never return. Inside the ironically named Grand Palais, it was still another world. The chatter in the stalls, which subsided only slightly when the curtain went up, the heckling, and the dialogue and songs on the stage were all in Yiddish. Walter later confided that he had felt much as he had done when he went as a schoolboy to see

Aristophanes performed in the original Greek in an Oxbridge college garden, and being a poor classicist had dutifully chuckled along whenever the scholars around him laughed at the ancient jokes.

*The King of Lampedusa* recounted the real-life exploits of an RAF pilot – in his former life a tailor's cutter from Hackney – who had run out of fuel over the Mediterranean and crash-landed on the islet of Lampedusa, whereupon the resident Italian garrison had surrendered to him en masse. Like most Yiddish dramas, it offered a *zing*, a *lach* and a *trer*: a song, a laugh and a tear. In the invented part of the action, the snobbish north London parents of the pilot's fiancée, the AllRightniks, decide that he might just be good enough for their daughter after all. Poignant and pantomimic by turns, it had at first been poorly received by the regular Jewish theatregoers. Then the author, a journalist, prevailed upon the *Daily Express* to review it, which it did, enthusiastically. Thinking, as the last surviving member of the play's cast puts it, that 'if the *goyim* [gentiles] say it's good, it must be good', London's Jews flocked to see it, along with some curious but uncomprehending *Express*-reading gentiles. Its celebrity earned the play a mention in one of Lord Haw-Haw's broadcasts from Berlin: the Jews of the East End, Haw-Haw avowed, would not be laughing for long. It was the longest-running of any of London's Yiddish hits, a miniature Jewish *Mousetrap*, which played for seven months with ten shows a week, before touring to Leeds, Manchester, Glasgow and Dublin. It was also the last. The Yiddish theatre struggled after the war; the virtuoso who had played the lead, his glory fading, criss-crossed Whitechapel, selling theatre tickets to the businessmen who came in from the suburbs to work in the East End during the day, introducing himself as the King of Lampedusa. By taking Walter, conspicuous in his three-piece and pince-nez, to see it, and allowing Walter to see him backslapping and *shmoozing* with his old associates, Henry was letting his friend in on a secret.

*The King of Lampedusa*'s reign ended when the Grand Palais, like most of London's other theatres, closed after the V1s – the 'doodlebugs' – began to strike the city in June 1944. Rumours that the Nazis were 'up to something' had been circulating since the previous autumn. Just after D-Day, the something turned out to be a flying bomb. 'Thanks for wire which put my mind at rest,' Walter wrote from Cornwall on 16 July 1944, 'and I'm anxious to hear from you. My thoughts are continually with you, and the very peaceful life I'm enjoying gives one plenty of time for reflexion and meditation.' In particular, 'I'm terribly worried about the "doodle bug". The very fact of evacuation of thousands from the southern areas certainly shows that the authorities consider it from a serious aspect. I'm not ashamed to confess I've really got the wind up & having to comfort Cissie who is far more nervy than usual does not help matters. However, we all live from day to day.'

At first, the Germans struggled to find their range, and some of the V1s overshot London, landing in the northern suburbs and the green belt. Londoners soon learned that, if they saw the ghastly flares and heard the rattle of the motor overhead, sounding like a stick being drawn across iron railings, they were going to be OK. Whenever Henry saw or heard one, he willed it to keep going long enough to miss Harpenden and Miriam as well. That was one of the doodlebug's especial torments: the self-loathing that it left in its wake, as those beneath its flight path involuntarily prayed for it to wipe out somebody else. Then there was the feeling of defencelessness, because the hitherto unpopular anti-aircraft guns had been withdrawn to the coast to shoot down the bombs offshore. The fact that they were pilotless – 'impersonal as the plague', as Evelyn Waugh put it – somehow seemed to preclude even the possibility of mercy, even if that quality had been in short supply during the manned bombings, and the occasional strafing of civilians that had accompanied them. There was the horror of dying at the war's end, or very nearly, and for nothing. More prosaically, there was the disruption of the constant bomb warnings. If his staff went down to the shelters for every single one, Henry quickly discovered, they would get no work done at all. So, like other businesses, he posted watchers on the roof of his building in the Lane to raise the alarm when a doodlebug did seem to be homing in on Spitalfields. People took to carrying whistles, in case they found themselves entombed in the mountains of rubble that the new weapons created, to help them let the heavy-rescue men know that there was someone alive inside.

The good news was that as the Allied troops flooded into France after D-Day, and weary civilians decamped again to the countryside, there was more food to be found in the London shops. All the same, better to be out of town if you could be. 'I intend to stay here another two weeks,' Walter's letter from Cornwall continues; 'nothing much to do except long walks & an occasional game of golf.' The West Country courses were not as disrupted as the south-eastern ones, which were still cluttered with obstacles in case of an airborne counter-invasion by the Germans, with the edges of the fairways patchworked by allotments. 'It is only a tiny place,' Walter explains, 'but the lady running it has a farm across the road so we have fresh butter, plenty of eggs & poultry and wonderful puddings etc. You are a great sport to share your home [Babs had moved in for an extended stay with her three children], but I know that you put your visitors right on top & house, garden & furniture a poor second.' At the end of the month, July 1944, one of Henry's conscripted employees, now advancing through France, wrote back to London encouragingly: 'Those days were happy days,' he says of his time in the cutting room, 'and I don't think that we shall have to wait much longer now before we will all be back at home once and for all, as the boys out here are doing a fine job of work. We shall soon be delivering the goods on Hitler's doorstep before the milkman arrives one of these mornings, and catch old Hitler with his pants down.' France wasn't too bad, he wrote, but 'give me good old London any time'. Like all correspondence to and from the forces, the envelope was stamped 'Passed by censor'.

Then the V2s began to arrive, supersonic rockets that obliterated whole streets without warning. They threw up flashes and fireworks and clouds of black smoke, and people wondered whether London could have 'taken it' if the Nazis had invented them five years earlier; a few people even referred to the 'good old doodlebugs'. On 10 November, at twenty past two in the afternoon, a V2 landed in Goulston Street, a little way down the Lane from Henry's workshop. Customers ran naked from the bath house that Henry had used as a boy; the old lady who collected the entrance money was blinded. The horses from the nearby tea warehouse lay dead in the street. In the evening it snowed, and flocks of starlings darted overhead, confused by the floodlights brought in by the rescue squads.

At the beginning of December, Henry took Miriam and the children to the Tregenna Castle Hotel, on a cliff overlooking the bay at St Ives. On 11 December, the day the Home Guard finally stood down, and a week before the nocturnal lights went on in Piccadilly for the first time in five years – the blackout was to little purpose against a blind and supersonic weapon – Walter wrote to his absent friend from the RAC. 'My Dear Henry,' he begins, 'So delighted to hear that you both are happy, well, & enjoying yourselves at "The Castle". I remember it as a delightful place in the summer & under any conditions a place for a restful holiday . . . I hope you find the Cornwall horses to your liking & are enjoying on horseback the very beautiful country at St Ives & district. The weather here has been awful & you are well away from the rain & frost.' It was the worst winter in living memory, and there was no booze to be had in London for love or money. 'Things generally continue to be difficult for me,' Walter concludes, 'but there is always the future. Love to you both.' Henry was back by Christmas, but he and Walter missed each other at the Eccentric on 30 December, so Walter left Henry a scribbled note with the doorman: 'So terribly sorry to miss you – I'm feeling bad & think it wise to go back to bed before I collapse. Been waiting for you since 1 o/c . . . I'll sit up until 12 o/c on New Year's Eve especially to remember you for all good wishes for '45. Yours Walter.'

There had been official days of mourning for the Jews of Europe in the East End, when the stalls and shops of the Lane had closed, and there had been questions asked and minutes of silence observed in the House of Commons. But it wasn't until the Allies liberated the concentration camps that Anglo-Jewry began fully to confront the slaughter of its relatives on the Continent. After she saw a newsreel about Belsen and Buchenwald at the Regent cinema in Harpenden, Leah hurried over to Milton Road to see her daughter. When she arrived at Miriam's she could only sit in the corner, put her head in her hands and cry. My grandfather and his brothers began long searches, via the various international refugee agencies that were hurriedly mobilising, for any traces of their families from Solotwina, Nadworna and Kalisz. The other preoccupation of the last few months of Henry's war was with his family at home.

Building up his business, and doing his bit to close the 'dollar gap' that was threatening to bankrupt the country, became, for my grandfather, a sort of substitute war. 'England has suffered very much in the past two wars,' Henry wrote to an acquaintance in America, 'and the tremendous losses of man-power, of wealth and time, are not so easily replaced by theorists and plans, but can only come by the struggle of the citizens of the state.' There was a craving for luxury, for palpable proof that it had all been worth it; but the workers who were needed to make the good things of life were still in uniform, and the lifting of wartime industrial controls proved even slower than demobilisation. The little fabric that was available for under-wear manufacture was earmarked for utility goods, or for export. Then, in March 1945, Henry's brother Sid and brother-in-law Solly left his company to set up on their own.

'Sid has felt an urge to become a Boss,' Henry wrote on 18 March 1945 to his other brother-in-law Morris, who was still encamped by the Red Sea. 'He owes me or the firm, nothing. He has displayed a strength of character which he feels is grand and mighty. He has become a man! He has gone. On a friendly basis, of course.' The reality was not quite so amicable. Sid and Solly had, with Mick, spent much of the war working in a munitions factory. Now with their own families to support, when they got out Solly and Sid wanted to be equal partners in the firm, rather than mere employees. But Henry had bossed the firm alone for the duration of the war, and had bossed his family for so long that it was the only way he knew. As they got older, and as Henry's grandiose ambitions faded, what he and his siblings had in common overcame their differences; even in 1945 they remembered Henry's childhood sacrifices too well to be truly estranged. But Sid and Solly saw a life as underlings stretching out before them, and instead set up their own busi-ness importing T-shirts, which had been popularised by the GIs. Henry was obliged to buy out their shares in the firm.

To him it seemed a mortal betrayal, a monstrous ingrati-tude. He thought and talked of himself and his four siblings as the five fingers of his mother Millie Freedman's hand: the wanton severance of any of them was sacrilege. 'No doubt the great urge [Sid] felt was real, was great, almost all-consuming,' he wrote to Morris. 'But how much greater would his strength of character have been if, despite the turmoil in his brain, despite the risk of losing his manliness, he had decided to

remain, and alleviate my burdens, assist the firm over what is just becoming a most difficult period, and then, after three or four years, part if he so desired. Solly! I pleaded with him to remain, which plea he chose to ignore' – though the business still bore his name. 'You know my pride in being head of my family,' Henry confides, 'how I have tried to carry each one's burden ... This has been a far greater shock than the loss of our dearly beloved Mother. That was inevitable. This was something I never expected.' Then he urges Morris to hurry home to Babs: 'You are the only person in her life, beside her children, and I doubt whether you are ever out of her thoughts even for one moment.' Finally, he offers some homespun philosophical counsel. 'Be simple and humble,' Henry advises. 'Make the most of what you've got. Every time.' Or almost finally: 'Let me thank you for the delightful Turkish Delight. I won't say no to another basinful.'

Morris replied diplomatically. 'The only feeling I have is one of pity,' he writes on 28 March 1945. 'I don't blame any of you, but it is a great shame to have split up a winning team.

However, each man must obey his own instincts. Who are we to say it is right or wrong?' Then he turns to the bigger picture: 'I am very gratified at the wonderful war news, is it possible that the end is at last really in sight? I have given up all predictions.' He and Henry differed over the so-called 'Jewish question', which had been accentuated by the ongoing, violent stand-offs between dispossessed Jews and the British sailors guarding the approaches to Palestine. My grandfather would admit no tension or contradiction between being a Jew and being an absolute Englishman; Morris wasn't so sure. 'Do you remember me telling you that we Jews will always be different?' he asks, 'that's one thing experience has taught me to be 100% correct.' Then he takes on Henry's philosophising: 'I do not agree with your interpretation of life . . . You advise a doctrine of Be Simple – be Humble, noble sentiments my friend, but are you?? I don't think so really.' Morris's own humble ambition is 'to return home and make up to Babs and the kids for our lost years'. He 'notes your observation re: the Turkish Delight, and have taken the necessary procedure to meet your request'. He ends with another gift – a little poem he had written on the subject closest to Henry's heart:

> As I do now – can you recall?
> Some vests and pants, our littered stall,
> Neighbours too, both left and right,
> Fruit and fish, your common sight.
> Who of us will e'er forget?
> The lady – who without regret,
> Toiled with you, in every clime,
> As now she rests in peace sublime.

Henry stewed. 'A moment of difference of opinion,' he wrote to his still-loyal brother Mick on V.E. Day, in May, 'and I was asked, with complete disregard as to the consequences to me, to divide the business, which has cost me so much, which I wanted for all, and to which I in despair agreed.' As he wrote in his little office at the factory in the Lane, with its bombsite view, his employees were out doing congas, hokey-cokeys and Lambeth Walks, accompanied by the pianos that had been dragged to the doors of the pubs, or whirling around the bonfires that were scorching the kerbs and roadways. 'Now Mick,' Henry exhorted, 'we have a wonderful future. We have young families. This has to be a better world for our children. Let us see what we can do.'

That evening, back in Harpenden, he and Miriam hung British, American, Russian and French flags from their windows. It had rained in the morning but it was a warm dry night. They danced to an open-air band on a local rugby pitch, and Henry tried to enjoy it. Children hung and burned effigies of Hitler, and GIs disappeared with ATS girls into the gorse on Harpenden Common. Everybody wore ridiculous paper hats. Harpenden Hall was floodlit, in modest imitation of the light show in Trafalgar Square. Chinese lanterns that had languished in attics since the Jubilee celebrations of 1935 were strung from the horse chestnuts on the village green. At the prisoner-of-war camp that had been erected up the road at Batford, the soldiers on guard fired flares into the night sky.

Walter, meanwhile, attended the service of Thanksgiving at St Paul's, then walked to the RAC, past the revellers in the fountains in Trafalgar Square, the torches blazing in celebration outside the Pall Mall clubs, the servicemen perched on scaffolds and secretaries who had somehow levitated to the tops of lampposts. In the summer of 1945, during Henry's family crisis, Walter was his greatest support. Walter knew only the energetic, generous, devoted Henry, not the sometimes impatient and authoritarian version. He saw only the focus that the childhood hardship had bequeathed, and not the scars and hardness. 'Forgive me for not writing before,' Walter wrote from Dorset in the summer of 1945, 'I've had such bad nights &

tired days & the weather has been so unkind that altogether I've been far from happy.' However: 'I'm coming back on Tuesday & should like to see you on Wednesday . . . I've been thinking a lot about you & your present difficulties & I'm convinced you will come through the black cloud into sunshine and that fairly soon.'

There was a general rush for the beaches in the first summer of peace, but Walter's consistent custom had earned him the loyalty of hoteliers along the south coast. In the evenings, dinner jackets were reappearing in the sorts of dining rooms that he and Cissie preferred, even if, incredibly, the food shortages were becoming more acute. 'You will pull through with flying colours,' Walter wrote to Henry from the Cliftonville Hotel in Margate later in the summer, '& the next months that mean so much to you will in a short time become a memory of something big achieved. It is very gratifying to know that our friendship has helped you even a little in, as you say, tempestuous times. Of course my thoughts are very often with you & it is my desire at any time to give you gratefully some practical help to lighten even if only by a few lbs the weight you are carrying. My belief in your great success & considerable position in the very near future cannot be shaken. You practically are already there – God bless you Henry.'

In the autumn of 1944, amid the flying bombs, my grandfather had begun to negotiate with the Board of Trade over the opening of a new factory in South Shields, a once-prosperous town at the mouth of the River Tyne. He later said that he had chosen the north-east for his biggest venture because of the poverty he had seen around the Tyneside docks, when he went north to peddle his wares during the Depression. The slump had wrecked the coal-mining, glass-making, shipbuilding and salt-mining industries on which South Shields had once depended. Men from the town had walked to London in 1936 with their neighbours from Jarrow in the most famous 'hunger march' of the thirties. Bringing the work to the workers, rather than vice versa, was one of Henry's guiding business principles. Naturally, the incentives offered by the government for setting up shop in one of the so-called 'development areas', and the cheapness of local labour, may also have influenced his decision. The government was supposed to put up the new plant, then lease it to Henry, with an option to buy it later.

Despite the quarrels and the shortages, in July 1945, between V.E. Day and the atomic bomb, my grandfather began to turn out knickers and nightdresses at 'Victory works', as he named his new South Shields factory. 'Production will start on Monday at Victory Factory – first of the new light industries scheduled for South Shields to get into operation,' reported the *Shields Gazette* on 12 July 1945 (the headline on the front page is 'Monty in Berlin as Western Allies take over'). The new factory, the paper goes on, 'will provide the nucleus of what promises to be a fairly extensive underwear industry in the town'. Later in the article, Henry Freedman relates how he 'came to Tyneside once during a severe trade depression and saw the lack of industries other than the heavier types and I felt it would be fairer to open a new factory here'. He explains that 'Our aim is to provide good class underwear of the dainty type, which the ordinary working woman can afford to buy.' The report notes that my grandfather 'emphasised that his firm is entirely British and employs only British labour'.

On 16 July 1945, in the presence of the town clerk of South Shields, with his brother Mick and Walter standing on one side of him, Miriam on the other and Leah glowering next to her, Henry declared the factory open – but not the state-of-the-art facility that the government had promised to build for him as a condition of his investment. The provisional factory was in a disused school in Cone Street. Henry's new employees, some of whom had emerged from the munitions factories or come home from the war, but most of whom had only just left school, entered through doors still marked 'Boys' and 'Girls'. The school had originally been built on a mountain of red ballast, disgorged by the generations of ships that had loaded up with coal at the staithes a few hundred feet upriver. At the back of the building was the mouth of the Tyne and a huge dry dock, and beyond that the North Sea. The shipbuilding industry was still active, and big tankers queued up in the river to be refurbished in the dock, though its employees seemed to be on strike as often as they were working. In the afternoon, columns of grimy miners walked past the factory with their billycans, on their way from the nearby mines to the town's back-to-back terraces with their outside toilets, or to the rows of pubs that siphoned off their wages before they could be handed over to wives. Glamorous Newcastle, now a short hop from South Shields on the metro, was then a distant metropolis. Swan Hunter, the giant shipbuilding firm, was next door to my grandfather's building; after them came a ship's chandler's

warehouse, the customs house and the Mission to Seamen. It was a very different England from the versions to be met in London.

'I am very glad to be able to report,' the manager of the new factory wrote to Henry on 21 July, 'that at the end of this first week, everything has gone splendidly. We have 21 girls on our books, and we can record a production of about seven dozen nightdresses . . . In view of the fact that with one exception, all the girls are absolutely inexperienced, [the output] is quite satisfactory.' Though Henry's deal with the government meant he could only hire jobless workers, 'we are being badgered almost every hour of the day by people who come up looking for work, some of them already employed'. The workmen were finishing up the last of the painting; the canteen cook was making scones. The only real concern was less tangible. The money to pay the wages had been late in coming from head office in the Lane; there had been enough in the kitty, but it mustn't happen again. What worried the manager especially 'was the fact that we are a Jewish firm', and that missing wages would be 'to some people a wonderful opportunity to express some anti-Semitic feeling'. In the future, writes the manager, himself a sympathetic gentile, 'if we behave in any way shabbily . . . undoubtedly the question of Jews etc. will enter into any discussion. In a town like London, so vast, and full of people all intent on achieving something or other, such incidents could be overlooked, but in this relatively small community, anything, whether it be good or a bit of scandal, would get out and be on everybody's lips in a very short time.'

The satisfaction with production didn't last long. Later, after a rollicking from London, the manager wrote again 'to try to impress on you that although the girls are on the whole very conscientious and very willing to try and oblige, they have not the machine knowledge nor the background of machining that is found in the South of England. Therefore, where the South country girl could be given a job and left to get on with it, making a first class job of it, the people here have to be shown every detail and given every attention that it is possible to give.' There were headaches over absenteeism, restlessness in the packing room, bottlenecks caused by the makeshift layout, and a shortage of wood to build a cutting table. The manager himself turned out to be a typically optimistic appointment: he was a gas-fitter whose diligence had so impressed Henry that my grandfather took him on as his deputy in the north.

But in South Shields on the afternoon of 16 July 1945, it seemed to Henry, and to Miriam at his side, that Walter's predictions of impending greatness were beginning to be realised. Henry was not a true captain of industry: he was not a Jack Cohen of Tesco, another East End graduate, or an Isaac Wolfson of Great Universal Stores, or a Michael Marks of Marks & Spencer. Still, between his northern and southern operations, Henry was employing nearly 400 people, turning out French

knickers, camiknickers, pyjamas, nightdresses, blouses and housecoats. He was almost thirty-nine years old and Miriam was thirty-five, and they were being lionised in a town Henry had visited as a virtual mendicant a little over a decade before.

'There are lots of seemingly very rich people here,' Walter wrote to Henry from the Cliftonville Hotel in Margate in September 1946, 'but nearly all so inconsiderate and almost brutal in their behaviour. It makes one think people generally should express some gratitude to their Creator for the fortunate position they occupy in the world by being Englishmen and Women. There are,' he laments, 'two young pups in the next room to me – of course they have a Rolls Bentley – but they nevertheless shout in the corridor late at night, slam doors & generally behave as hooligans – nice boys really (about 22) but so badly brought up – such a pity.' Still, the English seaside had not lost its charm entirely: 'The sun is now shining & we are going for a walk before tea. Love to Miriam & children. Your affectionate friend, Walter.'

Different as their backgrounds were, Walter and my grandfather had similar ideas about the way their country should be. In the years immediately after the war, the England that Henry had been brought up to admire, and Walter had grown up taking for granted, seemed to be disintegrating. The crime rate leapt, as deserters scratched a living in the black economy, spivs hawked nylons and whisky from the backs of lorries, and father-less children haunted bombsites, encouraged in their delin-quency, so the eternal advocates of censorship maintained, by James Cagney and the gangster cinema. The war's social level-lings had undermined the once-traditional deference to elders and superiors. The well-heeled hooligan pups with ('of course') their Rolls Bentleys, as well as the thugs who wielded coshes against unfortunate gentlemen in the West End, made it plain that England would never be the same again.

Henry and Walter's relationship evolved after the war too. In their letters, they are still more and more greedy for each other's company. Walter still provides pukka introductions – in the City; to Ciro's members-only nightclub in Orange Street – and he is perpetually extolling and exhorting Henry's accomplishments. 'My Dear Henry,' he wrote from the RAC on New Year's Day, 1946, 'My thoughts at midnight were with you and yours. At home – Miriam & the children – at your offices and works, the health and strength to carry your progress. May 1946 be the beginning of your great achievements. God bless you, Walter.'

But the equilibrium of needs was unbalancing. As my grandfather's life expanded, Walter was displaced from its centre. Their friendship became first a communion of equals, and then tipped the other way, as Henry became ever more immersed in the new world to which Walter had introduced him, less and less needy of advice and validation, and Walter, sixty-nine when the war ended, was increasingly beset by ill health. From late 1945, he was regularly laid up either on England's south coast or, when it became once again possible, in the South of France. 'Waiting typically continental, food good and plentiful, bathing excellent, weather perfect,' reports a contented postcard from his first foreign jaunt after the war.

Walter left nothing to my grandfather in his short, impersonal will. Instead, while he lived, every few months he would give Henry mementoes of himself, and of their short but intense friendship. Henry knew what these pre-emptive bequests meant, and was sometimes reluctant to accept them. 'My Dear Henry,' Walter wrote, again on RAC paper, late in 1945, 'Please accept with my renewed affection a small gift that I very much value, having won them [a set of cufflinks] in open competition, when I was captain of the Eccentric Golfing Society.' For Christmas, 1946, Walter scoured the art dealerships of Mayfair for a fitting token. It was the middle of an

% "AUTOMOBILE LONDON".

WHITEHALL 2345.

THE ROYAL AUTOMOBILE CLUB,
LONDON, S. W. 1.

*1945.*

*My Dear Henry.*
*Please accept with
my renewed affection
a small gift that I
very much value,*

apocalyptic winter: the country's fuel supplies ran out; men waving flares directed the London traffic through the freezing fogs. Bread was rationed, which had never happened during the war itself. Every morning Henry passed the German POWs – not yet repatriated from their camp at Batford, and recognisable in their dark overalls with a yellow diamond motif on the back – who had been detailed to clear away the deep snow in Harpenden High Street. After the snowdrifts, there were floods. Walter's gift took his friend away from the winter's grind, to a world of higher priorities and longer perspectives. 'I know you will value this 17th Century oil painted miniature,' his card reads, 'not because of its value as a work of art, but because it is given you by . . . Walter.'

As the generosity escalated, so the inhibitions about saying what they felt became less binding. 'My Dear Henry,' Walter wrote a year later, on New Year's Day, 1948, 'This letter is to thank you for your many kindnesses to me during the past year. What fond and very beautiful memories I have of our very happy friendship & the many kindly acts of hospitality I've received from your very generous self. May I misquote from one of our greatest poets, Robert Burns: It is my earnest prayer that "auld acquaintance shall ne'er be forgot & always kept in mind". At midnight last night I sat by the dying embers alone with a glass of the spirit that comforts and warms the soul, and you and yours were embraced in the thoughts and wishes of my own people. Yours, Walter.' Henry replied on 12 January: 'Dear Walter, I shall always cherish your letter of January 1st this year as one of my proudest possessions. No words of mine,' he protests, as he had once protested to Miriam, 'can express the gratification I feel at having such a great friend and that you too feel similarly about myself. As you know, you are always in my thoughts, and I am always praying that you should be given continued strength and good health to be with your people, and to allow me to share a small part of you for very many years to come. Yours, Henry.'

In the early summer of 1948 Walter and Cissie stayed again with my grandparents in Harpenden. 'We thoroughly enjoyed our short stay,' Walter wrote in his thank-you letter, '& felt it a pity to leave such a lovely garden on such a beautiful morning': there were beds of tulips and polyanthus, and aralias, yellow alyssum and anemones in the rockeries. Then, in July, Walter decided that the good things of life were in too short supply in England, and that his own life was itself too short to put up with the dismal situation any longer. 'Dear Henry,' he wrote a little tersely on July 5, 'Cissie wants a House Coat to take away with her. Have you one in stock that would suit *not heavy*? If so please have posted to White House Hotel Dorking.' Having caught the boat train and passed through Paris, he writes more expansively from Cannes. The hotel, he reports, is 'large, lofty, beautifully furnished and the comfort generally is superlative . . . The food is perfect & the chef knows his job (late second chef of the Carlton). Just finished lunch,' whose menu, perhaps a little insensitively, he proceeds to elaborate: 'melon, salade & jambon, baby lamb (not from Ciro's), pastries, cream & peaches etc.' There was no mention of snoek, an inedible relative of the barracuda, shiploads of which the Ministry of Food was then vainly trying to foist onto Britain's hungry population. The only drawback, Walter complains from Cannes, with the perennial hypocrisy of the tourist who wants to share his find and at the same time keep it to himself, 'is that too many visitors come to cocktail parties & meals.' He hasn't 'been to the Casino, but I'm told the gambling is very heavy & hundreds of millions (francs) won & lost nightly by such people as the Aga Khan'. At the end of the letter, 'Cissie sends her love to Miriam & considers a weekend with you is a happier time than the continual rush here . . . Yours affectionately, Walter.' Miriam and Cissie were trying to pretend, to themselves as well as to their husbands, that they were just as close as the men. Cissie's few imitation letters to Miriam try to transcend mere courtesy, and to overcome their own inhibitions, through terms of endearment ('dear' and 'darling') and meaningful underlinings ('<u>Many</u>, <u>many</u> thanks'), but somehow cannot help sliding back into well-wishing and polite inquiries about the children: 'I do hope you all had a very good Christmas time . . . I am sure you must have missed Philip very much . . . I shall look forward to meeting you again soon.'

Henry's reply to Walter's letter from France was typed on 20 July: 'Thank you very much for your most delightful letter, which warmed the cockles of my heart when I reached the office this morning. Frankly, I have been rather worried the whole of the week not hearing from you and when that morning

Miriam received a letter from Cissie, I felt quite jealous. I hasten to pen these few lines, so that when you arrive home they will be there to greet you, and I look forward to hearing you on Wednesday. Yours sincerely, Henry.'

Towards the end of 1948 Henry had a minor heart attack. He spent much of January and February of the next year recovering at Ruthin. The doctor, he reported to Miriam, 'feels there is every hope that I should live a normal life again'. 'My Darling Henry,' Miriam began her reply; she tells him about the garden and the children and the bad weather, and – suddenly autonomous – seeks his approval for a proposed visit to his brother Mick ('we will go at two, and get back about eight'), and about the piano tuner coming from Luton. Then, 'Philip, Michael & Amelia send their love to you, they think you are the most wonderful daddy in all the world . . . With all my love, Miriam.' Henry was an adoring and wildly generous father when his children were young. There was a pigeon loft for the boys, to complement the aviary and aquariums, upgraded, when they liked it, to a multi-storey pigeon palace at the end of the garden, and pigeon races and competitions. There were fireworks, and pantomimes at Christmas, trips to Whipsnade safari park and a grey pony called Pimpo for Amelia. Once, riding Pimpo on Harpenden Common, soon after a little girl had been murdered on it, Amelia stopped to pick some flowers and was late coming back. Miriam was in the streets looking for her; at home, Henry explained that he had to smack her, but then gave her a present afterwards. He was a less sure-footed parent when the children got older. Unexpected ambitions and adolescent insubordination were as unfamiliar from his own childhood as were gifts, and he turned to Walter to help him through them. For Miriam, the lesson of childhood was that rows must be avoided, and urgently soothed if they happened, and she would patiently mediate between aggrieved patriarch and tearful disenchanted offspring. She was that rare sort of parent who, when she said it didn't matter how well the children did so long as they tried their best, really meant it.

'Thank you so much for your letter,' Henry wrote back to Miriam from Ruthin after his heart attack. 'It is amazing, though we speak to each other 2 or 3 times a day, how welcome a letter is.' He was supposed to be there alone for a month, but he soon asked her to come down each Tuesday, and stay until Friday, to 'bring us together for at least half the week . . . I miss you and everyone very much indeed . . . with all my love and life, Your Henry.' 'I've always understood the castle & grounds are very fine,' Walter wrote to his friend on 28 January 1949. In their exchanges there is now a heightened, reciprocal urgency to see each other, as if, without too much discussion, both men knew the value of what they had to lose, and how soon, one way or another, they might lose it. He misses Henry badly, but 'I must be patient for your return.' On 8 February, Walter writes again from London: 'I thought of you continually during the week end.' Walter's brother Herbert has been ill, '& the doctors are not in any way optimistic . . . If you were in town I could see you & I know your encouragement would be very valuable to me . . . Of course I miss you but every day is one nearer to our next meeting.' Then, on 14 February, 'I hear that you look wonderfully well . . . I'm so pleased and shall be able to see for myself next week . . . Henry the time will soon go, as time does, all too quickly.'

The gifts were becoming more portentous. For Christmas, 1949, Walter sent Henry another miniature painting ('A signed late 17th Cent? Miniature painting by celebrated Dutch artist in original frame . . . A thing of beauty is a joy forever'). Henry sent Walter a souvenir programme from the Ryder Cup. Then on 17 July 1950 Henry didn't 'know whether to be pleased or otherwise on receiving your own evening cigar case with my initials . . . I deeply appreciate the sentiments, but hate to

deprive you of the usefulness and the joy of beautiful things which you have chosen for your use with such care and judgement. On the other hand, I have another treasure to add to the store of the many good things you have given me.'

Walter and Cissie finally moved into their new home in Surrey during the autumn of 1950. Finishing its much-delayed construction had become a quixotic mission, pursued with an oblivious English stubbornness despite, or perhaps because of, Walter's deteriorating health. The house was a sort of deluxe bungalow, with a long elegant driveway and a landscaped garden. But, as Walter explained on 21 November, in response to the housewarming flowers and telegram sent by Henry, at first the situation was chaotic, and he longed for the serenity of his provincial hotels. 'The road being constructed is a quagmire owing to tremendous hail and rain . . . the bedrooms are finished but the sitting rooms are in a state of great disorder.' Almost immediately, Walter fell ill and was out of touch with Henry for a week, after, so his next letter says, spending too long in the garden with a contractor. 'I am so glad I received your letter today,' Henry replied. 'I missed you as much as you have missed me.' As soon as Walter recovered, Cissie was struck by an unspecified but grave ailment. 'Walter rang me rather distressed as Cissie is very ill, and I saw him for lunch and did my best to comfort him,' Henry wrote to Philip, his elder son. 'He also gave me two wrought brass bowls, about two to three inches in diameter, which he had made for him in front of his eyes in North Africa some years ago.' As Walter relayed after he returned to Surrey from his London lunch, his son-in-law had 'sent down a specialist (of Swiss nationality) supposed to be very first rate', though they would also be going to Harley Street if Cissie was up to it. 'You can see by my writing I'm all upside down,' Walter says, and indeed he had foregone most of his habitual flourishes, though he still managed a beautiful, swirling 'D' for his opening 'Dear'; 'but I am hoping for everything to come right.' 'Walter,' Henry replies, 'if there is anything I can do, you have only just to ask and my time and energies will be at your disposal.' 'I am hoping soon to be able to go out & enjoy life once more,' Cissie wrote to Miriam when she was feeling better. 'It has been such a trying time feeling so ill & having my skin trouble. I cannot go into details, it would take too long.'

In the summer of 1951 Walter and Cissie fled to the Cavendish in Eastbourne. 'The weather has not been too kind,' Walter complained, but 'the food is wonderful . . . I'm enclosing menu for today's lunch. Unfortunately it's terribly expensive, which did not matter so much in the days gone by, but today a short stay is all I can afford.' More importantly, 'I think this will be the 5th week since our last meeting!' That Christmas, Walter sent Henry another pair of cuff links, with a note expressing his hope that they 'will still be going strong when I'm only a memory. God bless you and yours . . . ' The following summer was the last in which Walter could enjoy the gentlemanly diversions that he had lived for. On 10 September he wrote to my grandfather from the Metropole in Folkestone. 'My Dear Henry, A lovely morning! We have been sitting on our balcony which is as big as a tennis court overlooking the sea.' There were not too many other guests, though 'John Coke, Queen Mary's equerry is staying for a few days. You remember, I introduced him to you at the Ks of R.T.' Oddly enough, 'another old friend – Sir Clive Morrison-Bell – who I first met in 1898, is here recovering from a serious motor accident, both thighs broken, poor old man.' There was also a wealthy ship-breaker whose 'cousin Evelyn was God mother to my eldest Grand Daughter, and who tomorrow leaves America on one of the Queens. What a small world!'

By the end of 1952, although his writing had recovered its loops and swirls, Walter, now seventy-seven, felt that he was approaching his end. 'My Dear Henry,' he wrote at Christmas time, 'It has been my intention for years to leave you my pearl pin & I'm anticipating somewhat by asking you to accept it now. I assure you it will give me great pleasure to see you wearing it & hope I shall have this pleasure for many Xmases,' though in his heart he probably knew he wouldn't. 'Believe me Henry,' he goes on, perhaps inscribing as firm an insistence as might be considered polite, 'when I express to you my great happiness in our friendship, and may the Good God keep you and yours.' In return, Henry, who was striving to ignore the references to his friend's mortality, rather ambitiously sent down a poodle puppy to Surrey, hoping it would have a rejuvenating effect. 'He is a dear little fellow,' Walter wrote, 'perhaps a few weeks too young to leave his brothers & sisters, but full of life & at present spends most of his time (when he is not excreting) tearing up anything he can get in his mouth. I'm sure in a few weeks he will enjoy his new home as much as we shall enjoy his company.' But the following week Cissie wrote apologetically to say that they couldn't manage the puppy after all.

Walter's life, like most lives, did not end with a crescendo, nor exactly when he or his friends expected it to. He seems to have been incapacitated by the sort of demoralising sequence of ailments that can overtake the elderly, before finally succumbing to pneumonia in July 1954. The last of his surviving letters to my grandfather were written during the previous summer. They do not include any grand declarations of affection, or sage contemplations on how and why these two men from opposite ends of the class spectrum, and, ancestrally, from opposite ends of Europe, came, so swiftly, to prize each other so highly. They offer only the humdrum banalities of a friendship between two Englishmen, the sort of nothings people say to one another to let each other know that they want to say something. On 12 August 1953 Walter wrote from Surrey to thank his friend for the postcard he had sent from his holiday in Stresa. 'Just a few lines to acknowledge your card & to wish you the happiest of holidays,' he writes, leading off his note with a flamboyant dropped J. 'The heat in London & also here is over-powering & it's impossible to do anything but sit in the shadiest spot possible. Make the best of your time, even three weeks soon goes, Love to you all, Walter.' The final note from Walter to Henry was written on a scrap of office notepaper on the day before my grandparents were due to return from their break. 'Dear Henry,' he writes, plainly and frailly, 'A note to welcome you home & may the happy memory of your holiday be with you for many years. Walter.' In a postscript, underlined in emphasis of his determination, he adds, 'Hope to see you on Tuesday next.'

Henry always had a talent for friendship. He cultivated friends assiduously, corresponding for years with people he had encountered only fleetingly on business trips, and with former employees who had emigrated. He loved the clubs and institutions to which Walter introduced him because they were gentlemanly, and because they were Walter's; but also because of the opportunities they provided for meeting new people. He trusted easily and was often disappointed. At the end of his life, he told his children that Walter had been his only true friend. The day after his friend died, Henry wrote to his son Philip: 'Poor Uncle Walter passed away yesterday. It must have been a happy release. I shall certainly miss him.'

# FIVE:

# 'Living as in a dream'

160 *Cheapside*
*London* E.C.2

*2nd September 1947*

*Dear Mr Chandler,*
*For more years than I care to remember it has been my ambi-*
*tion to become a Liveryman and Freeman of the City of*
*London. My very great friend, Walter Sherman, has been a*
*Liveryman of your Company for many years and naturally it*
*has been my greatest desire particularly to join your worthy*
*Company. This desire has been more prominent in my mind*
*since I took over my new headquarters at 160 Cheapside, E.C.2,*
*which is the very heart of the City.*

*I have had the pleasure of meeting you on several occasions*
*and I have discussed this ambition of mine with you. I would*
*esteem it as a great honour and kindness if you would put my*
*name before your Court when you meet early in September.*
*Herewith are the various particulars relating to myself:*

*My name is Henry Emmanuel Freedman. I reside in*
*Milton Road, Harpenden. I was born in London, of British*
*parents, on the 10th August, 1906. I am married and have*
*three children. I am chairman of the board of directors of*

*S. Newman Ltd, 160 Cheapside E.C.2. My company has factories*
*at London, Harpenden and in the development area of South*
*Shields. We have 400 employees.*

*I can assure you that I will set myself out to be a true, loyal*
*and worthy Liveryman.*

*Hoping you are well, and with kindest regards,*
*Yours sincerely,*
*Henry Freedman*


'My Darling,' Henry began his letter to Miriam of 24 March 1946, 'The plane is most comfortable and is really the most wonderful sight – an aluminium bird.' It is, he records at the top of the letter, '7.15 Greenwich time, 2.15 American time, pitch dark outside.' 'Going west as we have,' he explains, 'we have been following the night which will be about 16 hours long against 11 hours if we were in England . . . it seems so strange to travel so far and so long without seeing daylight at all.' Henry was crossing the Atlantic to investigate new production methods for the South Shields factory, and the possibility of doing business in North America: an urgent mission, he had decided, if his company and his family were to prosper in the harsh post-war conditions. It was to be a daunting, thrilling, catalysing little odyssey, taking in New York, Chicago, Montreal and Quebec City. But at 7.15 Greenwich time on 24 March, what my grandfather primarily felt was lonely. 'As I write this and think of a whole month, four whole weeks without you,' he tells my grandmother, 'it makes me feel afraid to think.'

Five days later, ensconced at the Biltmore hotel, next to Grand Central Station on Madison Avenue, he described the journey in more detail. 'After leaving Prestwick aerodrome [just outside Glasgow] at 6.30pm Saturday we landed at Iceland [then a common stopover on transatlantic flights] at 11pm.

| **016**  23380 | IN CONNECTION WITH TICKET FORM $\mathcal{B}$ | NOT GOOD UNLESS VALIDATED BELOW |
|---|---|---|
| **PASSENGER'S COUPON** | NO. 3948 | APR 20 46 |
| | AGENT *DFB* | NEW YORK |
| **AMERICAN AIRLINES SYSTEM AAL** | LBS. 40 | VIA AIRLINE |
| | RATE PER LB. 1.70 | |
| **EXCESS BAGGAGE TICKET** | AMT. $ 68.00 | FROM *New York AOA* |
| "SOLD SUBJECT TO TARIFF REGULATIONS, AND IF AN INTERNATIONAL PASSENGER'S BAGGAGE CHECK HAS BEEN ISSUED IN CONNECTION HEREWITH, THE CONDITIONS AND PROVISIONS STATED OR REFERRED TO THEREIN WHICH ARE HEREBY MADE A PART HEREOF." | TAX $ | TO *London* |
| | TOTAL $ 68.00 | |
| | ATP ☐  GOVT. ☐ | |
| | OTH. *Cash* | TO |

After spending an hour there and having eggs, bacon, coffee
and tomato juice, we left again at 12.' Bacon and eggs: the
*kashrut* dietary laws had become almost unobservable during
the war, especially since forbidden foods – shellfish and game
– tended to be more obtainable than permitted ones. At reaping time in Hertfordshire there was still a glut of non-kosher
rabbits, trapped in the middle of the fields by harvesting farmers. In any case, divine wrath came to seem less awesome next
to the immanent and imminent threat of the Blitz.

'After an adventurous crossing,' Henry continues to Miriam,
with just a hint of his civilian's need to glamorise his exploits,
'we reached Newfoundland at 9am on 3 engines, setting down
on an iced runway at 20 degrees below zero. The 32 passengers
went along to a large hall which was previously occupied by
the American airforce, and had an excellent meal and a game
of gin rummy. We got under way in five hours and took the
last hop to La Guardia aerodrome, New York, landing again at
6pm.' Hundreds of thousands of people had flown as human
cargo during the war, but very few had travelled as paid-up
passengers. When my grandfather first did so, in 1946, the experience was slower but also more luxurious than it would

soon become, when the era of mass commercial airlines dawned. Airports were still glorified huts on the apron of the tarmac, but the few civilian planes that touched down on them were more spacious and comfortable than their cramped successors, and journeys in them resembled aerial safaris.

'On the last hop,' Henry records, with the amazement at the possibility of open abundance that rationing had instilled, 'we were served with lovely steaks, fresh fruit and "korfee". I helped the stewards to wait on the passengers and received the best bit of steak as my reward.' Even for a native Londoner, 'the first sight of New York was bewildering, the traffic coming at you from the wrong side of the road, at such a pace I felt like a little country mouse. I have never seen so many cars at one time in my life.' Writing a few days later, he is still thinking of Miriam, and still dazzled by New York, but between them she and the city have redoubled his resolve: 'Darling, to say I miss you is much too mild. I realise more than ever how much you mean to me, and what I see here, how the women are dressed and the luxuries of life, only urges me on, so that I can one day, do the same for you.' His yen to transform himself and her, involving night after night of *shmoozing* the powerful, would sometimes make my grandmother wish that they could go back to how they had been before the war; but not yet. Finally, 'we are off to Canada on Sunday . . . the Mayor of Quebec City has invited me to Dinner with him and has reserved a Suite of rooms at the Chateau Frontenac at the City's expense.' (Having received a slightly exaggerated impression of Henry's eminence, the

industrial commissioner of Quebec City had sent him a telegram just before his departure from Prestwick aerodrome, care of American Overseas Airlines: 'HIS WORSHIP THE MAYOR OF THIS CITY . . . HAVING BEEN INFORMED OF YOUR TRIP TO CANADA . . . AND OF YOUR INTENTION TO INVESTIGATE THE POSSIBILITY OF ESTABLISHING A PLANT IN THESE PROVINCES WISHES ME TO CORDIALLY INVITE YOU TO STOP AT QUEBEC CITY WHICH IS RICH IN POWER AND LABOUR . . . AN INDUS-TRIAL SURVEY WILL BE READY FOR YOUR PERUSAL WHEN YOU ARRIVE IN CANADA.') 'Darling,' Henry winds up his letter to Miriam, 'you know how much you mean to me, I love you dearly and long for you. God bless you and keep you my Sweetheart. Your Ever Loving Henry.'

In New York, my grandfather visited factories, union leaders, industrial colleges, fabric-makers, and the American Viscose Corporation, whose headquarters were in the Empire State Building, as well as the relatives of friends in London who forty years earlier had remained on the boats from Germany all the way across the Atlantic. 'What I have seen here confirms my opinion regarding business,' he told Miriam, 'and if only we could adapt the American methods to our produc-tion, we should be in the forefront of British manufacturing.' He rode the train to Chicago to visit fashion houses and machine manufacturers. He scoped out the latest pinking, ruffling, embroidery and laying-up machines, as well as new market research, advertising and training techniques. He kept everything: all the notes he made about his meetings and visits, complete with scrawled messages to himself ('American ambition is to capture world markets: must acquire machines to keep abreast of competition'); copies of all the thank-you letters he wrote to his new contacts, often accompanied by cheeky gifts of lingerie; long lists of people in London for whom he had to buy presents; hotel receipts; restaurant menus. He kept the letters that his colleagues and relatives wrote back to him, care of the Biltmore in New York. 'My Dear Gov,' Nan Jones began, 'What a wonderfully interesting time you must be having. You are always in our thoughts and we do appreciate how hard the going must be. Mrs Freedman and the kids miss you very much as do everybody here. The girls (Hilda, Daisy etc) feel very flattered that you should have thought of them whilst you are amidst the glamorous American women.' America meant Hollywood, Barbara Stanwyck, Bette Davis and Lana Turner. The idea of someone you knew actually going there was at the margins of the possible. 'Quite frankly,' Nan admits, 'I think we all envy your wonderful experiences.'

As well as his letters to Miriam, my grandfather wrote every day to Mick, his brother and last remaining partner, who had doubted the wisdom of the trip and been alarmed by its cost. Henry's report to Mick on 3 April is as wide-eyed about the efficiency of the American underwear industry as his letter to Miriam had been about the 'aluminium bird' and the New York traffic. 'There is so much to learn here,' my grandfather writes, 'and so little time to do it in.' The key factor in the Americans' success, he considers, is 'sectionalisation'. During the war, the power of the American unions had driven up the cost of labour. The manufacturers had responded by improving efficiency, attending to details – lighting; canteens; the colour schemes of shop floors – that their British counterparts were still neglecting. Most importantly, their operatives worked on scientifically segmented processes, using bespoke machines, with the result that even though they were paid more than their English counterparts, the garments they produced cost less to make and to buy. American manufacturers, Henry noticed, also tended to be more ruthless in their determination to cut waste and beat the competition: they 'work until their work is done, and with a thoroughness that frightens me'. He rhapsodised about the machines, the fabrics, the vocational training,

and the licence he had already negotiated to make a new
brassière-cum-fitted slip – 'the slip I have been hunting for . . .
a completely revolutionary garment so far as England is concerned' – that he thought might soon be the only thing they
made at South Shields. (By 6 April he had decided to forget the
licence and simply copy the pattern.)

He was also keen on 'the Latin Quarter, a night club with a
marvellous floor show', and Radio City Music Hall, and the
Hickory House, a jazz restaurant on 52nd Street, otherwise
known as Swing Street. He loved the outsize American cars
and the frank gluttony of the restaurants. 'I now say Au Revoir
to you, Mick,' he winds up on 3 April, 'and say how much I
wish you were here with me to share my experience. Give my
love to Freda, and remember me to each and every one of the
staff individually.' Finally, 'ring Miriam and tell her how with
all the attractions of this great city I am the loneliest man on
earth without her'. Next day, Henry writes to Mick again, with
the same combination of commercial urgency and unabashed

sentimentality: 'The only means of survival we have is to produce a standard article at the lowest and most economic selling price. The underwear industry in England is, although a comparatively new one, very antiquated. What I have seen here has opened my eyes and I sincerely feel that were we able and willing to follow the methods carried on here, we should be able to lead the entire industry in Great Britain' – and after Britain, no doubt, the world. Why not? Then, at the end, 'give my love to my Darling wife and kids. She knows how I feel, as she is feeling the same way . . . Au Revoir, old pal.'

My grandfather loved Canada. In New York he felt like an ingénue, 'a little country mouse'. He was dwarfed by the monumental architecture – the top of the Biltmore alone was higher than anything in London – and he was overtaken on the pavements by the relentless pedestrians. In Canada, he felt like a king. The Canadians still deferred to the mother country: to them, Henry was a visiting English dignitary, not a half-bred *arriviste*, as he was sometimes made to feel at home. The Chateau Frontenac, above the St Lawrence River, was the grandest private building he had ever been allowed inside. The whole place felt like one big opportunity, ready for exploitation by anyone with the initiative and hard currency to take it up.

'My Darling Miriam,' Henry began his letter of 8 April, 'Here I am in Canada. It is very different to what I have seen in New York. We took the plane to Montreal at 11.15 and were here at 1.25. It is just like a miracle. It's no use repeating how much I wish you were here but believe me, what I have learned, if only I can get it all into the business, should make it possible for us to travel all over the world.' To that end, 'today I have seen a large Canadian chain store executive, who is most anxious that we make up the best hand-made lingerie in Quebec City . . . I should very much like to have a letter from you,' he tells her, recalling his appeals of sixteen years earlier, when she had been away in Poland and he at home in London, 'so please write me at once at the Biltmore.' (Letters remained – and would always be – an agony of insecurity for my grandmother. 'I only wish that I could write better,' she would lament to her son Philip, whom Henry later sent to study fashion at a college he had visited in New York: 'I have to have a fight to make myself do it . . . my pen will not write what my thoughts and heart want to say.' She managed letters as a child approaches burdensome homework, stretching them out by writing only a few words on each line and leaving gaps between paragraphs. Your mother, Henry told his son, 'writes from the heart, and each word from her is a kiss'.) 'Tell me darling,' Henry winds up from Montreal, 'how are my lovely children getting on? Do they miss me? Does Amelia ever ask about me? You can tell them I miss them all very much, and cannot wait until I see them again.' Finally, the paramount question: 'Have you got the nylons yet?'

Mick's letters to Henry make it clear that he is still not convinced about North America. He knew that his brother was a skilful deal-maker and natural entrepreneur, but he was worried by the grandiosity of Henry's schemes and the liberality of his spending. On 9 April 1946 Henry tried again to persuade him. 'As you can see,' my grandfather begins, on paper headed 'Canadian Pacific Railway', 'I am penning these lines to you in the Pullman, at a writing desk, on the way to Quebec City.' He had almost as much space to himself in the Pullman carriage as he and his brothers once had between them in New Castle Street. 'Please understand once and for all,' Henry went on, 'that I would not under any circumstances persuade you or coerce you into a decision . . . Don't think for one moment that I shall be carried away. I have a clear picture of what we want, and what is best for us, and our whole future depends on the wisdom of the decisions made. I am more convinced than ever that this trip of mine was well timed, and with your support, of which I have no doubt whatsoever, we should continue to

MOUNT ROYAL HOTEL
MONTREAL 2, CANADA
VERNON G. CARDY, PRESIDENT

*Monday 8th April 1948*

*My Darling Miriam, Here I am in Canada.*

make the most of the future, as we have succeeded beyond our wildest dreams in the past.' This appeal to history was Henry's argumentative trump card: Mick knew, as only a sibling could know, just how far they had come. 'The weather here is fine,' Mick's still-sceptical letter of 11 April reports, 'and Miriam is bringing the kids up to town tomorrow for a day out. She sends you her love and is anxiously waiting for your return.'

On 12 April Henry cabled excitably from Quebec City: 'HAVE SEEN TREMENDOUS OPPORTUNITY FOR ESTABLISHMENT OF RAYON PLANT IN ONE MILLION SQUARE FEET OF MOST MODERN BUILDINGS NOW AVAILABLE IN THE PROGRESSIVE CITY OF QUEBEC STOP ALL POSSIBLE FACILITIES STOP MUST HAVE INTERVIEW LONDON HIGHEST POSSIBLE LEVEL STOP ACT AT ONCE HENRY'. 'This is virgin soil,' he expanded in his next letter, 'and if we were lucky and big enough to break in, it would be equal to the diamond and gold boom in South Africa.' Back at the Mount Royal Hotel in Montreal, he shared with Miriam the private sense of astonishment that seems always to have shadowed his vaulting self-confidence. 'I am living here as in a dream. Never have I met such influential people, even ministers of the state have invited me to lunch': me, an erstwhile seller of inedible chocolates, as well as me, Henry Freedman, heir to all the privileges and opportunities due to a British businessman in a Savile Row suit. 'Darling,' Henry writes, 'I have been a good boy and am longing for you. I show your photographs and the children's with pride. My

INDUSTRIAL COMMISSION

work is very hard but the thoughts of you sustain me. I am off to New York on Saturday. God bless you my sweetheart . . . Ever yours, Henry.'

He promised his new Canadian friends that he would alert Sir Stafford Cripps, then the President of the Board of Trade, to the risks to Britain and the Commonwealth of leaving Canada to the Americans, whose businessmen, Henry concluded, would be quick to corner the Canadian market in the absence of proper competition. When he got back to London, again via New York and Iceland, he tried hard to fix meetings with Cripps and several other government ministers, but he never got beyond the lower ranks of officialdom. Nor was he able to persuade the authorities to let him take out of the country the cash he would need to open a plant in Quebec City: strict criteria governed the expatriation of capital, and Henry's idea didn't satisfy them. So he had to write to the Canadians to explain that he wouldn't after all be expanding into their country. For their hospitality they got only several nights of stories of the Blitz and Henry's explanation of Churchill's defeat in the 1945 election, and some gifts of lingerie sent with his apologies that they had nothing else to show for their suite at the Chateau Frontenac.

There was another disappointment: Arthur Warburton. Arthur was a Manchester 'converter' – he bought loom-state cloth from the Lancashire mills, dyed and finished it, and sold it on to the manufacturers – whom Henry seems to have met by chance on the plane to America. By the end of their trip, Henry had secured a handsome slice of a consignment of German parachute silk that Arthur was expecting; they had already begun to talk about the great things that they would accomplish together in the future. When they got home, Henry invited Arthur and his wife to the party he and Miriam threw at a hotel for their son Philip's *barmitzvah*. 'This being the first time I have attended a function of this sort,' Arthur wrote periphrastically, 'I would be glad if you could let me know if we should bring dress clothes with us.' He and Henry met regularly in Manchester or over lunch at the Albany Club, and their letters and telegrams shortly began to concentrate more on their friendship than on their business interests. 'Twelve months have not dimmed the memory of the very happy time we spent together,' Arthur wrote in 1947, 'and have cemented our friendship, which I know will go on and on.' He found out the date of the Hebrew New Year from his Jewish associates in Manchester, and wrote to wish 'my dear friend a very happy New Year and well over the fast', which, as he had touchingly ascertained, was the traditional salutation before the fast of *Yom Kippur*, the Day of Atonement. At Christmas, Henry wrote to thank Arthur for the 'very great and pleasant surprise [of] your charming gift [a picnic rug], and what I appreciated even more, just those few words, that little card tucked away for only one who seeks to find. Our friendship,' he writes, susceptible as ever to the dream of instant communion, 'though not of very long duration, seems to me to have been for so many years past that we are as closely linked as only many years of friendship could accomplish.'

Not closely enough, it turned out, to withstand the divisiveness of the textile drought of the late forties. In April 1946 the Board of Trade had announced that frills would be permitted on non-utility underwear, and promised the disgruntled, drab masses 'new, non-austerity trimmings'. But where the material to make them was supposed to come from was a mystery to the industry. An ill-advised government pledge of 'nylons for all' proved tough to fulfil: there were riots in some shops when new batches of stockings arrived. Then Christian Dior redefined glamour with his 'New Look'. The Look had a cinched waist and a long, full skirt. It required petticoats and flounces, was worn with a slim-line corset known as a 'waspie', and scandalised MPs denounced its irresponsibly lavish use of fabric in the House of Commons. Even Henry's energetic distribution of cigars, of which he had a curiously inexhaustible supply, could not ameliorate the textile dearth. The more acute it became, the more the fabric cost, while the government-imposed ceiling prices for the underwear itself were kept the same. Less imaginative manufacturers went under. Henry trekked to St Gallen, Zurich and Geneva, hunting for ribbon, silk and lace.

Arthur let him down. 'Dear Arthur, It is a long time since I have heard from you, and I am wondering how you are getting on,' Henry wrote; 'the position between us has deteriorated to a tremendous extent, inasmuch as not only do I not get any offers of fabric, but also I have not had a word from you at all, and I am wondering whether it means that you are satisfied with this state of affairs and that you wish to allow our association to die out.' For Henry's part, 'this is the last thing I would like to consider, as I have always thought that we should be able to do big things between us'. 'I am the first to agree,' Arthur replies, 'that an explanation regarding the supply of cloth to you is what you can rightfully expect, especially as I am very appreciative of the confidence you have always expressed in me and the many kindnesses you have shewn to me.' After gratitude, he tries flattery: 'I shall do my best to explain the causes in detail, without withholding anything from you because I know quite well that this is not necessary with your gift of understanding.' He then expounds in numbing detail the various regulations and mishaps that have disrupted his supplies. 'I am sure you will believe me', Arthur optimistically concludes, 'when I state that I honestly regret more than I can find words to express the unfortunate position I find myself in, and I hope you will agree that I am just another unfortunate victim of circumstances over which I have no control.' 'I cannot induce you to do other than that which is your policy,' Henry answers, 'but I can say that I am rather disappointed things have not turned out as we had planned. Wishing you the compliments of the season . . . ' – compliments that, in their tepid formality, cauterised my grandfather's short-lived friendship with Arthur Warburton. In every life there are people who appear and look for a time as if they might become something lasting and important, only to slip away, leaving almost no trace. Arthur was such a person in Henry's life. They never spoke again; Walter remained his one true friend.

In practical terms, Mick was right to have been doubtful about the American trip. It cost a lot of money, and the best contact it turned up was an unreliable Mancunian. It didn't make my grandfather the global industrialist that he hoped it might. On the other hand, along with Walter's friendship, his adventures in the New World helped to shape his ambitions and to transform his life. The parameters of his universe, which had expanded across London from his parents' East End stronghold, then darted across the North Sea to Scheveningen in 1936, now spread across the globe. The scale of his dreaming stretched with them. He would soon set about becoming the confrère and confidant of earls and lords and ladies, and a familiar of the royal family. But, after he came back from America, he first set his heart on becoming Lord Mayor of London.

My grandfather kept the invitation for the first formal City occasion that he ever attended, as he kept all the invitations for all his balls and banquets. It was a dinner of the Worshipful Company of Poulters, of which Walter was a member, held at the Vintners' company hall in Upper Thames Street on 22 October 1946. 'Uniform or Dinner Jacket – Decorations', the printed card instructs, and in handwriting up one of its vertical edges is written '*At the invitation of Mr W.J. Sherman*'.

In October 1946 the City was still a wasteland. The Gothic porch of the Guildhall, the heart of the Square Mile, had survived, but the roof had collapsed amid the firebombs. Gog and Magog, eighteenth-century statues of the City's folkloric guardians, were lost. Intact buildings were considerably outnumbered by scaffolded casualties and out-and-out wrecks. Eight Wren churches had been incinerated in the great fire-bombing of December 1940. Many of the livery halls, seats of the City livery companies, had been destroyed: the Poulters were borrowing the Vintners' hall for their dinner because their own had been bombed. Unexpected blooms – red clover, larkspur and toadflax – had appeared amid the rubble.

Sitting next to Walter in a newly acquired dinner jacket in October 1946, Henry was enchanted by the worldly politesse the company mustered amid the destruction. The evening felt like a sort of social laundry: money-making men like him mixed with professional and military types, and no one talked about so-and-so being 'in trade' with that faintly disparaging air that some gentlemen put on elsewhere. At the end of the meal the diners drank from the 'Loving Cup', a tradition, so his other neighbour informed Henry, that dated from the time of King Edward the Martyr, reputedly slain while drinking. It was a three-man job: one to lift the cup's ornate cover; one to sip from it; and one (in Henry's case, Walter) to protect his back against imaginary assailants. The Lord Mayor of London sat at the top table, next to the master of the company and the other leading liverymen, dressed, as the Lord Mayor always does on such occasions, in black breeches, black silk stockings, patent leather shoes and various elaborate jewels of abstruse historical significance.

My dear Henry, Walter whispered to my grandfather between the toasts, one day that could be you.

Money, for Henry, was never really the point. Of course he wanted enough of it to provide for his mother while she was still alive, and then to give Miriam and the children the luxuries of life that he had seen in America. But money alone could never compensate for all the times a policeman had told him to move his barrow on, or a gentleman in a silk hat had ushered his wife across the road when they saw Henry coming towards them, grimy, on his way back from a day's selling. He wanted something less tangible and more elusive than money, even if money could help him get it. He wanted to be someone in London; he wanted to be someone else.

He wanted to look different and sound different, and he wanted his name to look different too, to sprout ornamental letters like those of the other men he met at City dinners and at the Knights of the Round Table, who had advanced degrees and daunting acronyms emblazoned on their place names, whereas my grandfather had to make do with a bald 'Esq.'. He began to amass his own private alphabet when, in June 1947, he became a fellow of the Zoological Society of London, on the strength of the collection of tropical fish that he was assembling in the conservatory in Milton Road. Thus he became an 'FZS'; soon afterwards he added an 'FRHS' (Fellow of the Royal Horticultural Society). In the hope of a less advertisable sort of distinction, at Masonic meetings at the Café Royal and the Connaught Rooms he ascended through the ritual ranks of wardens and deacons towards the mastership of the Titan Lodge. In April 1947 he tried to speed up his promotion by presenting a new, embroidered banner to the Lodge. A programme choreographed the dedication ceremony: 'The Dedicating Chaplain says: "Wor. Bro. Director of Ceremonies,

kindly unveil the Banner" . . . The brethren sing "So mote it be"
. . . The Brother who has presented the Banner says: "Wor.
Master, deign to accept this Banner, which I present to the
Lodge." The Wor. Master replies: "I accept it with great pleas-
ure, Bro. H.E. Freedman."' Eventually, the Brethren join in
singing the Dedicatory Hymn:

> *Great Architect, to Thee we pray,*
> *This Banner bless and us always,*
> *May Titan Lodge for ever prove*
> *A home of loyalty and love. So mote it be.*

Henry bought guides to public speaking, and honed his
oratorical skills at meetings of the Apparel and Fashion
Industry Association (AFIA), a trade body with whose efforts
to correct the irrationalities of government policy he had
become involved during the war. The AFIA's bulletins and
annual reports, all of which he kept, document his ascent up
the letterhead, as he scales its little hierarchy and chairs ever
more influential committees. The association was based in a
building at the upper end of Regent Street, and the committees
held their sessions in the middling hotels around Portland
Place. Henry laboured over his chairman's opening remarks
and other addresses to his colleagues, which may have
bemused the assembled underwear manufacturers with their
Macaulayan grandiloquence and expansive, metaphor-laden
sentences. 'It would be a brave man,' he told an annual meeting of the Women's and Children's Underwear, Slumberwear
and Dressing Gown Section, as if grasping for a bigger stage
and a more illustrious audience, 'who would dare at this stage
to express with any confidence his view as to what is likely to
occur in the future.' He opines on the shortage of fabric and
the invidious ceiling prices, then closes by wondering
'whether, in meeting the storm which has already broken upon

us, we shall be able to come through with that element of stability in our industry which we have learnt in recent years to treasure so much.'

But in the late forties the Whittingtonian dream Walter implanted that night at the Vintners' hall was Henry's main preoccupation. It didn't last for ever, but for a few years Walter's prophecy drove my grandfather's life. He couldn't be a doctor, and he couldn't be a cabinet minister or a high court judge, but he could – why shouldn't he? – be Lord Mayor of London: King of the City, the nearest thing to royalty to which a commoner like him could aspire, and the final, most irrefutable accolade of a self-made English man.

In the spring of 1947 Henry returned to the kerbside car dealership in Warren Street and traded up the Daimler he had bought during the war for a Sedanka Deville Rolls-Royce. My uncles and cousins who rode in that Rolls still recall its enormous, bug-eye headlights, the spare tyres mounted on either side, the beautiful running boards and the partition between the driver's cabin and the passengers'. But the Rolls weighed a ton, had a primeval gear system and was almost impossible to drive. So Henry hired a chauffeur named Eric, who had

advertised his services in the *Daily Telegraph*. Eric was tall and good-looking – just like Danny Kaye, said the girls at the factory in Harpenden – and had an ever-expanding family. In June and July 1947, making good on his American pledge to show my grandmother the world, Henry got Eric to drive the two of them to Paris, and then across France to Cannes.

For all the new airs they were assuming – it was around this time that Henry dispatched Miriam for elocution lessons with a snooty but impecunious lady in Holland Park – my grandparents were never very good at having servants. As well as Eric, these included an odd-job man who had been in the abortive airborne assault on Arnhem of 1944: he had three holes in his left leg that he would allow the unsqueamish Freedman children to finger, and could play a wood saw using a fiddle bow. There was Harry, a gardener from Somerset who had fought at Ypres, which he called 'Wipers', who would give the children rides on the handlebars of his bicycle while singing 'Gee up Neddy to the Fair'. There was Bessie the cook, a widowed Jewish East Ender, who had lived near the comedian Bud Flanagan when he was Reuben Weintrop, and remembered him as a 'big *lobos*' (rascal). Bessie had bought a brooch in a market for a few shillings that turned out to have real diamonds, and she kept it in a special pocket that she had sewed into her knickers. Her three children had emigrated, and she came back to my grandparents' house for Jewish holidays long after she had stopped supplying Henry with chopped liver and gefilte fish. Amy was a Jamaican housekeeper whom my grandparents poached from a displeased couple at a hotel in Bournemouth. She sent most of her wages back to Kingston, and would mutter, 'Have a good stare at a black person,' when parochial eyes tracked her along the high street in Harpenden.

With all of them, my grandparents were always more inclined to generosity and inclusiveness than was strictly proper, as Eric's letters from France to the children back in Harpenden

attest. 'I don't know how to begin to tell you of all the beauty we have seen,' he wrote on 3 July 1947. 'I went to the opera one evening and am sure that nothing could be finer or more grand . . . On Sunday we went to the races at Auteuil to see the French Grand National, what a sight! Masses of people beautifully dressed, enormous grandstands and grand colour, and to complete the thrill my horse nearly won': only nearly, but that was good enough for Eric. 'We went last night to the Monte Carlo ballet'; this time he 'saw the whole show from the balcony, it is no use trying to describe it . . . ' In Cannes, they stayed at the Carlton. Dora, proprietress of Chez Dora, the city's only kosher restaurant, sauntered through the lobby bearing platefuls of pickled herring for the Jewish guests from London. It was Miriam's first time out of the country since her visit to Kalisz in 1930. She missed the children and her mother, but she liked the opera and the ballet, and she loved the time with Henry, just the two of them and Eric, and no Walter and Cissie or weekend calls from the factory managers. It was like Canvey, but with better weather.

When they returned from France, Henry acquired an office in the City, the very first thing he needed for his Lord Mayoral quest; he kept his workshop in the Lane, along with the factories in Harpenden and South Shields. The new office was near the junction of Cheapside and St-Martin-Le-Grand: just around the corner from where he had scrounged the cloth to make up his first knickers in 1933, next to a bombsite and with a close-up view of the miraculously preserved dome of St Paul's. Today, the premises would be unaffordable to anyone but investment banks, corporate law firms and high-end accountants. But in 1947, when some people thought the City would never recover, Henry got it fairly cheap.

Then he wrote to a Mr Chandler, a friend of Walter's, whom he had met at that first dinner and at a couple of other City events, and whom Walter said was willing to second Henry's nomination to the Poulters' livery company (only a liveryman could become Lord Mayor). 'For more years than I care to remember,' Henry dictated to his secretary, 'it has been my ambition to become a Liveryman and Freeman of the City of London. My very great friend, Walter Sherman, has been a Liveryman of your Company for many years and naturally it has been my greatest desire particularly to join your worthy Company . . . I would esteem it as a great honour and kindness if you would put my name before your Court [the company's governing body].' In the summer of 1947 Zionist extremists were rebelling, murderously, against the British forces occupying Palestine. In the first week of August anger transferred from the Middle East onto Britain's Jews, and the older prejudices it liberated exploded in now-forgotten anti-Semitic riots, from Glasgow to London. Cemeteries were desecrated, synagogues vandalised and Jewish-owned shops smashed. So it is understandable that, in his personal particulars, Henry tells the truth, but not the whole truth. 'I was born in London,' he writes, 'of British parents, on the 10th August, 1906.'

Soon afterwards, he wrote again to Mr Chandler to say that 'Walter has seen me today and has told me of the honour you are doing me in being my seconder to a Livery and the Poulters' Company, and that my name will be coming forward at the next Court . . . I will uphold the confidence you have placed in me.' According to the Guildhall's archives, Henry became a freeman of the City – a separate procedure from the livery – on 28 May 1948, swearing before the Chamberlain of London in his ermine-trimmed gown, and with Walter standing next to him like a parent on prize day, to 'keep this City harmless . . . know no gatherings nor conspiracies made against the King's peace, but I will warn the Mayor thereof, or hinder it to my power'. He formally joined the Poulters' company, so its registers record, on 6 July 1948.

As Henry learned to his disappointment, freemen of the City of London are not, as urban myth has it, permitted to drive sheep over London Bridge. Nor are they entitled, if convicted of a capital crime, to be hung with a silken rope, or beheaded with a sword instead of an everyday axe. But the City and its ancient livery companies do boast some of the oldest and quaintest rituals and customs of any British institution. The livery companies are the descendants of the Saxon craft guilds (though their members are no longer expected to practise the eponymous professions), and had traded favours with the monarchy since the Norman Conquest. In return for their royal charters, the companies once helped to raise the Crown's armies, and welcomed the King back to London from his foreign adventures. The City banquets and ceremonies offered endless opportunities for bonhomie and graceful gestures, each dinner and handshake a test of Henry's metamorphosis that was its own reward. There was lots of dressing up, which he always enjoyed: the look of himself in black or white tie or a ceremonial gown was always a kind of vindication.

The Lord Mayor takes the lead role in these performances. He still has a large retinue of medieval functionaries: the Common Cryer; the City Marshal with his cockade of white plumes; the Sergeant-at-Arms with his mace; the Sword-Bearer with his fur hat and sword. The Lord Mayor is Admiral of the Port of London, and is entrusted with the password to the Tower. He is entitled to a share of the venison from the royal forests. He entertains kings and queens and is entertained by them; when a British monarch dies, the Lord Mayor attends Privy Council and signs the proclamation of the succession to the throne. He has an inexhaustible supply of theatrical gowns and robes, along with a dazzling array of hoods, wigs, seals, coaches and other accoutrements. On Michaelmas Day, 1947, Henry watched as Walter and the other liverymen elected the latest Lord Mayor, who emerged from the Guildhall to the sound of the state trumpeters and the pealing of bells from St Lawrence Jewry.

The path to this apotheosis is long, demanding, expensive and competitive. Many more freemen were and are gripped by my grandfather's ambition than can ever realise it. The Lord Mayor must previously have served as an alderman (a sort of local councillor) and as one of the sheriffs (the Lord Mayor's deputies), so that, as an ordinance of 1385 explains, 'he may be tried as to his governance and bounty before he attains to the Estate of Mayor'. He would usually have spent time on the City's main decision-making body, the Court of Common Council. The common councilmen, in their turn, were and are elected by the voters of the wards in which they live or work, and sit on the council in their special mazarine gowns, along with the sheriffs, and the aldermen in their scarlet robes with fur edging and black braid. The Lord Mayor would often have served as well on the courts of one or more livery companies. A lack of a high-class education was not an automatic disqualifier, but a shortage of liquid funds was: aspiring Lord Mayors had to hobnob enthusiastically, entertain generously and give bountifully to charity.

None of which deterred my grandfather. Henry thought, as he always thought, that there was bound to be a way, somewhere, to side-step obstacles and slip down shortcuts. He hurled himself into the City, with its strange traditions and frequent carousing, neglecting his business and sometimes, though she pretended not to resent it and almost never complained, my grandmother too. He joined a series of City clubs that enabled him to cultivate and impress liverymen from companies other than his own, storing up goodwill and impressions for when the critical electoral moments came. On 8 July 1948, right after his formal acceptance by the Poulters, he wrote to Walter, then making his escape for Cannes, to say that he was 'sending you this application for membership of the City Livery Club and I shall be very grateful if you could find a proposer and seconder for me and return the form so that I can send it to the secretary'. He joined the United Wards Club and the Farringdon Ward Club, volunteering to be its social secretary and winning plaudits all round for his indefatigable and imaginative efforts in that post. He arranged for the club to dine with the Lord Mayor and Lady Mayoress at the Apothecaries' hall; to visit Dr Johnson's House; to see beer being brewed, newspapers going to press and Beaumont and Fletcher's *Phylaster* performed at the Guildhall drama school. For old time's sake, he organised a tour of the J. Lyons and Co. factory, where his club saw Swiss rolls and ice cream being made, and were afterwards entertained to a tea ampler than the ones Henry had bought for Miriam at the Lyons Corner House in Coventry Street, when they were walking out.

He seized every chance of office and responsibility, however minor and time-consuming. 'On Friday I took the secretary's place at the Committee meeting of the [Farringdon] club,' he wrote to his son Philip, 'and was congratulated on all sides on my first occasion in this capacity.' He found seconders in the Poulters' company for the nomination of relatives and associates, who after their admission would be entitled to vote in City elections. He joined a second livery company, the Worshipful Company of Carmen, which met at Whittington Hall in Paternoster Row. His face was becoming known; he had developed a nice reputation as an off-the-cuff speaker and a generous contributor to charitable appeals. He confided to a

policeman friend from the Poulters' company, who had left London for a job in the Bahamas, that he was 'going along very nicely in the City', but, alas, 'so far, the Common Council is eluding me'. There was the rub.

Every time, Henry thought that the council hustings he had attended, known as wardmotes and held on St Thomas's Day in September, had gone rather well. 'Oyez oyez oyez,' the Ward Beadler would yell at the beginning: 'All manner of persons having anything to do at this Court of Wardmote . . . draw near and give your attendance.' When it was Henry's turn, he referred to his respect for the City traditions, and the importance of education, and when he was well enough Walter came along to finesse his friend's delivery with subtle hand gestures: a little louder, Henry, now a little slower, now a little more gesticulation and now less. But somehow he could never quite muster the votes to become a councilman. The City's archives have not retained the results of council elections for the period of my grandfather's Lord Mayoral campaign, so it is impossible to know how close or otherwise he came. Perhaps his background limited his appeal to the City gents who made up the bulk of voters in his ward; it is said by some who remember his City career that it was block voting by the big legal firms that kept him out, and put their men in instead. Had he been able to run in the ward of Portsoken – which flanks the Lane at the City's eastern extremity, and, with its seven synagogues, had returned Jewish councilmen and aldermen since the nineteenth century – things might have been different. But his office was in the ward of Farringdon Within. Each time he stood, he was convinced he would make it; but for whatever reason and by whatever margin, he never did.

As many people say of their thwarted ambitions and abortive schemes, maybe my grandfather would still have become Lord Mayor, had circumstances – in his case, business troubles – not intervened. There had been, it was true, some happy developments: in April 1949, shortly after Henry returned from his post-heart attack stay in Wales, the government finally abolished clothes rationing. British women became more and more able to follow fashion in their high streets, rather than only vicariously in American magazines. Henry wised up early to the selling power of Hollywood in the glamour-starved post-war years, and in the late forties, under his new brand name of Slenderella, he marketed a series of nighties based on blockbuster costumes. The first was *The Dancing Years* nightdress, 'designed in Empire Style and made from pastel georgette with small puff sleeves and satin ribbon', which was 'inspired by the ballet dress worn by Patricia Dainton in the film' of the same name, itself an adaptation of an Ivor Novello musical, which Henry had taken Miriam to see at the Adelphi theatre in London in the darkest days of 1943. *The Dancing Years* nightie was followed by garments modelled on Ann Vernon's attire in *Warning to Wantons*; a Delilah nightdress that paid profitable homage to 'Exotic Hedy Lamarr

"The Dancing Years" nightdress

Patricia Dainton

IVOR NOVELLO'S "The Dancing Years"

# Slenderella

OBTAINABLE AT YOUR LOCAL STORE

as Delilah in Cecil B. DeMille's masterpiece *Samson and Delilah*'; and a range of nightwear patterned on that of Elizabeth Taylor and her fellow *Little Women* ('they have the appeal of the demure Victorian miss, brought up to date with a dash of modern devilment'). Henry sewed up some useful export deals, including one with Iceland, which he visited again and where he was interviewed by the newspaper *Visir*. He sent the cutting to the Icelandic legation in London to be translated. 'Recently a British businessman,' the journalist wrote, 'a man well known for his industry and enterprise, Mr Henry Freedman, was here in the course of his travels.' Then Henry shares his mildly presumptuous views on Iceland's 'hospitable and bold' people, and on Reykjavik's schools, hospitals, sanatoria, swimming baths, electricity station, hot springs and geysers.

For all that, the tail-end of the forties was a lean time. Partly, it was all the shenanigans over the new factory. Shortages of cash and steel, then the requirements of the government's rearmament push, plus assorted other 'hitches', as the Board of Trade described them, conspired endlessly to delay the construction of the new building that Henry had been promised for South Shields, leaving him stuck in the ill-suited surroundings of the Cone Street school. The government tried to fob him off with a site outside town on the Jarrow Road, but he declined. By the end of the decade, ingratiation gave way to vitriol in Henry's correspondence with the local council, the Board and with Chuter Ede, the MP for South Shields, who also happened to be the Home Secretary. 'I would be more of a mouse than a man,' Henry told the Board in January 1948, 'if I did not write to you in protest at this very gross injustice which

has been done me.' The machinery he had bought for the new factory was sitting idle, he complained to the town clerk of South Shields; this 'dilly-dallying' had inflicted 'incalculable damage'. He had run the plant at a loss for two years, and now was only scraping into the black. He had accepted assorted proposals for other sites and layouts, but each had been retracted

229

after it was advanced, 'and so it has gone on like this until today I have nothing'. The town's honour was at stake, he argued, as well as his business. Anxious that Henry might cut his losses and, with his firm, leave altogether, the town clerk petitioned the Home Secretary in March 1948 in support of my grandfather's claim, copying Henry in on his letter in a bid to abate the flood of remonstrations. The company, he writes, 'have proved to be excellent employers'; the workers 'seem to be very happy'. In May Henry himself wrote to Ede, warning that 'we may be forced to reconsider more drastically our invidious situation, for which any business concern could be held liable for heavy damages, by virtue of those breaches of faith and contracts that have been made between us and the Board of Trade'.

Eventually, Henry was granted a meeting at the House of Commons with Ede and Sir Hartley Shawcross, then president of the Board. He took Mick with him, and they walked along the river from Cheapside, past the skeletal hulk of the new South Bank arts centre on the river. As they went through St Stephen's Gate into the Palace of Westminster, Henry felt much as he had done when he paid his thankless call on the bank manager in Liverpool Street to ask for his loan. He and Mick stood in a central lobby and whispered like two school-boys outside the headmaster's office in the Jews' Free School. Then a functionary appeared and ushered them past a bored policeman and into a surprisingly small office, off an upstairs corridor, all wood panelling and green baize. Ede, whom Henry had met before in South Shields, was waiting for them behind a desk; Shawcross arrived while the tea was poured into House of Commons china cups. The ministers seemed to listen as Henry talked; someone's private secretary kept notes. They were sorry for his inconvenience; they would give the matter their fullest consideration. The Freedmans left. Absolutely nothing happened as a result.

There were two other major glitches: Eric the chauffeur, and Henry's increasingly fraught relationship with Mick. 'Surely you appreciate,' Henry wrote to Mick after a stand-up argument between the brothers, in front of the other Cheapside staff, 'that as managing director of the firm I am entitled to a measure of respect from you as well as any other employee.' In the end, 'it is naturally impossible for two captains to be at the helm'. The only way to avoid the rows, Mick replied, seemed to be 'for me to say absolutely nothing about anything that happens . . . You know yourself there is no question of two captains, but as between a captain and a senior lieutenant – there is something missing which is very serious.' The fact that they were brothers was 'a continual embarrassment to me, and because of it I have accepted from you more insults and humiliations than I would stand from anybody else'. Their conversations and their correspondence were grim, ominous tirades of unforgiving 'you's.

Eric the chauffeur's story ended in tears, mainly his. So impressed was Henry by Eric's ability to keep the cumbersome Rolls on the road, mechanically and literally, that he promoted him to be the manager of the factory that he had opened during the war in the converted cinema in Harpenden. If Eric could drive that Rolls, he reasoned, he could certainly run an underwear factory. But Eric couldn't. Of all my grandfather's leap-of-faith appointments and promotions, this was the most optimistic, and the most disastrous. Eric struggled with new garment lines and was too soft with the staff, and after several months of trouble Henry wrote with some stern instructions, though he also reassured Eric about his position: 'I refute completely the statement Elsie [Eric's wife] made that I have turned against you – far from it. You never had a greater champion, or will ever find one in the future, than in me.' However, 'for some unknown reason you have not been able to grasp the requirements for the present circumstances ... and the more I have tried to assist you, the more you have evidently become confused'. He must delegate more; he must be stricter with the machine girls; he must spend a fortnight in South Shields. But Eric couldn't take the criticism, couldn't live with the thought that he might be letting his benefactor down, and not long afterwards he called my grandfather from the converted projectionist's room in the factory to resign.

Henry went straight down from Milton Road to see him, feeling half-relieved and half-betrayed. Eric was disconsolate and wouldn't be talked out of it, or talked to much at all. But, that evening, he tried to explain his feelings in a letter. 'It felt like a lash on my inner self,' he writes of my grandfather's advice, 'it twisted and tormented deep within me, I stood up to it only because it was you, and for the respect I have always tried to give you, I would rather die than feel like that again.' Loyal to the last, he implores Henry to 'please confirm that I did not leave you high and dry'. He is going, but he doesn't know where: 'God only knows what I shall do, I feel I have had to leave my very life behind, even my dreams are there. I could carry on writing for another page or two,' he says, writing only painfully, and painfully to read, 'were it not for the utter emptiness in me . . .' Henry was a generous employer, sometimes, as perhaps in Eric's case, to a fault. But if someone he had trusted let him down, he could be unforgiving. 'The first time he was really tested,' he wrote of Eric to his son Philip, 'he has failed.' At the factory, Henry observes, 'there was terrible tension in the air. The girls as you know like Eric very much . . . [they complain] that I raise my hat to them and say "good morning", but I call them all the bastards under the sun behind their backs. So I do. Mind you this conversation with Eric took place in the upstairs office, so if they heard anything at all you can imagine how much noise their machines were not making.' But there was no harm done, other than to Eric: 'I went into the factory on Thursday and Friday and the girls were all smiles again. The lesson here is that discipline is most necessary and kindness is misplaced and taken advantage of'; also that 'people are ready to kick the underling and lick the boots of those that succeed'.

The film tie-ins, the growing export trade and the old factory in the Lane kept the firm from going under. In the end, however, it came down to this: Henry would never have a chance of becoming Lord Mayor if he didn't have a thriving business to bankroll his ticket; but his business would never thrive so long as he dedicated himself to the pursuit of his dream, spending more of his time in the office writing election manifestos and invitations to club outings than thinking about apparel, and more lunches and evenings politicking in the City than buttering up clients and suppliers, or at home with Miriam and the children. He confided his dilemma to another

City friend, a knighted dressmaker to the Queen who lived in Buckingham Gate. 'My advice to you,' came the reply, 'is to give up all ideas of public service. For a business man this is a waste of time, and only distracts your attention from the important occupation of earning a living.' My grandfather marked the envelope 'very important', then tried to ignore its contents. He would stand in elections again when business picked up and, he told himself until long after it had ceased to be plausible, he would still be Lord Mayor of London. Before long, however, his ambitions were transferred to another milieu that, with Walter's help, he and Miriam had managed to infiltrate.

## SIX:

# 'Quite a success in society'

*10, Downing Street*
*Whitehall*
*9th October, 1953.*

*Dear Mr. Freedman,*
*Thank you for your letter.*

*I am afraid it will not be possible for my Husband and myself to lend a room in Downing Street for a Committee meeting for the Ball to be held in aid of the National Spastics Society. I wish I could help to publicise the Ball in this way, but since I saw you at Lady Heald's house on Tuesday I have been considering the circumstances.*

*When Sir Winston was Prime Minister during the War we lived in small quarters, and the larger reception rooms were rarely used. I did then hold a few meetings here for charities in which I was personally interested. When my Husband became Prime Minister for the second time we began to live in the bigger rooms, and we felt we should open them all up for Coronation Year, and we are still using them. But looking through my letters I find that I have recently expressed regret to several charitable organisations that I cannot lend a room on the floor which has now become our private residence.*

*I do hope you will understand that I cannot very well do as you ask without hurting their feelings.*

*I am so sorry.*
*Yours sincerely,*
*Clementine S. Churchill*


Just before 4.30 in the afternoon of 20 May 1953, my grandparents arrived for a meeting at 11 Lyall Street, a grand, stucco-fronted mansion in the heart of Belgravia. The other invitees included seven 'Ladies', two 'Honourables', a pair of countesses and a Parker-Bowles. The hostess was Lady Irene Astor, daughter of Field Marshall the Earl Haig ('the Butcher of the Somme') and wife of Gavin Astor, who would later inherit *The Times* and Hever Castle, in which Henry VIII once courted Anne Boleyn. Like Henry's fruitless colloquy with Ede and Shawcross in the Palace of Westminster, this was not the sort of meeting that was likely to be recorded in newspapers or show up in history books. But, for my grandparents, the afternoon was momentous.

The Lyall Street get-together was the first session of a committee formed to organise a garden party on 8 July 1953 in aid of the Sunshine Homes for Blind Babies. Henry retained the minutes that Lady Astor distributed afterwards, which, not intended to be read fifty years later, unselfconsciously record the tics of top-drawer fifties Society, and hint at the combination of altruism and one-upmanship that animated the meeting's participants. 'It was suggested that there should be two stalls,' the minutes record, 'one for toys and sweets which Lady Caroline Waterhouse kindly agreed to look after, and a miscellaneous stall with the assistance of Mrs Freedman.' The ladies and the odd gentleman present proposed their ideas for boosting the party's revenue – rides, raffles and so on – but baulked at any proposals of questionable taste: 'It was agreed that there should be a Puppet Show, but unanimously decided that we should not have Tony's Performing Dogs as it was felt that many of the Public would not approve.' One attendee announced that she would endeavour to procure, via her officer husband, the band of the Grenadier Guards. Another volunteered a brace of pipers. Then my grandmother, dressed in a new suit by Norman Hartnell that my grandfather had given her for the occasion, spoke up.

She hadn't wanted to. Speaking in public daunted her as much as it excited Henry. As well as polishing her vowels, by May 1953 her elocution mistress had taught her to avoid many of the little vocabulary solecisms that might have embarrassed her in polite company. She had learned to say 'pudding' instead of 'sweet'; 'looking glass' for 'mirror'; 'wireless' rather than 'radio; 'what' in place of 'pardon'; 'napkin' not 'serviette'. 'Toilet' was, naturally, an abomination. She knew that she was supposed to make 'Ralph' rhyme with 'safe', slur the last three syllables of 'formidable' and use 'telephone' as a verb. She could just about manage all that in the comfort of a tête-à-tête at the Albany Club in Savile Row. But talking in front of a dozen titled strangers, all listening and looking and judging, felt not right, not for her. Couldn't Henry do it at Lady Astor's? He, after all, loved it, loved the frisson of impersonation, the secret feeling that his life had become a perpetual heist, and at the same time the sense that he was sloughing off an old skin that had never really been his, emerging as the Henry Freedman he had always known he could be.

No, she must do it. The other ladies would be offering their wares on behalf of their husbands, and so should she. Anyway, he would be there with her, so what could go wrong?

They planned it like a *coup de théâtre*. Let them all rattle on about their tombola prizes and home-made jams or the children's slide they would bring up from the country. Then, as the minutes record, 'Mrs Freedman offered to obtain an elephant.'

'Wherever will you get it, dear?' had been Miriam's response when Henry had first come up with the elephant idea.

But fellowship of the Zoological Society, it turned out, had its benefits. Henry had begun his correspondence with the curator of mammals at London Zoo well before the committee meeting. By 9 June, when Lady Astor's team reconvened at Lyall Street, he had secured the services of Lakshmi the baby elephant, along with those of a Shetland pony, two rideable donkeys and a llama cart. There was some anxiety about the llamas: 'I am not quite sure how [they] will behave in strange surroundings,' the zoo's curator of mammals wrote to my grandfather, 'and if they give any trouble either as we attempt to move them or when they arrive, then I am sure you will understand if I cancel them and just supply the other animals.'

The minutes of the second meeting record Miriam's announcement of this herd, as well as the hostess's own countermove: 'Lady Irene announced that Mr Jack Hawkins [according to a 1953 opinion poll, the country's favourite screen actor] had kindly agreed to open the Garden Party, and Mr Douglas

Fairbanks had consented to give the prizes.' Unfortunately, 'the Balloon Race had been forbidden by Scotland Yard, owing to it being in the Metropolitan area and illegal'. The minute-taker had a nice line in casual hauteur, almost invisible to the un-tutored eye: 'Mrs Claremount also announced that we had the promise of a Mrs Barnett, who calls herself a super-sensory medium, to read hands, etc.'

Showers on the morning of the garden party – held in the grounds of a villa in Regent's Park – kept some of the ticket-holders away. Still, apart from the committee members, a satisfying number of viscounts, duchesses, marquesses, earls, countesses, sirs, lords and ladies, as well as a scattering of ambassadors, turned up. So did the promised film stars, Hawkins and Fairbanks. But, at least according to Lady Astor's thank-you letter, sent from the Astors' home in Sussex, it was the animals who 'made the party . . . I just cannot thank you enough.' The party and the elephant were hits, and Henry kept

Lady Astor's letters, the minutes of the meetings and his correspondence with the zoo for posterity.

Looking back on the unlikely social career that my grandparents came to enjoy in the fifties, there are two surprises. The first is that this country-house, lady-in-waiting set could be so easily joined by a hustling couple such as they were. The second is that this (to Henry and Miriam) brave new world of titled ladies and paternalistic benevolence and private balls, which seems to belong more to the eighteenth century than in post-war Britain, was still so vibrant and, for my grandfather especially, so seductive.

In some accounts of the decline of the British upper classes, the slide began with the First World War, continuing until the recent ejection of the hereditary peers from the House of Lords. The cull of the officer class in the trenches; falling agricultural prices and the land sales they led to; death duties; the extension of the voting franchise; and the falling credibility of gentlemanly amateurism in what had once been blue-blood-dominated professions: all these drove the aristocrats out of government, off their ancestral estates and, in some cases, into self-imposed exile in East Africa or on the Riviera. By the thirties many titled gentlemen had been obliged to take up careers in the City. In 1939 those grand families who still maintained commensurately grand London establishments knew that the game was nearly up. There was a run of house-cooling parties in the still-functioning first-rank homes of Piccadilly, Park Lane and Grosvenor and Berkeley Squares; after the war, those that hadn't been bombed were mostly sold and demolished. Many of the corresponding country houses had been requisitioned for use by evacuated schools or as hospitals, or, if their owners were particularly unlucky, by the army. Afterwards there wasn't the money to put them right, and many were either pulled down or turned into country hotels or boarding schools. Or, still more unthinkably, their owners consented to let in paying guests, to admire the porcelain and speculate on the value of the furniture. Anyone who persevered in trying to maintain an old-fashioned establishment was afflicted by 'the servant problem': the reluctance of underlings who had left jobs in service to fight in the war to return to their below-stairs lives – which, in many cases, left no one to light the fires, wind the clocks, answer the door, dust the furniture and polish the silver. And even if the money could be found for a new hunting coat, the garment would also cost eighteen valuable clothing coupons.

Yet after the worst of post-war austerity, and before the taxes introduced during the sixties delivered the *coup de grâce* to the old lifestyle, the aristocracy and its fellow-travellers managed a kind of nostalgic coda, which, even as they were enjoying it, everyone knew couldn't last. 'Society' was no longer as influential or exclusive as it once had been. By the end of the nineteenth century, those industrialists too rich to be refused, a few Jews (the odd Rothschild or Sassoon), plus the American adventuresses who had crossed the Atlantic to trade their inheritances for titles, had already arrived in even the most rarefied drawing rooms, house parties and family trees. It helped if they had a house or three to throw parties in themselves. After the war, the charmed circle was stretched further. London Society – which before the emergence of pop stars, still provided the fodder for gossip columnists and daydreamers – took in writers and artistes, plus Frank Sinatra, Eric's *doppelgänger* Danny Kaye and other beautiful people from America when they were in town. But at its heart were still the old families, old Etonians and officers of the household regiments. Old-style hostesses cultivated salons and strove to design the perfect dinner-party list: even if future prime ministers were no longer decided upon over the brandy, the hostess might at least receive the credit for a glamorous marriage.

The return to Downing Street of Churchill – himself an authentic toff – for his own swansong in 1951 contributed to the upper-class Indian summer. 'We were at Claridge's for a Ball on election night,' my grandfather wrote to his son after the Tory poll win, 'and the excitement was immense.' Henry had grown into one of those instinctive conservatives that immigrant communities often produce, alongside their radicals and egalitarians. No resentment seems to have clouded his esteem for those born with the privileges he had fought for. Having got by without them himself, he was always sceptical about the virtues of government handouts. He was, in particular, a devoted Churchill enthusiast, who seemed to him to epitomise the indomitability and rhetorical dash that England was supposed to be all about. He was briefly involved in the United Europe Movement, a proto-integrationist group that Churchill founded in 1947.

The succession of an appealing young Queen in 1952, and romantic talk of a new Elizabethan age, contributed to the retro-chic atmosphere. There were practical fillips in the early fifties too: land values rose, and the art market boomed as big-time American collectors crossed the ocean to acquire auctioned heirlooms. Labour-saving gadgets helped hard-pressed country ladies to make do more easily without servants, provided someone came up from the village to help out on a couple of afternoons a week.

So, for a few years, it was almost possible to pretend that nothing had really changed, even though everything had. There was no longer a London summer 'Season' in the formal, nineteenth-century sense, with three dances in town every night between the opening of the Royal Academy Summer Exhibition and the Goodwood races. Young ladies no longer drove around Hyde Park with their chaperones in barouches and landaus. But there were still coming-out balls for débutantes to meet eligible bachelors, and plentiful opportunities for riding and shooting animals, playing croquet and dressing up. Ascot, Henley and many of the other institutions of the Season endured, as they do still.

Entry to this charmed if fated world was managed in much the same way as it had ever been. There were venerable rituals of acceptance and rejection – a sort of courtly romance between the initiates and those whose favours they were cultivating. Transgression of the unspoken but strict rules of the social game could still result in a 'cut'. The aspirants' best hope was to be 'taken up' by an established patron, who considered them sufficiently amusing or interesting to sponsor their social advancement.

This is what happened to my grandparents. Alongside Walter, their sponsors came to include Lady Victor Paget, ultimately known to them as Mavis. A one-time Bright Young Thing, she had dabbled as a dress designer and modelled her own creations in the pages of *Vogue*. She had acquired her third husband, a First World War hero and lord, in 1935. During the Second World War she had thrown a party for a visiting American actress, at which Noel Coward had given a famously moving rendition of 'London Pride'. There was also a jovial Polish émigrée princess with an unpronounceable surname, who organised musical soirées at her Kensington home, and was less solvent than she was popular; and a Belgravia lady who had survived the *Titanic*. These four orchestrated my grandparents' introductions. Then it was up to them to impress, and their new acquaintances to extend invitations to 'At Homes' or cocktail parties. (For the ingénue to do the inviting would have been a definite faux pas.)

The pretext for many of these introductions was charitable fundraising. Along with hunting, charity was a traditional base from which serious social climbers staged their ascent. An energetic involvement in good causes demonstrated a consciousness of the duty that accompanied one's social superiority.

It also clarified precisely how superior one was: there was an order of precedence among the charities one could support, determined in part by the eminence of their royal patrons. There was also a hierarchy within each organisation, from ordinary committee members through honorary treasurers and up to vice-presidents; ranking on committees and the social rank of the members themselves tended to be proportionate. The outsider would begin by making a donation, on the back of which he or she would volunteer to help organise one of the charity bazaars and balls that were an established part of the calendar. With charm and luck these endeavours would bring in invitations, which would in turn provide new introductions to yet more elevated acquaintances. The bazaars and fêtes were themselves a sort of skit: part of the fun came from the incongruous loftiness of the sales assistants, politely hawking their donated knick-knacks and toffee.

In this world of amateur retailers, Henry and Miriam had a powerful advantage: they were pros. My grandmother had first learned how to sell on her brother's stall in Hoxton, then honed her technique on her husband's. She knew that customers never bought from the first stall in a row, and how to guide their gaze to the most expensive merchandise ('your show's your takings'). She knew the cardinal rule that as near to nothing as possible should be left at the end of a day. She had helped out at fundraising sales for local charities up in Harpenden throughout the forties. Now, under the tutelage of Mavis, Walter and the rest, she deployed her skills in Regent's Park and Park Lane. She refrained from ribald and coercive patter, but then she had never much gone in for that in Hoxton or Spitalfields.

Her new, naïve friends thought she was a natural saleswoman. They were not, perhaps, entirely taken in by the elocution lessons. Even at the peak of their efficacy they could only partially camouflage Miriam's Hoxton twang, which sometimes overwhelmed the pretence altogether during the familiar bustle of the bazaars. Perhaps they noticed how she often said funny things without intending to. But seeing how she carried herself in her Hartnell and Hardy Amies dresses, her charity collaborators presumed that, though she may have come from trade, it was very likely the grander sort – department stores, big-time manufacturing, that sort of thing – and that Miriam herself must have been at a finishing school, when in fact she had been through a millinery sweatshop and then another apprenticeship in the Lane. Some of them clocked that she was Jewish, and reflexively reinserted the 'i' into Freedman when they wrote to her; it must have seemed suitably Germanic.

After every record-breaking charity sale, letters of admiration and gratitude arrived in Harpenden from impressed ladies with noble surnames. 'You have been quite wonderful and such a brilliant saleswoman,' the chairman of the Marie Curie Memorial Foundation's appeals committee wrote to Miriam after a Christmas fête; 'we should never have achieved half what we did if it hadn't been for you . . . do write to the Ladies Carlton [the female equivalent of the elite gentlemen's club] & when you have filled in the application form send it to me.' After the Royal College of Nursing's Spring Fair, its president 'cannot thank you enough for the way you have worked for the Fair, sitting in the little box taking numerous half-crowns, giving everyone such a charming smile and a word of encouragement in spite of the weather . . . I hope you are not too exhausted today after all your efforts.' At a meeting to plan a bazaar for the National Association of Mixed Clubs and Girls' Clubs, so the event's boss informed Miriam, 'several people said how much they missed the lovely stall of Undies etc, which you had two years ago. It was unanimously agreed that I should write to ask you if you will very kindly have a similar Stall at this year's Bazaar, which is to take place at 45 Park Lane . . . Mrs Attlee [wife of Clement, by then the ex-Prime

Minister] tells me she will be delighted to be joint Stall-holder with you this year if only you will have a Stall. Please say yes.' The Park Lane ladies never knew the full truth.

Henry loved watching Miriam's mock haggles with earls and ambassadors, and loved it when her sales trounced those of the other stallholders. But decorum dictated that, being a gentleman, he himself did not practise the art he had mastered in the Lane at these ersatz markets, however much he inwardly cringed at the sloppiness of Miriam's colleagues ('not like that,' he was always thinking, 'not the real price first'). Instead he contributed a talent for obtaining saleable goods at cost price or for nothing, and an amazing energy with ticket sales. Where other members of his committees sent polite notes to their acquaintances inquiring whether, should it be convenient, they might care to attend this or that ball or garden party, Henry sent out the tickets first. It was a variation on the old scam of placing the pyjamas or stockings into the customers' palms before the deal was done, letting them feel the fabric, feel themselves already inside it, understand that they had to have it.

Under scrutiny, good deeds can often seem to derive from mixed motives, and so perhaps does my grandparents' zealous charity work. Some of the motives were noble. Knowing how it could be to be poor, when they came into some money they always gave a lot of it away. While he was doubtful about government handouts, Henry approved of hand-ups from elsewhere, like the one that had set his mother up with her stall in the Lane in 1917. He was a tough man in some of his dealings and with some of his family, but part of his heart was soft. Miriam was soft all the way through, and was too accustomed to hard work to be deterred from a worthy cause by a spot of rain or a few hours' turgid labour.

But some of the motives were more complicated. In return for their efforts, my grandparents earned something intangible that to them was more valuable than time and dearer than money. After a while, their social sponsors and their charity efforts opened the way to a dizzying prize: royalty.

Henry and Miriam had first laid eyes on a king during the Silver Jubilee tour of 1935, when the loyal immigrant poor serenaded George V through the East End with choruses of 'For He's a Jolly Good Fellow.' In 1936 Henry saw the same king's coffin, lying in state before the public on its catafalque, with its orbs and sceptre and imperial crown, which was the last time he had been inside the Palace of Westminster before he went to see the ministers about the factory with Mick. During the abdication crisis, when supporters of besotted, beleaguered Edward VIII marched through the streets of east London, Henry – a paid-up romantic as well as an ardent monarchist – had been squarely of the King's party. In 1948 he saw another living monarch at the London Olympics: 'We were there on the opening day & it was truly an impressive sight,' Henry wrote to his elder son. 'After leaving the stadium we strolled along outside and saw the King and Queen and other members of the Royal Family,' though the impressiveness was mitigated by the crush and the huge crowds, which meant it took him and Miriam two hours to get to Baker Street station from the stadium at Wembley.

Through Walter, Mavis and the rituals of charity, in the early fifties it became possible that Henry and Miriam might actually meet and speak to members of the royal family: that the royals would shake their hands and talk to them and maybe remember their names. This prospect mesmerised a part of my grandfather that was still, and would always be, singing 'Rule Britannia' and saluting the Union Jack in the playground of the Jews' Free School in Spitalfields. It was as if, by pressing royal flesh, he hoped a little bit of the immortality of the throne might rub off on him, transforming him from a Galician frog into an Englishman prince. More so even than the Lord Mayoralty, the pursuit of royalty became for him a kind of addiction. Every thrill had to be succeeded by one still greater, a more illustrious princess or more intimate introduction, en route to the main event: a formal presentation to a reigning monarch, which, after her accession to the throne in 1952, would mean the new Queen, Elizabeth.

'We were full of excitement when we arrived at the Empire,' Miriam wrote to her son Philip in America on 1 November 1950, 'just a few seconds before the King and Queen with the princess Elizabeth and Margaret.' This was the Empire cinema in Leicester Square rather than the Empire music hall, and the occasion was the Royal Film Performance of 26 October 1950. Through his tie-in lingerie deals with the film studios, Henry had got himself invited to some post-war film premières. Once, when he took his friend Walter along, Walter had introduced Henry to an acquaintance who sat on the committee of the Cinematograph Trade Benevolent Fund, which set up the royal film shows. Henry had offered to help organise the festivities, and received two tickets for his pains. 'We were just next to them,' my grandmother writes of the royals, 'they were very beautiful and stately, it was quite a thrill . . . The film we saw was called *The Mudlark* [a soppy drama about Queen Victoria and a pauper, starring Alec Guinness and Irene Dunne], which was most enjoyable. I was dressed in my best evening gown with my beautiful necklace, and daddy in full evening dress.'

Like dances and cocktails, in London Society people drifted in and out of fashion. You could swim in invitations one year, and be ostracised or forgotten the next. In the early fifties my grandparents found themselves *in*. 'On Wednesday we went to a Ball at the Dorchester,' Henry wrote to Philip on 3 February 1951, 'and this morning we received an invitation from Mrs Attlee to an "At Home" at 10 Downing Street.' Miriam and Violet Attlee, then the Prime Minister's wife ('pretty, well-dressed . . . very self-possessed, very much the lady', according to Sir Henry 'Chips' Channon, the bitchy chronicler of mid-century high society) had met and hit it off at another charity 'At Home'. 'On Monday we are going to a Ball at the Mansion House, and we are going to a special concert at St James's Palace.' At the Mansion House they met the Lord Mayor and Lady Mayoress, and later that week Miriam went to a charity meeting at the Empress Club in Dover Street, the grandest ladies' club in London, whose drawing rooms were said to resemble the salons at Versailles. Then, in the second week of February, my grandparents went together to the 'At Home' in Downing Street, to help plan an auction in aid of the children's charity the NSPCC.

Because the security was so much looser, visiting Number Ten seemed much less daunting than it might today. 'We enjoyed our visit to Downing Street,' Henry wrote the following week, 'and found Mrs Attlee a most charming person.' Churchill aside, politicians and their spouses were too work-aday and sublunary to appeal to my grandfather in quite the way hereditary notables did. All the same, he kept the letter that Mrs Attlee sent, on Downing Street paper, after the NSPCC auction. She had bought a housecoat made in South Shields and donated to the cause by Henry, along with assorted slips and pyjamas. But it didn't fit, and although she hadn't really wanted it anyway, he insisted on replacing it. 'Dear Mr Freedman,' she wrote, 'It was indeed kind of you to make such a lovely house-coat especially for me, in place of the one I bought at the auction on March 21st. I like it very much – especially the collar. It fits me perfectly except that it is a little too long – a fault on the right side. Thank you very much. Yours sincerely, Violet H. Attlee.' Soon afterwards, Miriam helped out again at an NSPCC bazaar at the Dorchester, where, as Henry reported proudly to Philip, she 'took £160 at the Toy Stall, and when I came for her at 6.30, she looked as fresh as a daisy. The previous day she went to a meeting which was held at the House of Commons, and Mr and Mrs Attlee came up and shook her hand': both of them this time, though Miriam thought at first that it must have been another gentleman, since this one seemed so nice, and not at all the vandalistic socialist villain about whom some of her new acquaintances complained so relentlessly. 'I cannot tell you how popular she is,' Henry told their son, and 'with the new charity angle she is having a really exciting experience.'

Popular, definitely; exciting, perhaps. Yet my grandmother was slowly growing discontented with her reinvented self, silently at first, and then more openly as the make-believe took over their lives. All these *grandes dames* were friendly enough. But Miriam worried that they would lose the feeling that used to envelop them: the feeling that Henry and she together were the real world, and the rest was incidental, shadows on the wall of a cave. 'I have been having a busy time with all my social work,' she wrote to Philip in April 1951, but 'I wonder if daddy is doing right. I think it may be a little too much, for we have no time for anything.' She wanted to want what her husband wanted, and she enjoyed the compliments about how beautiful she looked, and being told what a remarkable and first-rate fellow her Henry was; but she couldn't quite persuade herself that everything new was better. The following week, 'we went to see a wonderful film *The Tales of Hoffman* [a fantastical ballet featuring Moira Shearer as a clockwork doll]. It was the premiere Queen Mary was there and we took with us Mrs Marks from the Lane she looked very nice and really enjoyed herself. Also we took Ida, Solly, Nita and Sid.' (But they didn't take Leah: Henry saw to it that when the Society crowd came to one of his own 'At Homes', Leah was in her own home, above the shop off Harpenden High Street, rather than in his. 'She is just the same granny,' he wrote to his son, 'who lives in a shell, a world of her own.') 'We are having a very nice time at all our social affairs,' Miriam pretended after *The Tales of Hoffman*, 'but I think daddy is spending a little too much shall we say over doing it.' There was another dinner at the Mansion House, but 'it was only for men, so I did not go with him'.

Spending too much money, too little time with her, and, once again, paying too little attention to his business. Slenderella, Henry's underwear brand, brought out a new seersucker nightgown, available in Exotic Flame, Azalea Pink and Peacock Blue, and a nightdress based on Deborah Kerr's tunic in *Quo Vadis*, a 1951 sword-and-sandals blockbuster. Giggling machinists from the Harpenden factory modelled a new range of Slenderella housecoats in the local parade for the Festival of Britain – that optimistic 1951 bid to cheer up and advertise the nation after over a decade of war and austerity – while short-trousered schoolboys, men (still) in uniform and women in sensible coats looked on. (Henry's Rolls also appeared in the parade, decorated in ropes of daffodils from the Milton Road garden along its running board and across the bonnet.) But my grandfather had made a bad hedge when

war in Korea looked imminent, buying up more material than he could use at inflated prices. When the utility scheme eventually ended, as he explained to his son, 'many new cloths and garments are in demand, and prices have gone to hell'. Between the recession, Korea and the outing of the Cambridge spies, 'our little island is going through a tough time, and its position in the world is most precarious . . . Our people are tired after two great wars, and the threat of annihilation hanging over our heads.' It was only, he reckoned, 'by an all out effort by the people that we shall pull through. Unfortunately, everybody is leaving it to everybody else . . . ' His prognosis for the garment business was bleak: 'The whole of the textile industry is in jeopardy . . . It is the survival of the fittest, and about 30% of those engaged in clothing manufacture will have to drop out.' Factory work was hard to come by; only the foolhardy spurned it once they had it. The mother of a Harpenden employee who had resigned wrote secretly to beg Henry to take her daughter back: 'Pam tells us she gave her notice on Monday would you be kind enough to try to get her to stay . . . her daddy has been at home with his nerves since November he is just getting better & now this will upset him again I know she is sorry from the bottom of her heart that she gave notice. Please do not let her know I have written to you but I feel sure she would stop if you would let her.'

Henry, meanwhile, was having the time of his new life: Covent Garden, with the seemingly ubiquitous Moira Shearer in *Giselle*, followed by a buffet supper; a pageant at St George's Chapel, Windsor Castle; drinks on the terrace at the House of Lords; balls at the Savoy and banquets in the City. There was a charity preview of *Much Ado About Nothing*, and an auction during the interval, and Henry bought a rare print of Irene Vanbrugh, an actress whom he and Miriam had once seen in *Catherine the Great* at the Troxy cinema on Commercial Road,

for more than he could afford, though for less than the knight and the viscount who had bought it before him and put it up for resale. A weakness for the spendthrift gesture, for living it up and beyond his means, was one legacy of his costermonger days that chimed with the have-a-care indulgence in his new circle. 'There was an article in the Londoner's Diary in the *Evening News*,' Henry reported to Philip, 'and one in London by Night in the *Standard*, in which my name was mentioned.' There was 'an At Home when I proposed a vote of thanks to the Countess of Dudley & the previous day we were at Lord Rothermere's home to meet the Countess of Athlone'. On 15 April 1951 he tells of a visit to St James's Palace: 'Queen Mary was there, and Lady Engleigh, who used to be Lady in Waiting to Queen Mary, spoke to Mummy and made a fuss of her. After that in the evening we went to Derby House invited by the Duchess of Beaufort and met many people we knew. We have become quite popular.'

*Quite* popular: Henry had assimilated the upper-class tendency towards understatement, which dictated that important things must be downplayed, while trivial things commanded apocalyptic adjectives such as 'beastly', 'ghastly' and 'frightful'; most damning of all was 'boring'. In 1950 and early 1951, the phase of his Society apprenticeship, my grandfather also learned the proper way to reply to invitations in the third person. He learned that while it was right to acknowledge the fine furniture and valuable art in a drawing room, gushing wouldn't do. He committed to memory the prescribed forms of address for ambassadors and the various ranks of the aristocracy. He understood that, when asked to an 'At Home', it was wrong to stay for long, even or especially if you were enjoying yourself. He learned to listen compassionately when acquaintances who still had them were distressed about their servants leaving or dying. From her home on Regent's Park, Lady Victor Paget confided to Miriam that she was 'very unhappy because my old and much loved maid Kate has had a second stroke & is on the danger list. I go to the hospital, but she does not know me. This, I know, must happen because she is 89, but after 28 years of faithful and devoted service to me it is still a shock when it comes . . . I hate writing to Henry for anything,' she goes on, now in her capacity as a committee member for the Greater London Fund for the Blind, 'because I know he is the most generous man in the whole of England'; but she asks for his help all the same.

So when Henry and Miriam met their first royal, they were ready. On 22 May 1951 the Sunshine Fund, on whose behalf Henry would two years later procure the elephant, held a fundraising ball at Claridge's. When Princess Margaret, the ball's patron, swept in with her entourage, Henry and Miriam's hands were among those that she inattentively shook. My grandmother had practised her curtsy, and they both knew the rules: don't be too obsequious nor too awed (they hate that); but on no account be too familiar (they hate that even more). Later, during the dancing, they manoeuvred as close to the Princess as they could, as unobtrusively as they could, hoping for an exchange of smiles or pleasantries.

Next day, the *Daily Mail*'s photo of the occasion depicts, in the foreground, the beautiful Princess – more beautiful than those too young to remember her in her prime might now credit – flirting on the dancefloor with a young aristocrat, tall and with his hair slicked back. In the background is another couple. She is wearing a silk dress and long gloves; he is in white tie, and looking neither at Margaret nor at his own part-ner, but straight into the camera. Henry phoned the *Mail* and asked for a copy of the negative, and when the print was ready he put it in a silver frame and on the middle of the mantel in the stippled Harpenden dining room, where it stood for several years, proclaiming my grandparents' arrival to the world and to themselves. 'We have had some wonderful adventures,'

Henry wrote to Philip, two days after the ball, 'being presented to Princess Margaret on Tuesday. Mummy and I are making quite a success in society generally.'

On 22 September 1951 my grandfather met Princess (not yet Queen) Elizabeth. It was at a gala performance of *The Lady with the Lamp*, in which Anna Neagle played Florence Nightingale, put on in Leicester Square in aid of the Royal College of Nursing – an evening that, as treasurer of the committee, Henry had helped to arrange. 'I was presented to Her Royal Highness Princess Elizabeth and the Duke of Edinburgh on Saturday night,' Henry wrote to his son. 'The Countess of Mountbatten presented me, and it was televised to millions of people . . . Since then I have been congratulated on all sides.' (Joseph Diener, a Polish refugee to whom Henry had given a job in the thirties, but who had later emigrated to America and opened a window-cleaning business, wrote to offer his 'sincerest congratulations it is certainly a very great honor and I am very pleased to hear from your success may God help you you should always be successful'.) In a surviving newsreel of the occasion, my short, by now slightly portly grandfather can just be made out, shaking hands with the Princess, who was wearing a diamond tiara and carrying an oversized bouquet of white roses, after she ascends some stairs. This, for the future Queen, must have been one of dozens of handshakes that were part of every official engagement, one of countless forgettable half-acquaintances that blurred into one another each year. For Henry, it was a triumph. His bow is perhaps just a little too low, and he clutches the Princess's gloved hand for perhaps a moment too long, before she withdraws it and moves on with Prince Philip to speak to the Mountbattens, Anna Neagle and Elizabeth Taylor.

By November 1951 it looked as if the final conquest – a meeting with a current monarch – was imminent. The Countess of Athlone had promised to introduce Henry and Miriam to the Queen (later the Queen Mother) at a charity concert. But the Queen caught a cold, and Princess Margaret came instead. There was some consolation: the Princess appeared to remember Henry and Miriam, and 'took the opportunity of having a nice little chat'; it seemed to Henry that if Miriam were 'the Queen herself, people couldn't be more anxious to speak to her'. Then, at the beginning of 1952, King George VI died in his sleep. Princess Elizabeth flew back from Africa and was met by Churchill on the tarmac. 'The King is dead,' Henry wrote to his son in America three days later, 'and now we have a Queen on the throne. She is a wonderful person, and will carry out her duties to the full . . . It is said that when a Queen reigns there is peace; let's hope that these words become true.' A week later he records that 'Everything has been overshadowed by the funeral of the late King . . . The loyalty of the people for the monarchy is stronger than ever. I think it would do the USA a lot of good to be able to have someone through whom they could show their allegiance to their country, who was above party, self and politics.'

Business had begun to look up: 'The wheel has turned, and we are on level ground again.' But for the rest of the year, the charity scene was bereft of monarchs and first-rank princesses. Henry had to make do with another, now almost-forgotten blue-blood, Marie Louise, a granddaughter of Queen Victoria and a cousin of Elizabeth. He, Miriam and Marie Louise organised a fundraising film show for struggling artists, and a hospital ball at the Dorchester ('Her Highness would be glad if you and Henry would sit at the top table . . . White ties for the men').

Mick Freedman finally walked out of my grandfather's business at the beginning of 1953. After the decisive phone call, Henry rushed into the sitting room in Milton Road, flopped onto the sofa and wept. He and Mick loved each other, but it couldn't work. Miriam phoned Freda, Mick's wife, but it was no use. My uncle Philip came back from America and joined the firm at around the same time, as my other uncle, Michael, would do later. Henry sold the factory in the converted cinema, and in May he wrote sternly to his northern manager, explaining that he had 'burned my boats by giving up my Harpenden factory and I am now completely reliant upon the success of the factory at South Shields . . . Unless we can live up to the reputation of Slenderella, we shall soon cease to trade.' But in the new part of Henry's life, a part that then mattered to him most, 1953 was an *annus mirabilis*.

After the formal mourning, Elizabeth was crowned on 2 June. In the sort of company in which Henry and Miriam now found themselves, there had been much gossip about who was and wasn't 'Abbey happy': invited to sit in Westminster Abbey among the tiaras, sceptres and coronets, the crimson robes of the peers and dark velvet cloaks of the Knights of the Garter. Like most people, my grandparents watched the Queen arrive in the golden coach, saw the fireworks and heard the guns at the Tower of London sounding their salute only on the television. They went to a coronation party at the Zoo, thrown by the Zoological Society and overseen by Field Marshal Viscount Alanbrooke. Then, on 23 July 1953, two weeks after the elephant garden party, the new Queen presided at my grandmother's own coronation.

Henry had assumed that shaking hands with a princess in the foyer of a West End cinema or hotel was all that was meant by 'presentation'. In fact, as he became aware by the spring of 1953, true presentation to the Queen involved a very specific, arcane process. A presentation at Court occurred when, through the sponsorship of a married woman who had herself been presented (or was the wife of an ambassador), a lady was introduced to the Queen at a gathering convened for that purpose. You could not apply for presentation yourself: the sponsor must apply for you, via the Lord Chamberlain's office. Most of the names thus submitted were those of youthful debutantes. Before the war, the debs had decorated their hair with three ostrich feathers – an eighteenth-century tribute to the Prince of Wales's crest that had somehow stuck – and worn long trains and veils. Presentation parties were suspended during the hostilities, and afterwards the lavish evening ceremonies were swapped for humbler afternoon gatherings. The debs emerged from rows of limousines lined up on the Mall, entered the palace, curtsied to the monarch, then huddled on the lawn for tea and cake.

The 'levées' at which men had once been presented had already been scrapped; the understated afternoon parties for ladies would themselves be abolished altogether in 1958. They went partly because they were increasingly oversubscribed, and too often by the wrong sort: down-at-heel ex-presentees, including the odd dowager peeress, had wised up to the commercial value of their status, and were selling their access to the palace to moneyed fathers who wanted to gentrify their daughters. Sometimes these entrepreneurs paired the applications and attendance on the day with preparatory instruction in palace deportment: the proper way to enter and leave the royal presence; the perfect curtsy.

The woman who presented Miriam was not a courtly mercenary but the daughter-in-law of an eminent doctor, whom Henry had befriended in the City. At the beginning of July, she sent down my grandparents' card for the presentation party, but declined their offer of lunch for the following weekend. It was haymaking season, and she and her husband couldn't leave their Herefordshire farm. 'Thank you so much for the card for the presentation party,' Henry replied. 'Being country folk ourselves, I can fully realise how busy you must be. You must take advantage of the weather to make hay while the sun shines. I look forward very much indeed to seeing you and your husband on the 23rd . . .' Miriam curtsied until she ached. They bought a dress. They parked the Rolls on the Mall.

The date and occasion of my grandmother's moment were punctiliously entered in the records held at the Royal Archives at Windsor Castle. The Court Circular in *The Times* on Miriam's day, and on the following one, mention the party and supply some details. 'The Queen and the Duke of Edinburgh gave an Afternoon Party in the garden of Buckingham Palace,' the circular says, 'at which the attendance of certain married ladies constituted presentation at Court.' It was the last garden party of the coronation season. In the morning the Queen had received a delegation from Thailand, and conferred a batch of knighthoods. The Duke of Edinburgh, Princess Margaret, the Duke and Duchess of Gloucester, my grandparents' old ally Princess Marie Louise and Princess Marguerite of Baden attended the afternoon party with her. Adlai Stevenson, fresh from his failed American presidential bid, was there too. The presentations took place in a marquee after tea. The bands of the Royal Air Force and the Metropolitan Police played.

The climax of my grandparents' metamorphosis, the end of their high road from the Lane, was a routine moment in an unexceptional royal function. There is no account in the newspapers or in the archives of the way Miriam's gloved hand shook as she gave her card ('Mrs Henry Freedman') to the footman in the marquee, and how she flattened her dress as she walked up the red carpet to where the Queen was sitting in the formal crimson chair. Nor of the way Henry felt as, from the side of the tent, he watched the girl he had brought out of the Boot Street basement, now a woman of forty-three, but with the same smile and almost the same figure, shake the young Queen's hand, curtsy impeccably, then retreat backwards as she had been told to. Nor of the short set-to they had in the garden afterwards about whether Elizabeth had recognised Miriam (Henry insisted that she had; Miriam told him not to be silly), and the way he scolded her for not being able to recall precisely what the twenty-odd words were that Her Majesty had uttered. But the contretemps was soon forgotten. Sometimes my grandfather felt that my grandmother hadn't changed as much and as fast as he wanted her to; that there was still a little too much Hoxton about her, an indelible mark of Kalisz that would never be washed out; sometimes Miriam knew that he felt that way. But on 23 July 1953, so Henry thought and told her, she too looked like a queen.

By the autumn of 1953, thanks in part to the elephant, my grandparents had ascended high enough in the charitable hierarchy for my grandmother to be made chairman of the organising committee for a ball at the Savoy, a fundraiser for the National Spastics Society. After being introduced to her at an 'At Home', Henry wrote to Clementine Churchill, Winston's wife, by then reinstalled at Number Ten, to ask whether the ball's committee could meet in Downing Street. 'Dear Mr Freedman,' Clementine replied on 9 October 1953, in a disappointing

*Clementine S. Churchill*

letter that nonetheless itself became a treasure, 'I am afraid it will not be possible for my Husband and myself to lend a room in Downing Street for a Committee meeting . . . I wish I could help to publicise the Ball in this way, but since I saw you at Lady Heald's house on Tuesday I have been considering the circumstances.' At the end, after a circuitous explanation, 'I am so sorry. Yours sincerely, Clementine S. Churchill.'

There was no Downing Street meeting, and no introduction to Churchill, but there was a ball, at which Miriam, as chairman, had to make a little speech between the dinner and the dancing about the work of the society and the guests' generosity. Until the very last moment, she thought she couldn't; but then she did, and it went off quite satisfactorily. *Tatler* carried a full page of pictures of the event. Miriam had first appeared in *Tatler* in April 1951, alongside Mabel, Countess of Airlie and two other grave-looking ladies, in connection with Her Majesty's Needlework Guild. In April 1953 she was photographed with Mrs Attlee, sipping drinks at a cocktail party. But the photos after the Savoy ball were the best. In one, Miriam, in a shimmery dress, elbow-length gloves and three rows of pearls, talks to a Lady Bennett. In another, she is chatting with the Duchess of Gloucester. Standing behind them, wearing white tie and a grin is Henry, looking into the camera.

Today, in a different Britain, and to later generations who take for granted what my grandfather felt he had ceaselessly to prove, some of his ambitions can seem strange, quaint, perhaps even a little silly – though also, at least to me and in their own way, a little bit heroic too. Three months after my grand-

*H.R.H. the Duchess of Gloucester was talking to Mrs. Henry Freedman, chairman of the ball, Mr. Henry Freedman and Col. R. H. Russell. The dinner ball was given at the Savoy Hotel*

mother's presentation, Henry's quaint, silly, heroic royal mission reached its ultimate objective.

Medieval historians have identified a way of thinking about royalty that is known as the doctrine of 'the king's two bodies'. According to it, a monarch is at once a discrete, corporeal human being, and something more eternal, a transubstantiated idea. Though he might have described it differently, my

*Mrs. Attlee, wife of the Leader of the Opposition, with Mrs. von Neurath and Mrs. Henry Freedman*

HER MAJESTY THE QUEEN

and

HIS ROYAL HIGHNESS THE DUKE OF EDINBURGH

have graciously consented to honour with their presence

# The Royal Film Performance

at the

ODEON THEATRE, LEICESTER SQUARE

on

MONDAY, OCTOBER 26th, 1953

in aid of

The Cinematograph Trade Benevolent Fund

Patron : HER MAJESTY THE QUEEN

President and Chairman : REGINALD C. BROMHEAD, Esq., F.C.A.

★

*World Premiere of Walt Disney's "Rob Roy", also Stage Presentation
in which famous British and American stars will appear*

★

CHAIRMAN :

The Marchioness Townshend of Raynham, J.P.

VICE-CHAIRMEN :

The Counties of Inchcape

Henry Freedman, Esq.     Miss Monica Michell    Mrs. Bernard Sunley

HON. TREASURER :

The Marquis Townshend of Raynham, D.L.

---

grandfather felt something similar about the royal family. He had met Elizabeth when she was a Princess; but now she was a Queen, the night he was himself introduced to her in Leicester Square – 26 October 1953 – meant something different and more. As the programme for the event shows, Henry Freedman, Esq., had ascended the letterhead to become a vice-chairman of the Coronation Royal Film Performance. The chairman was the Marchionness Townshend; a fellow vice-chairman was the Countess of Inchcape; and the organising committee boasted a baroness, ladies, knights, countesses, earls, generals and HRH Princess Frederick of Prussia. 'I have pleasure in advising you that you are included in the introductions to be made to Her Majesty, the Queen, and H.R.H. The Duke of Edinburgh at The Odeon Theatre, on Monday next, the 26th instant,' wrote the president of the Cinematograph Trade Benevolent Fund the week before the event. 'The introductions will be made on Her Majesty's arrival at approximately 8.20pm, and I should be grateful if you would kindly arrange to be at The Odeon Theatre not later than 7.45pm.' A postscript specifies the dress code: 'Full Evening Dress. No Decorations. No Gloves for Gentlemen. White Gloves for Ladies.'

The Court Circular records that the Queen and the Duke were attended by 'the Countess of Euston, Lieutenant Colonel the Hon. Martin Charteris, Captain the Lord Plunkett and Wing Commander M.G. Cowan.' A black-and-white newsreel captured the evening's highlights. The film opens with the glamour-hungry crowds outside the cinema, straining for a glimpse of British royalty and American talent. The new Queen arrives with Princess Margaret and Prince Philip, and they are introduced to the lines of impatient officials and celebrities in their regulation white tie or strapless satin dresses. Philip shares a joke with Gary Cooper; Richard Todd, Alec Guinness, Jack Hawkins and Dirk Bogarde are also in the line-up. Then, in the last round of hand-shaking, the royals are introduced to Henry's committee. There is more of my grandfather on the film than there is in his earlier newsreel appearance. He is there, beaming contentedly in the background while nervous children present bouquets, and as the Queen and her entourage sweep into the auditorium to watch *Rob Roy*. But, perhaps appropriately for a life lived on the periphery of epochal events, on the threshold of grand but elusive success, the victorious moment when Henry takes the Queen of England's hand has been cut.

My grandmother's transformation from market girl to lady is immortalised in a form less ephemeral than this distress-ingly edited newsreel. In 1952 Henry met Flora Lion, an elderly and distinguished portrait artist who worked from a studio in Kensington. She and her husband came to Harpenden for lunch, and Henry drove them back to Kensington, and 'it was really like one of the studios that you see on the films in Paris,'

he told his son Philip, 'so lofty with many lovely pictures around the walls.' Flora Lion had painted the Queen Mother and her two Bowes-Lyon sisters in their youth, and Henry commissioned her to paint his wife as well. The resulting portrait was displayed in the Summer Exhibition at the Royal Academy before Henry took it home. Miriam sits in front of a half-drawn curtain, with a pigeon perched on the windowsill in slightly clumsy homage to the pigeon loft that Henry had fitted in Harpenden for his boys. Her hands are in her lap, and she is wearing a beautiful ivory gown, an ethereal chiffon wrap and her most prized jewellery, in which Henry had invested as an alternative to a pension fund. She wants to look poised and patrician, and she almost does. But, true to her calling, in the slightly over-stiff posture and the lines around the eyes and mouth, the artist has perhaps captured the tension of imposture, the anxiety of not quite belonging.

For a while, Henry was an Englishman first and second, and a Jew only vestigially and rarely in public. He had given his three children a religious education, but not from the store of learning that his own firmly orthodox early childhood had bequeathed. Instead, an impecunious rabbi who lived near Harpenden station came up to the house in Milton Road once a week. The children received their secular education at a nearby private school (for 'the sons and daughters of gentlemen'), which offered much rugby and heartiness and some casual anti-Semitism alongside the classical curriculum. Henry remembered Passover and *Yom Kippur* – the lowest level of observance before outright apostasy – but otherwise serviced his own hibernating faith and salved his conscience mainly by making donations to his old synagogue in Old Castle Street, and to a new one in St Albans.

Then, little by little, as he became more comfortable in his new self, he let his old one incrementally re-emerge, switching between Englishman and Jew, as, in the East End, his conversation had once alternated between English and Yiddish. In April 1951 he told his son in America that on 'Thursday we went to the Home of the Countess of Middleton. These Society people are really charming and friendly.' In the next sentence, 'I took Michael to *shool* [synagogue] again this morning, and after had *kiddush* [a post-service snack] at Mrs Marks': he took the boys to fish pickles from barrels and have their cheeks pinched by Mrs Marks as his had once been; he took them to eat salt beef sandwiches in the Lane, and to buy chickens from the kosher butcher in Goulston Street, who slaughtered them in the yard behind his shop. In the autumn of 1951, after the Jewish New Year, Henry wrote that he 'went to synagogue and I had a really enjoyable time, and I have been asked to be *Chozen Beraishit* on

*Simchat Torah.*' To be *chozen beraishit* on *Simchat Torah* – a festival that celebrates the end of one annual cycle of readings from the Torah, and the beginning of the next – is the most prestigious of the many ways in which lay Jews can participate in synagogue services. Then, in the next sentence, Henry explains how he had come to be introduced to Princess Elizabeth in the cinema: 'it was on account of my being Honorary Treasurer and I was the only person except those connected with the film who was presented'.

He also used the skills and contacts he acquired in the English charities to raise money for the Jewish Lads Brigade, for a Jewish orphanage, and in particular for a club for deaf Jewish children. He arranged a boxing match at the Albert Hall, cocktail parties, a film première at the Marble Arch Pavilion, and a ball at the Grosvenor House Hotel. He tried to recruit Jack Hawkins as the ball's celebrity turn: 'You may remember me,' he wrote to the film star, 'my wife and I with Lady Brabourne gave a cocktail party at Claridge's for the Royal Film Performance.' He solicited the support of the great Anglo-Jewish families (the Sassoons, the Rothschilds, the Mishcons, Sebags and Montefiores), and of the newer Jewish aristocracy: the (Tesco) Cohens, the Ratners and the Wolfsons. Gathering prizes for a raffle at the Grosvenor House, he wrote to Emmanuel Shinwell, another Jewish boy who hadn't done too badly, in his case as Labour's Minister of Fuel and then as Secretary of State for War. 'I regret that owing to far too many other commitments which arise from my position as an MP,' Shinwell replied, 'I am unable to respond to your request however deserving it is. You have no idea what demands are made upon us.'

Then, at the zenith of their social careers, my grandparents' old world caught up with them, dramatically and unrefusably.

If they managed it at all, it took many British Jews a painfully long time to track down their surviving relatives on the

Continent. There was a baffling array of refugee agencies to negotiate, and often only old and defunct addresses to work from. Until January 1952 Henry had no word of, or from, his parents' extended families. Then, at breakfast on 18 January, he was reading the *Jewish Chronicle*, then as now the main weekly organ of Anglo-Jewry. Scanning the 'missing relatives' column, he read the following among the other abbreviated narratives and pleas, unmistakable for all its mistaken conflations: 'Amalia Freedman, about 67, of Nadworna, Poland, whose last known address was Newcastle Street, Catford S.E., is sought by Carl Kurt Meyer, in London.' Carl Meyer, it turned out, and as Henry explained to the *JC* in his thank-you letter, was acting for 'a cousin, a Mr Troper, who is now in Paris'.

Philippe Troper, it turned out, was the son of Millie Freedman's sister Rifka, and the cousin with whom Henry had wrestled in Stanislau in 1913, when my grandfather had travelled to Galicia with his mother. At the beginning of the First World War, as rumours of atrocities by the invading Russians and their peasant accomplices swept across the region, Philippe's family had buried many of their belongings and fled, by foot, cart and cattle wagon, through the Carpathians and across Hungary to Nikolsburg, Czechoslovakia: 'all over by *Chanukah*,' a coachman had assured the young Philippe on the way. Millie Freedman kept in touch, and sent money, for as long as she could trace them. Her brother Herschel enlisted, was captured by the Russians and spent much of the war working as a waiter in a Siberian hotel. Back in Stanislau after the armistice, Philippe was kept out of higher education by Poland's anti-Semitic quota system, so had returned to Nikolsburg to study, then moved to Vienna where he worked as a bank clerk. He emigrated to Paris with his new wife Amalia in 1936. In 1939 he had joined the French Foreign Legion; during the retreat of 1940 he was demobilised and dispatched to a work camp for foreigners. His wife fled Paris with their two young children and her mother, winding up in Brantôme, a small town in the Périgord region. There, via a relative in Switzerland, Amalia learned of her husband's whereabouts. She also discovered that farmers could request labouring help from camps like the one Philippe was in. So she rented a small plot of land under her maiden name, and recruited her own husband as forced labour. Philippe was delivered during the night by two gendarmes, and his family spent the rest of the war disguised as peasants in Brantôme. His three siblings were killed soon after the Germans reached Stanislau, as was much of the rest of Millie's family. Philippe had been trying to find his English cousins for years, at one point appealing to Scotland Yard for help. In the summer of 1952, thirty-nine years after their wrestling match, Henry and Philippe met again in Paris.

Tipped off by the Tropers, the daughter of Millie's Uncle Kaswin – the well-to-do fur merchant of Stanislau – traced Henry too. Illa Kaswin had married a Viennese banker named Rohatyn. The husband had been sent, early, to Dachau, but somehow, apparently through her good offices, he had got out. They had divorced, whereupon Illa remarried, this time to a Frenchman, survived the war in France, lived in Paris for several years and then returned to Austria. When she first wrote to Henry, on 6 August 1952, Illa was in a sanatorium in Bad Ischl: 'Dear children of my cousine Malca! Philippe Troper told me of his happyness to find the whole family – and how kind you are. I too am very glad, because we have searched for you all these years. I remember cousin Malca who came with her four children to visit us in Stanislaw and we admired the beauty of you all girls and boys.' Her typed English is studded with crossings-out and corrections, and punctuated by the occasional German or Yiddish expression that defeated her powers of translation. 'I was very tuched that you still remember us,' she writes, 'although you have must been a child of 5–6 years? I am sorry your mother is dead – she

was still young – write me abaut her. I too remember your father – he was a very clever fur-marchand like my father Mr Kaswin. Philippe told me you are quite nombreuse family – and so I too am happy after the terible loss of the whole family – to find you all at last.' This 'terible loss' is a rare glance at atrocity in Henry's correspondence with his parents' rediscovered relatives. To a twenty-first-century eye, most of these letters seem stricken with a sort of amnesia, by a need not to talk about the obvious thing, perhaps out of speechlessness, maybe out of an obscure shame. 'Especialy I am delighted to hear,' Illa goes on, 'that you all kepp together like in bible times . . . Are you too in the same business as you and my father? I should be very pleased abaut it. Please send me some photos and tell me all about your life – you sisters lives and the children. Now I am the only membre of the old Generation, So I beg you to drop me some lines – I stay here still two month in the sanatorium because I am ill, but withaut pleasure in Austria . . . Your old aunt, Illa.'

On 24 August 1952 Henry replied to her in the sanatorium: 'Dear Tante Rohatyn,' he begins, addressing her as 'aunt' in Yiddish. 'It was a great surprise and pleasure to have your letter . . . My mother passed away in 1940 at the age of 53 and had unfortunately very many difficulties after my father died in 1915. My memory of Stanislau is very vivid and I can remember you and your children almost as though I were with them today. You were undoubtedly the most beautiful person I had ever seen,' he tells her, 'and I have followed your life from a distance.' In answer to her question, Henry is 'not in the fur business, as none of the friends who knew my father were willing to help me and I have had a hard struggle, but thank God am now manufacturing ladies' underwear and I am very satisfied . . . Please do write to me again, when I shall write to you once more. With love from my wife Miriam, myself and my children . . . '

The following August – the summer of Miriam's presentation, and of the holiday in Stresa that followed it – Illa is again in the sanatorium: 'My dear Henry, Since I imagine you are returned of your short holidays (a business-man has no time for long holidays!!) I try to drop you some lines. Thank you for your amiable card of Stresa – I am very glad that you did not forget the oldest member of our family. Even when you are so "*vernommen*" [well known: German] try to find a moment for the old-new family . . . I hope you and your wife and children enjoyed the beauty of Italy and recovered you all.' She apologises for her English, and wishes him a happy *Rosh Hashanah*, the Jewish New Year. 'Let me say what a pleasure it is,' Henry replies on 3 September, 'to have letters from you in English. They are written very well indeed and I only wish I could write as well in German or Yiddish.'

In the autumn of 1952, by means that are now unknowable, Henry and his siblings found a surviving cousin from their Solotwina family, another Miriam, the daughter of Fishel Freedman's sister Basse. She was living with her husband

Abraham Gonic and their children in a wooden hut in a refugee camp in Israel. On 24 September 1952 Henry's first extant letter to them began by wishing them a happy *Rosh Hashanah*, and a new year 'which will bring peace to Israel, to yourselves and to this world'. Next, lest they think that their sometimes importunate attentions were unwelcome, he writes that 'I count myself fortunate in having found cousins – children of the flesh and blood of my father's family.' This Miriam had also made an impression in 1913, if a less striking one than Tante Rohatyn: 'I think I can remember you, Miriam, when you came with Tante Basse from Rumania to meet my mother and we met at a railway station not far from the border and it stands out in my mind still. Of course, we too have suffered very much but, thank God, we have been spared the many dreadful things that have happened to the families in Europe; but our lives are made not to look back but to go forward and we must therefore shake our shoulders and do all we can to make the lives of our families better and more secure.' This tendency of Henry's to assume that every problem, including those more crushing than any he had encountered, could be faced down with a shake of the shoulders and a stiff upper lip, may perhaps have galled his almost-desperate correspondents. Still, he offered some compassion alongside his homilies: 'if there is a possibility to help you, please ask me, and if it is possible I will do so, and if not, I know you will understand.'

'Of course, I can vividly remember that border scene,' cousin Miriam replies from the camp (via an anglophone amanuensis) on 18 October 1952, 'and especially you! I shall never forget our meeting at the railway station.' Then, 'because you are asking, I must admit that the valuable presents you are good enough to send us are *badly* needed, as you are our only help, and my husband can't find *parnusse* [sustenance: Yiddish], nothing to say of the hut we are living in. But it never occurred to our minds to think that you were obliged to help us: you just send if you please what you want and when you can. I'm glad and happy to have found you again,' she reciprocates, 'and must insist only on your writing more often, you and all the other families. I've read about a dreadful accident,' she adds, 'a collision of 3 trains in the South of England [at Harrow]. I'm so stupid as to tremble for your lives, and am praying, my husband and myself, for your health and well-being. God bless you and believe us, Your most sincere, Miriam, Abraham and children.' Henry's reply, written on 17 November 1952 – the day of the charity ball at the Dorchester with Princess Marie Louise – is humbler, elegiac, maybe even tacitly apologetic: 'It is sad to think of the years that have passed and the many changes that have taken place, and memory unfortunately becomes so dim and the mind adjusts itself to present conditions and one must be forgiven if we appear to each other at such great distance.' Nevertheless, 'we are sending you parcels each week and I shall be sending you along some clothing for the family . . . We all wish you good health and hope that Abraham will soon find something to make a living, and also that you will be out of the camp very soon.' Abraham did find something, training to be the camp's *shochet* or ritual slaughterer. 'My wife, whose name is also Miriam, and my children join me in sending our love and best wishes . . .'

How did these blasts from a ravaged past make my grandparents – and the many other British Jews who made similar reacquaintances – feel? Guilty, for not having done more and not being able to do more now? Lucky, because decisions made by their parents before they were born meant that they were alive and comfortable in London, while these other lives, which could so easily have been theirs, were wrecked? Awkward? Embarrassed? Inconvenienced? Whatever they were, these feelings must have been most acute for my grandparents when, in July 1953, they received a letter from their most bereaved, most inconsolable and, to begin with, least helpable new-old relative:

Miriam's cousin Jakob Erlich, the son of Leah's sister Tauba, whom my grandmother had met on her trip to Poland in the summer of 1930.

In one of the episodes of extravagant inhumanity that have somehow been eclipsed by the war's other calamities, between the partition of Poland by the Nazis and the Soviets in September 1939, and Hitler's invasion of the Soviet Union in June 1941, around 1,700,000 people were deported eastwards from Poland to work in mines, quarries, farms and forests, from the Arctic Circle to Vladivostok. A few of the deportees had committed some confected political sin, and been deemed 'enemies of the people', counter-revolutionaries, anti-Soviet, anti-something. But many were simply seized at dawn by secret policemen with fixed bayonets, who gave them half an hour to gather their things and their families, just to make up the numbers. Among the deported were several hundred thousand Jews, mainly escapees from Nazi-occupied central and western Poland, who had scrambled east when the Germans arrived, diving into ditches and under wagons or crouching in forests when exuberant Luftwaffe pilots strafed the chaotic columns of eastward refugees. A few of these Jews went to Siberia voluntarily – because they were believing communists, or simply to get further away from the killing. For some, 'voluntarily' meant only assent when the alternative was dispatch back to the German side. Voluntary and involuntary were packed into the cattle wagons that stood at the railway stations, bolted from the outside until the trains were full. As they rolled through the Russian tundra, steppe and taiga on eerie, single-track railways, the deportees were fed water and stale brown bread, cut holes in the floors of the wagons for sanitation and, whenever the doors were opened, threw out the corpses of the old, young and sick who had succumbed to the cold or disease or starvation.

It is not clear how 'voluntary' Jakob Erlich's deportation with his sister Hannah was. When the invasion began, they had fled east from Kalisz, separating from their four other siblings, their nieces and nephews, and from their parents, Leah's sister Tauba and her husband Abraham. (Leah's brother, another Abraham, seems to have escaped to Switzerland.) The others had at first not wanted to abandon their homes and businesses and leave their lives behind. Perel, whom her mother Tauba had tried to pair with Miriam's brother Paul in 1930, had married a man named Zygmunt: in photos from their wedding, Zygmunt has thick wavy hair and Perel looks like my grandmother. Perhaps, deciding quickly in the tumult, like many other Polish Jews they had thought that these Germans would be like the Germans in the last war: not pleasant, but better than the Russians if you had to choose. Maybe, like many others, they put their faith in the Polish army; maybe they put it in God. Jakob's fiancée had also stayed. Whatever the reasons, and whatever the circumstances of the deportation, from the postcards and letters sent to Jakob and Hannah by their family left behind in Poland – correspondence that Jakob eventually carried back with him to Kalisz, and ultimately to England – it is certain that by January 1940 Jakob and Hannah had been sent to Kopeysk, a mining town near the city of Chelyabinsk on the Siberian side of the Urals, just north of Kazakhstan. The others had not been able to remain long in Kalisz.

These postcards have been franked with swastikas and 'General Gouvernement', the Germans' name for their administration in Poland; their stamps depict the Nazi eagle and icy Bavarian castles. The script is crammed onto the cards, along the edges and around the addresses. The 'sender' entries chart the Erlich family's wanderings around occupied Poland. The first card Jakob and Hannah received, written on 28 February 1940, explained (in Polish) that a neighbour in Kalisz 'has forwarded your postcard which you sent on 24th January we were

overjoyed what was most important to us was that you were together'. The family has for ten weeks been in Cracow, already far from home. 'Why were you silent for such a long time and did not let us know where you were day and night our thoughts followed you . . . Now our beloved children you must tell us everything about yourselves, what happened to you, are you happy with your life, how are you coping, have you somewhere to sleep, do you get enough to eat, are you working and where? . . . Fate has driven you so far away.' As for the writers themselves, 'do not think too much about us, we are in good health, thank God, the worst thing is that we cannot be with you'. Only at the end does the card say a little about the family's situation: 'we all live together, 4 families in one room, the room is large and sunny'. Contradicting, perhaps, the injunction not to worry, they are frantic to know 'when are we going to see each other again, write to us, tell us where you are, do not forget about us, we think about you all the time'.

'We can't wait to hear from you,' they write again from Cracow on March 7th, 'how are you doing, all this waiting for news from you is so awful! But we are so helpless.' How is Hannah coping with the Urals winter with so few of her things ('you went as if to town')? 'We are going out of our minds here, there is no space left on the card I will write again in a few days . . . I wonder if I wrote the Russian address correctly.' Finally, 'You must respect each other as the only ones left in the world, bye for now, your parents and siblings.'

In the earlier of these cards and letters, and, it seems, in the lost ones from Kopeysk that answered them, there is a sort of delicate, tactful dance: both sets of correspondents – Jakob and Hannah in Russia on one side, and the rest of the Erlich family in Poland on the other – want to shield their loved ones, as long and as much as possible, from their reality. 'Listen, it's not bad in Cracow,' reassures a letter from Poland of 26 March 1940, 'because it is a big city and you can cope ... it is not as bad here as you are imagining, we do not go hungry.' As for Hannah and Jakob, 'do not worry and do not cry, do not lose your head, the main thing is that we are alive and that you can feed and clothe yourselves ... Dear Hannah write a letter yourself and tell me everything so that we have something to read. I cannot describe how much we miss you but we think this will be over one day.' Two little nieces send their kisses; they are said to remember the chocolates that Jakob once brought them from Poznań.

But even as they wish to protect their recipients, between their lines these letters to Siberia witness that the reality they are finessing is unbearable. So, it is clear, did the missing replies from Russia. Jakob and Hannah were living in a wooden barracks. A tailor in pre-war Kalisz, Jakob was working in a coal mine. Life was appalling if you chose not to co-operate with the Soviet authorities, and terrible even if you did. 'Who does not work,' they were told, 'does not eat.' But work brought only starvation rations, which the workers supplemented by foraging for mushrooms and berries. They fashioned sandals for themselves from the bark of trees. They were in theory free to leave the camp occasionally, but in practice they were imprisoned. The dogmatic official atheism meant that Jewish prayers could only be said in secret. The frost could be lethal in the interminable winters. The family in Poland wanted to come to Kopeysk and be together in Russia; but, lunatic as it now seems, well into 1940 Jakob and Hannah were thinking and writing about going back to Poland, which, they must have imagined, couldn't be any worse than the mines.

Tauba and the others try gently to dissuade them. 'You should not cry and despair over our letters,' they write from Cracow on 4 June 1940, 'it is not so bad here but as for your living here with us if it was compulsory for you it is a different matter, but if not then it might be better for you there . . . If you do not have to leave, stay, and if you can, take us in, and if you cannot then that's fine too do not worry when the time comes we will soon invite you here.' Being together again somewhere is the most important thing: 'all this waiting for your letters is so awful, you think about us and we think about you . . . Our hearts are calling out for you like yours are calling out for us, but what can we do?'

On the road to Warsaw at the end of the following month, the delicate dance could no longer be sustained. 'We arrived in Skierniewice yesterday,' the Erlichs in Poland wrote on 20 July 1940, giving the address of the town's Jewish community centre, 'but unfortunately there is no room for us, we can only stay for a few days, and what next we do not know, we are homeless.' There is no more equivocation about who should come to whom: 'we only have one favour to ask of you, please do what you can to save us . . . no town and no village wants to receive refugees, one town sends people to the next one . . . there is only one thing left for us to do, and that is to join you, there is nothing else.' They are young, the family say, and they can work.

In the end, they found a patch of space on the fourth floor of a refugee centre in Warsaw. 'We have been in Warsaw for over 2 months now,' they write on 20 November 1940; 'it's not bad, we only worry about you, we are very concerned because we haven't heard from you for such a long time, we have one wish only, to see a few words from you very soon, our hearts are aching for you and missing you.' Can Jakob and Hannah send a package of something to sell? Everything sellable from Kalisz has already been sold to buy food. (Deportees to Russia were permitted to send food packages back to Poland, to demonstrate the abundance purportedly enjoyed by the blessed guests of the Soviet Union.) Can they help with a visa application that has been submitted to an agency in Berlin? Above all, can they please write to Warsaw with their news as soon as possible? 'We carry you in our hearts all the time, we think about you all the time.'

There are some later letters. A family the Erlichs know has made it to the Crimea; others have been less fortunate. There are a few recriminations and many self-recriminations. Hannah and Jakob should eat plenty of potatoes and herring, and Hannah should look after her figure. A sister misses sharing a bed with her. A neighbour from Kalisz has turned up in Warsaw with Jakob's violin, and to hear him play it is excruciating.

These letters that Jakob cherished – letters that outline the fate that might have been Leah's – came to an end in the spring of 1941. 'Operation Barbarossa', the German invasion of the Soviet Union, began on 22 June. It cut off Jakob and his sister from their family, but it also had an unexpectedly positive consequence for the Poles in Russia. After Stalin came to terms with the Polish government-in-exile, most of the deportees who were still alive were 'amnestied'. Though some were kept in ignorance and in bondage, and there were special rules for Polish Jews, most escaped. Some joined the free Polish army that was gathering in Persia; others simply went south in search of warmer weather, better diet and less gruelling work, which they found on the collective farms of Central Asia. They mingled with the new waves of refugees who were spilling east-wards across the Russian continent, until their money or their momentum or their luck ran out.

From the letters their family sent from Poland in late 1940 and early 1941, it is evident that Jakob and Hannah had tried to leave Kopeysk at least once, but hunger or capture brought them back. So it is surprising that, when they could have left, they seem to have stayed in the barracks and the mines until the very end of the war. Maybe they hesitated when the amnesty was announced, and were then trapped by the new restrictions on the Poles in Russia that came in when the two governments fell out again in 1943, after the discovery of the

Soviet murder of 21,000 Polish officers at Katyn. Hannah lost the husband she had met in Russia, but in 1945 she somehow found her way to Brest Litovsk, where she had a daughter, and from there she made it to England. Jakob went back to Kalisz to look for his family.

Most of the Jews who, like him, came back from Siberia, or out of hiding or the camps, and returned to what had been their homes to find nobody there, their property expropriated and their neighbours as hostile as ever, quickly left. They headed for the displaced persons camps in the British and American zones in Germany, where they hoped to secure passages west. Or they contacted the underground networks that conveyed people through Greece and Italy to Palestine. On 4 July 1946, there was a pogrom in the Polish town of Kielce: new-old rumours spread about Jews using the blood of Christian children to make *matza*, and a mob of soldiers and civilians ransacked a hostel inhabited by Jewish survivors, killing more than forty of them, plus two gentiles who went to their aid. After that, most of the few Jews who had tried to settle back in Poland fled, conjuring up the money to get around the emigration bureaucracy and get out. But, just as he had earlier stayed in Russia, after the war Jakob stayed in Poland. It is said that he wouldn't contemplate leaving his country until the construction of the Warsaw ghetto memorial, and there is indeed a photograph of him standing on the steps in front of the memorial's grim façade in a sombre coat – though that picture may be the source of the story rather than a corroboration. When the borders were definitively closed by the Soviet-backed regime, Jakob was trapped in Poland.

So it happened that when, on 4 July 1953, he wrote to his cousin Miriam, my grandmother, Jakob was still in Kalisz, marooned in a city of ghosts. 'This letter writes to you your cousin Jakób, and asks you not to be angry for such a long silence. I suppose you will excuse me, considering my very difficult conditions in which I have been living since so long. I am quite alone, you are sure to know that all my family was brutally burned by Hitler fascists in Ghetto in Warsaw. Of all so enormous family only two survivors were left, I and my sister, who is with you.' Henry had offered Hannah a job in South Shields, but she had declined and made her own way in London. 'I am fully conscious of all that you have been doing for my sister,' Jakob writes, 'when she was so very ill and now you help her and her poor orphan child. God bless you and may He give you health, happiness and long life. I also wish you everything that you may desire.' What he himself desires is pathetically undemanding: 'Dear Miriam, please write to me as soon as you get this letter . . . I wish I could see you again in my life.' Jakob had been a boy, just past his *barmitzvah*, when Leah took her children back to Kalisz in 1930, whereas Miriam, though only a few years older, had been a marriageable young woman; so he may have made less of an impression on her than she on him. 'I have to stop now,' Jakob winds up, 'but I shall live with hope to hear from you and to know that you have not forgotten me . . . With heartiest love, your cousin Jakób.' His letter must have arrived in London around the time of the elephant garden party. My grandmother wrote back on 14 July 1953, perhaps with a little help from Henry: 'We wish it were possible for you to be able to join your sister Hannah in England . . . I do remember you when I was in Kalisz although it was so many years ago, and I wish it were possible once again that we should meet.'

'Your precious letter reached me safely and I thank you most heartily for your kind heart,' Jakob replied on 23 August. He writes again about his losses, and his sadness ('I am also a man, who has a heart'). He apologises for the month-long hiatus, due, he says, to his 'loneliness and psychical break-down', and the fact that 'the professor who translates my letters into English was away'. He has requested exit visas for both

England and Israel, but 'Fate was against me and did not let me go, which I longed for so much . . . if only I could I should go on foot to my nearest relatives, and to my only sister . . . Best love to my Aunt Leja. Yours ever, cousin Jakób.' This desolation prompted an uncharitable response from Henry in the autumn of 1953: 'you must live your life and make as much of it as is possible and do not trouble yourself with thoughts that make you unhappy'. Even Henry's encouragement seems to contain an implicit rebuke: 'I am glad to say that your sister Hannah is looking very well indeed and she is a different person and has very much courage.' But Henry does offer some hope, and some affection: 'you will one day be united with your sister and her daughter and live many many happy years together . . . we shall always be happy to hear from you whenever it is possible for you to write. Aunty Leah joins in sending our love to you . . . '

Henry was right about the reunion, if maybe less so about the happiness. Jakob's escape from Russia to his new life was halting and indirect, but he made it. Stalin's death, which curtailed his crypto-genocidal campaign against 'rootless cosmopolitans' (that is, Jews), also seems to have eventually benefited the few Jews stranded in Poland. Some time after his anguished correspondence with my grandparents, Jakob managed to obtain an exit visa – to Israel, since direct migration to Western Europe or America was still impossible. Once he was in Israel, Henry sponsored Jakob's application to come to Britain, offering the necessary guarantees of financial wherewithal and moral oversight. So, finally and exhaustedly, and bringing little with him apart from the letters his family sent to him in Kopeysk, Jakob made it to London.

He was so grateful, and so awed by Henry's bureaucratic know-how and his worldliness, that he would probably have done whatever my grandfather advised. What Henry recommended was that Jakob move to South Shields, where a job was made for him in the factory's cutting room. Perhaps Henry thought that a smaller town would be better for Miriam's disoriented cousin. South Shields had a little Jewish community of its own, a spillover from the bigger one in Newcastle, where some of the North Sea ferries had deposited their emigrant passengers fifty years earlier. There was a synagogue near the Victorian town hall, to which Henry donated an ornate curtain for the Ark (a sort of sacred cupboard in which the Torah scrolls are stored).

Jakob Erlich lived in a terraced house on Ocean Road, the long main street running away from the seashore. At the end of it was the Ocean Beach funfair, and next to that the sort of English sandy beach that can feel grand when the weather is fine, but most of the time attracts only dog-walkers. Jakob's home was surrounded by a colony of bed-and-breakfasts, and by the end of his life faced a row of curry restaurants. It was a fair-sized house, and Jakob took in lodgers to fill it; but sooner or later he would always become convinced that they were plotting against him, and throw them out. He was likewise paranoid about his colleagues at the factory. He so spooked the layers-up, markers-in, trimmers and the other cutters in the cutting room that, after a while, Henry made him a sample cutter and gave him a little workshop of his own. It was a prized and highly skilled job, which involved cutting out the sample versions of each new style; the garments would then be made up by the factory's top machinists, and distributed to the travelling salesmen to show to the department stores and other big customers. Henry would have liked to give Jakob more responsibility on the shop floor, but too much communism had rubbed off on him for Jakob to become a manager. With his tailoring background in Kalisz he was good at his work, but he kept erratic hours, absenting himself for long stretches, then reappearing without apologies or excuses. He is said to have had an arrangement with an usherette at the picture house further up Ocean Road, who kept him a seat and would let him stay on when the cinema was cleared between shows.

He always had a nice smile for pretty South Shields girls, but he never courted anyone after his fiancée in Kalisz. He became more and more stubborn and reclusive, and fanatically ascetic. He made all his own clothes and slept on a couch in his front room. Nothing but instant coffee and condensed milk was ever to be found in his kitchen. His hair grew wild and unkempt. When relatives from London visited or phoned his conversation rambled unpursuably into distant reaches of Judaism and philosophy. On his rare visits to London for weddings, *barmitzvahs* and funerals, resentful children would be ushered towards him by adults mumbling something about 'poor Uncle Jakob' and his hard life; the children would manage a few minutes of awkwardly dutiful pleasantries before they escaped. For a short time Jakob talked half-heartedly about moving south to be nearer to my grandmother, but he never did. By the time he died in 1998, aged eighty-two, his sister, his aunt Leah and his patron Henry were all long gone, and Miriam was too frail to travel. The South Shields synagogue had closed. The Ten Commandments are still inscribed above the old synagogue's door, and the Hebrew dedication stones remain set in the brickwork, which is enlivened still by the original stained-glass windows. But inside, the building is now a community arts centre: only the pillars that once propped up the upper gallery for female worshippers recall its former use. To make up a *minyan* – the quorum of ten Jewish men required to hold a service – the *yeshiva* in Gateshead sent a posse of its students to Jakob's burial, a long way from home, in the small Jewish section of a cemetery in South Shields.

# SEVEN

# 'Identifying myself'

'The newly arrived Russo-Jewish immigrant is, in all essentials,
a mediaeval product, and his children grow up into something
like the type of modern Englishmen.'
From *The Jew in London* by C. Russell and H.S. Lewis

'There is only one race better than the Jews, and that is the Derby.'
Attributed to Victor Sassoon

I have only one, slight memory of my grandfather, and it is the sort of untrustworthy recollection that may in truth be a compound of fragments of family history, details discovered later and wishful thinking, which over time can come to seem real and whole. In it, I am sitting on an uncomfortable blue stool in my parents' kitchen. I swivel round to face the front door as my grandparents arrive at our house. Miriam is carrying the leather gloves that she methodically put on and took off before and after every motoring trip, at what, to the impatient grandchildren she was driving, seemed intolerable length. She always drove with the awe and crossed roads with the anxiety of someone who had grown up in a still horse-drawn age. Henry is there only momentarily in my memory, grey and frail-looking, but kindly and smiling.

**S. NEWMAN**
LTD.
UNDERWEAR MANUFACTURERS.
WHOLESALE AND EXPORT.
*94, Middlesex Street,*
*& 4, Strype Street,*
*London, E.1.*
*& Victoria Works, Amenbury Lane, Harpenden.*
9th January, 1943.

*Telephones*
BISHOPSGATE 7637 & 2840
*Telegrams*
BISHOPSGATE 7637 LONDON

DIRECTORS:
N. FREEDMAN
A. GREEN
S. NEWMAN (Governing Director)
S. FREEDMAN
M. FREEDMAN, B.A.

**S. NEWMAN LTD.**
DIRECTORS: N.E. FREEDMAN · F. FREEDMAN · M. FREEDMAN · L. LEVENE
MANUFACTURERS OF LINGERIE, BLOUSES AND HOUSECOATS.
WHOLESALE AND EXPORT.
HEAD OFFICE:
*160, Cheapside,*
*London, E.C.2.*
*Telephone:*
METROPOLITAN 9027
PRIVATE BRANCH EXCHANGE.
31st May, 1949.

*Telegrams:*
IMPULSE, CENT,
LONDON.
*Cables:*
IMPULSE, LONDON.

HN/BH

FACTORIES:
VICTORY WORKS,
SOUTH SHIELDS.
VICTORIA WORKS,
HARPENDEN.
94, MIDDLESEX STREET,
LONDON, E.1.

**S. NEWMAN LTD.**
DIRECTORS: N.E. FREEDMAN · M. FREEDMAN · F. F. FREEDMAN · G. BENNETT · A. BOWIE
N. A. FREEDMAN · M. BROWN · G. BROWN · D. RIDDIFORD
MANUFACTURERS OF LINGERIE AND SLUMBERWEAR.
WHOLESALE AND EXPORT.
HEAD OFFICE & SHOWROOMS:
*Dumbarton House,*
*68, Oxford Street,*
*London, W.1.*
*Telephone:*
LANGHAM 6231/2/3/4
STD

*Telegrams:*
IMPULSE,
LONDON, W.1.
*Cables:*
IMPULSE, LONDON.

FACTORY:
VICTORY WORKS,
COMMERCIAL ROAD,
SOUTH SHIELDS.
TEL 4263/4/5.

If this unexceptional but somehow impressive entrance occurred, it must have been in 1978, when I was three. Because in November 1978, aged seventy-two, Henry died. His health had been damaged by his accident during the Blitz, and by too much too hard work at too early an age – though perhaps because he started working in a different way before it was too late, the hardships of the markets didn't kill him so prematurely as they did his mother. He worked until the end, with his two sons, in the business he had started. On 28 November Miriam drove him to Moorfields Eye Hospital, on City Road, for a check-up. He was wearing a smart suit for the trade exhibition he was going to visit that afternoon. While Miriam was parking, Henry had a fatal heart attack in the waiting room.

Deep into my efforts to resurrect him, my uncle Michael rediscovered a recording made at the party thrown for his *barmitzvah*, at a suburban hotel, in June 1951. The set of thick 78s, only playable on an antique gramophone, must have been the fifties equivalent of today's celebration videos. Beneath the crackling, the records are narrated by a woman with an impossibly cut-glass accent, who roams the party, interviewing the sometimes reticent, sometimes extrovert guests. Daisy Ritherford, Henry's first employee, tells my thirteen-year-old uncle, via the recording, to 'be a good boy'. Morris Feltz, Henry's soldier-poet brother-in-law, compares my grandfather's merchandise unfavourably with the rival underwear brand that he had set up when he came back from the war. Some of the contributions are barely decipherable through the speakers' heavy Eastern European accents. Miriam's voice is straining to be posh, but her pronunciation of 'darlin'' keeps giving her away. The narrator describes the dancing like a genteel sports commentator ('Everyone is enjoying the first waltz of the evening . . . Everyone is enjoying the ever-popular Charleston'). When a pair of professional ballroom dancers entertains during dessert, 'she is dressed in a lime-green ankle-length gown, and he, of course, in tails'. The band leader tours the hall to serenade the guests with his violin. Mrs Marks from the Lane sits at the top table.

There is a noisy toastmaster, and there are lots of speeches. 'What I lack in stature,' begins Henry's brother Sid, 'I hope to make up for in velocity.' Next comes the rabbi from Old Castle Street, the synagogue in which the ceremony had been held, and in which Henry had himself been *bamitzvahed* in 1919. In his preamble the rabbi explains that he will 'direct my speech to the *barmitzvah* boy in English, and after I will speak in plain Yiddish.' Not everyone will have understood the plain Yiddish: Walter was there, and he offers the loyal toast with tasteful brevity ('Ladies and gentlemen, the toast is – the King!').

When my grandfather speaks, his voice surprises me. It somehow doesn't have the timbre I was expecting, nor quite the plumminess I thought he would have honed by the summer of 1951. He still sounds as much like the East Ender he was born as the West Ender he was struggling to become. He says 'me-self' for 'myself', and along with the residual cockney lilts there are some sub-liturgical, sing-song inflections that advertise his Yiddish pre-history. His voice made me wonder how far he really did confound the subtle, instant judgements that English people made and make about each other's accents (and demeanour, and shoes, and haircuts); how far the Astors and the rest were truly fooled; and how often they may have sniggered among themselves at my grandparents' airs and graces. But then perhaps one of the lessons of their lives is that, in the middle of the last century, the seriously posh were less possessively defensive of their rank and privileges than nervous middlers like the members of the Harpenden Bowling Club. The startling curve of my grandparents' identities hints that England then was not quite the starched and stratified place that popular history depicts it as, and as it is still depicted today.

By the autumn of 1953, when Henry met the Queen in Leicester Square, my grandparents had reached the top of their curve. After that, it levelled off for a few years at its vertiginous altitude. In September 1954, following a decade of strife with the Board of Trade, Henry's new purpose-built factory opened in South Shields, right next door to the old Cone Street school. Today, the big building is almost derelict, and may soon be demolished to make way for blocks of flats – part of an effort to emulate the trendification of dockside neighbourhoods in other struggling northern towns. The original school-turned-factory was long ago knocked down: only one of the walls is left to show that it was ever there at all. Upriver, the coal staithes are gone; the dry docks on the south side of the Tyne are silent; the mines are closed. In the fifties there was a big showroom at the side of the

new factory, alongside the thrumming shop floor with its battalions of machinists, and behind that a packing room that backed onto the river and the dock. Cheap imports would strangle the British apparel trade before too long, but when my grandfather's factory opened, freed finally from the grip of rationing and austerity regulations, the industry flourished. 'Frou-frou' and 'Can-Can' petticoats were in, made of muslin and taffeta with frills and ruffles. Underneath them, knickers were shrinking towards vanishing in emulation of Bardot. Later in the decade, the factory expanded. 'Shields factory expands again . . . It will mean an extra 100 jobs,' was the headline in the *Shields Gazette*. There was a new quilting room, a new cutting room for Jakob and a mezzanine floor for storage. 'In an area starved of new industrial developments,' the paper predicted, 'the expansion of S. Newman Ltd [still that old, hard-to-explain misnomer] will have far-reaching effects. Its prosperity will be reflected immediately in the town, where more people will be given work.' More than 300 women and girls were already employed at the plant, says the report, plus 26 men, and the goods they made were exported to South Africa, Jamaica, Persia, Jordan, Germany, Norway, Sweden and dozens of other countries. 'It would be hard to find a more attractive opening for the school leaver,' observes the journalist, citing the annual staff dinner dance and summer excursion as incentives. 'Nothing succeeds like success,' he concludes, 'and that of Newman's may prove more effective in attracting new industries than all the pleas that have been made.' Henry kept the speech he made at the extension's opening, along with his cheque stubs, club bills, annotated factory reports, Masonic summonses and lecture notes (which, in turn, have led me to other people's memories, other people's attic and bottom-drawer papers, and sites and archives from South Shields to London to western Ukraine). He told the assembled mayors, town clerks and MPs that 'the North East, too long neglected, and South Shields, are blossoming, to take their share of the prosperity of our great country'. He thanks Daisy, and he pays 'a special tribute to my dear wife Miriam, for the great inspiration she has been throughout the last 30 years'.

There were more social triumphs and feats of chameleon-ism: even if there was never quite another thrill to match the Royal Film Performance of 1953, nor does Henry seem to have tired of clasping a begloved royal hand by the proffered finger-tips or of bowing to tiaras. That shadow sense of half-disbelief in who he had become never faded. In response to a last-minute

panic about the protocol for introductions at a charity concert at St James's Palace, in December 1954, which Henry helped to organise along with a viscountess, a lord, an earl and Princess Alice, one Lady Beddoes Rees wrote to say that 'of course *your* name has been included on the list of those to be "presented" to Her Majesty the Queen Mother on her arrival at the Palace . . . The presentations are to be made in the Boudoir just beyond the Throne Room.' Supplications of help and letters of gratitude from aristocrats and the occasional princess rolled in throughout the fifties.

After ascending through the finely gradated ranks of Masonic wardens, stewards and deacons, Henry became master of the Titan Lodge in 1955. He never made it onto the Court of Common Council in the City, but he was elected to the governing body of the Carmen's livery company, explaining in the circular he sent to the liverymen voters that he sought office 'because I believe so strongly in the great traditions of our City and of our ancient Company'. He catalogues his affiliations and accomplishments, adding that he had been born 'within the sound of Bow Bells' and had 'traded as a merchant in the City for a quarter of a century', understandably not specifying the precise location of his birth, a hovel on Whitechapel Road, or the exact nature of his enterprises during the first decade of his commercial career. 'Could you please advise me,' inquired a recipient of one of my grandfather's City circulars, 'if it is indeed your wife, the Mrs Henry Freedman, who does such good work for the NSPCC and the National Playing Fields Association? Should this be so, I should be very happy to assure you of my support, and to do anything I can to assist you in your endeavour to become a member of the Court.' In the margin of the letter, Henry has scribbled 'YES'. Had he stayed on the company's governing body, he would have become Master of the Carmen, and from there he might have made a bid for the Lord Mayoralty. But by the end of the fifties that dream had finally died.

Henry and Miriam cherished Canvey, but they holidayed instead in Venice and the Caribbean, and took breaks at the upmarket kosher hotels of Bournemouth, where, after dinner, Henry would treat the other guests to his practised interpretation of 'My Yiddishe Mama'. They visited Israel, and met the relatives they had helped in the early fifties. But unlike many British Jews of their generation, my grandparents never considered doing more than visiting. London was the centre of their universe. It contained all their possibilities, their dreams of distinction and their nightmares of indigence. London was part of them; and the story of struggle, success and transformation

that they lived is at the heart of London. Away from its grime and grandeur, my grandfather would have suffocated.

In 1964 he and Miriam finished an old London cycle – from inner-city squalor to suburb, and back to inner-city stateliness – that generally takes immigrant families several generations to complete. Henry had decided that he needed to live closer to the head office and showroom that he had by then opened in Oxford Street: he had quit his premises in Middlesex Street and finally left the Lane. He bought a flat in Clarence Terrace, one of the swish alabaster crescents that enclose Regent's Park.

For eighteen months, while the new flat was being adapted to his exacting specifications, Henry, Miriam and their daughter Amelia, who had infuriatingly resisted her father's plans for her to become a debutante, moved into a townhouse in Sloane Avenue, just off the King's Road in Chelsea. Leah Claret – or Levine, as her last relationship had left her – was corralled, old and cantankerous, into a little room in the attic, where Miriam could keep an eye on her. But Leah hated the indebtedness and the semi-incarceration, and she kept escaping back to the independence of her doll's-house flat above the discount shop in Harpenden, with its questionably come-by antiques, from which Henry would have to retrieve her. She must obscurely have understood that he would resent these recapture missions even more than she did, because Henry wanted her under his Chelsea roof even less than she wanted to be there. But for him it was an ineluctable duty, as was taking his mother-in-law along for the Mediterranean holidays on which, as Henry saw it, she contrived ever more ingenious social humiliations for him. When the new place on Regent's Park was ready, Leah moved into the basement, where, at an unknowable age, she died in 1967. (Henry said all the necessary prayers for Leah on Miriam's behalf, and in her will Leah left, as a last-gasp token of reconciliation, 'to my beloved son-in-law Henry Freedman, the Italian painting of flowers'.) Above her in Clarence Terrace

my grandparents' grandest home had an L-shaped first-floor living room, with a head-high Adams fireplace, Persian carpets and elegant tall windows overlooking the Regent's Park boating lake. There was a terrace that looked down Baker Street, and a panelled library, and the erstwhile Earl of Hertfordshire was as proud of it as any aristocrat of his inherited pile.

Henry's hardness towards his mother-in-law was one of the harsher by-products of his ambition. He never shook off the habit of autocracy that he had picked up as the pre-*barmitzvah* head of a slumland household. He was the sort of person, I suspect, who can be easier to admire than to live with. He was intolerant of people who seemed to him to be content to finish where they had started, and not to share his philosophy of life as a perpetual struggle for something better. Sometimes, along with Leah, those people included my grandmother. He almost never forgot, on their anniversary, to give Miriam an arrangement of lilies-of-the-valley, which had been her bouquet at their wedding in Philpot Street in 1932; but he did not always impeccably observe the oaths of devotion that he swore in his early love letters. My grandmother could not always live up to his idea of her, and of himself. Perhaps she became an avatar for everything that Henry hadn't achieved, for the part of himself that was beyond transformation.

There were costs for him too, in his declining health, and his unstable finances. Eventually, his heart went out of Society, and he resigned himself to a slower life. He quit the livery companies, and even his beloved Honourable Society of the Knights of the Round Table, and he and Miriam moved out again to the suburbs, to a comparatively modest flat overlooking a golf course in Stanmore, stuffed with books and dominated by Flora Lion's portrait of my grandmother, where tea was only ever served in a proper china cup and saucer. The Rolls had been traded in for a Humber Hawk, and that for something humbler still. 'Happiness can only spring from yourself,' Henry had written to his son Philip in 1952; 'you can take a situation comparing it with one set of circumstances and be the unhappiest person in the world, but if you look a little farther and compare it with another set of circumstances, you can consider yourself to be the most fortunate and should be, therefore, the happiest of people.' This intuitive relativity helped my grandfather to survive the hardships of his early life. His talent for accommodation also helped him to come to terms with the comedown of his last years. He rediscovered his father's faith, delighting the rabbis who had accepted his donations or gifts of new ornaments for their Torah scrolls but despaired of his soul, and in the early seventies wrote to congratulate the sudden revival of his orthodoxy. He tracked down a copy of a kabbalistic tract written by one of his ancestors, published in Lemberg in 1848. He tried hard, though in vain, to recover a silver ornament for his *talis*, or prayer shawl, which his father had left him along with the bowler hat, and which Henry had given away in his high English phase. 'I never believed that I would need it,' he wrote to a relative whom he had enlisted in the search, 'but now I am 66 years old, I am longing to see it again & wear it.' He did not altogether eschew his pursuit of greatness: he produced a family tree, which purported to trace the Freedman/Friedman line back to Maimonides, the famously polymathic medieval scholar from Spain, a sort of Jewish version of Aristotle. But towards the end my grandfather no longer concealed his East End background. He no longer minded that Boot Street was more detectable in my grandmother than the Lane was in him, or that she was sometimes awkward in polite company, and was less easy with witticisms than some quicker ladies of his more recent acquaintance. He loved her again, so his last letters to her say, without all the complications.

My grandparents lived many lives in one: poor and comfortable; liminal and straight; immigrant and English; extraordinary and what you might call ordinary, though no one who came out of the sink of Edwardian east London, or lived through the two world wars, can by today's comfortable standards be said to have had an ordinary life. The extinct Belgravian world into which they temporarily insinuated themselves now seems almost as strange and distant as the Yiddish enclave in which Henry was born, or the other-worldly Galician life that he visited in 1913. (He never went there again: there was nothing left to go back to, and today there is very little left even to feel. What remained of the old civilisation in Nadworna and Solotwina after the war was lost to the general Soviet erasure of history. Now the only, almost invisible, traces of centuries of Jewish life in Nadworna are a few faint indentations left behind by unscrewed *mezuzahs*, the door-post emblems of Jewish households. With the aid of old birth certificates retrieved from Ukrainian archives, a Habsburg-era map, and the good offices of the chain-smoking, phlegmatic rabbi of Stanislau, now Ivano-Frankivsk, when I went to Nadworna I found it possible to identify the place where Millie Freedman was born Malka Kanfer in 1886. The site is now occupied by an optician; around the corner there is a car park where the *mikveh* used to be, and a tatty playground where the synagogue with its hidden entrance once stood. The Jewish cemetery in Solotwina, on a slope behind a little farm, is used to raise goats, and choked by tall grass and wildflowers, from which the worn

Hebrew gravestones protrude at jauntily improbable angles. But it is in better condition than the one in Nadworna, where a few plain shelters have been put up to keep the plants and the elements and the vandals away from the graves of the illustrious rabbis to whom I am very distantly related.)

Miriam lived for another twenty-two years after Henry died, a time that for her, as for many long-lived widows, was like another life again. For nearly half a century Henry had chosen their friends and ordered her drinks and dispensed her housekeeping money. She never stopped revering him, and could burst into tears when inquisitive grandchildren too clumsily tried to find out what he had been like. But, alone, she was as unpretentious as she was ladylike. She gave up the extant affectations like a tired fancy-dress costume, and dropped or was dropped by the remaining Society friends, eventually even losing touch with Walter Sherman's children and grandchildren, whom Henry had kept up with until the end.

Senility overtook her in her seventies and eighties, and by the time I realised I wanted to, it was no longer possible to talk properly about her past: maybe we only see what we are losing, and the fact of loss, when it is already too late. Still, for most of those years she had sporadic accesses of clarity, in which she would recall the Hoxton firewood sorties, the shoe-shop heist of her girlhood or the love songs of her courtship, even if, as she did so, she had forgotten whom she was talking to or whose house she was in. Almost to the end, and after both were dead, she asked after her brother Paul and after 'poor Uncle Jakob'. At dinner on Friday night, the Jewish Sabbath meal, when the women of the family intone a Hebrew blessing as they light the ritual candles, she would gamely mumble along in an undertone, hoping, as she had hoped when she first moved into New Castle Street in 1932, that nobody would notice that she didn't know the words. Amelia, my mother, grew up to be an accomplished classical musician and the director of a chamber music ensemble. Miriam came to every concert, and each was 'the most wonderful ever, darlin''. Then once, driving her back to Stanmore after a concert that included a *lieder* recital – and perhaps also after she had allowed herself her occasional half-glass of sweet sherry – we asked her what she really thought of the concert. She liked it, Miriam said, but she wasn't sure about the singing. Why not? Well, why couldn't they sing something that everyone could join in with, like 'Roll out the Barrel' or 'The Lambeth Walk'? She lived for her afternoons at the community centre, where they laid on a pianist and fish and chips. She loved a sing-song, and she loved dancing, and later the illusion of dancing that could be had by standing still with a gentle sway. I sat with her, in Stanmore, through the night between her death and her burial next to Henry, as Jewish custom enjoins relatives of the dead to do.

So my grandparents finished their lives more or less where, according to the rules of British sociology, they might have been expected to: industrious children of hard-working immigrants, they had ascended a few rungs up the social ladder, from the lowest of the law-abiding rungs to somewhere in the nuanced and elongated middle. But in between they had swapped Petticoat Lane for Park Lane, ghetto for gentility, rollercoastering almost to the very top. They lived, in a way, outside of the fabled class system, inhabiting so many of its niches in succession that, looked at in retrospect, their lives defy categorisation. With no inhibiting pride in the fortitude of poverty, no meek resignation to what might have been their fate, they remade themselves in an image of their choice. Class, their story suggests, exists mainly in the mind.

Yet at the same time as he triumphed over its predestinations, Henry was for most of his life in thrall to class, obsessed with ascending through the system's echelons. At bottom, what he wanted was to be a new-minted person, on whom no trace of poverty or obscurity remained. Perhaps he abandoned the high life and moved to Stanmore because he came to understand that his race against the past was unwinnable. Maybe he found out that even if he fooled all of the people in Sloane Square all of the time, he would never fool himself, and lived out his life feeling that he could never have been what he wanted to become.

Or perhaps, as I would prefer to believe, some time in the sixties Henry instead understood that no one would ever again speak to him like the bank manager who had perfunctorily denied him the loan in Liverpool Street, or like the Home Office bully who had petrified a newly widowed Millie Freedman with his talk of repatriation, or would ever again write to Henry in the exclusive doublespeak used by the bowling club's secretary. That no one, including himself, would ever again think that Henry Freedman was less than any other Englishman. He had the evidence to prove it. In November 1958 he wrote to the Gaumont-British Picture Corporation in Wardour Street, Soho. The company had, Henry believed, made a film during the coronation year that included some footage of the Queen arriving at the Royal Film Performance in Leicester Square. He was momentarily in the film too, my grandfather explains, 'although I am not sure whether I am actually talking to Her Majesty'. If possible, 'I would very much like you to send me either still shots or a cine film of this particular scene.' Gaumont wrote back, requesting a photo of Henry to help them find him.

Eventually, they sent my grandfather a negative that showed him dressed in a tailcoat, wing collar and white tie. In it, a smart little boy is presenting a bouquet almost as large as himself to the young monarch. In the background, Henry is looking past the Queen and into the camera, committing this moment of consummation to posterity.

Old black-and-white photos can be melancholy, even a little maddening. Like the letters Henry sent to Miriam when she went to Poland, or those from Auguste Claret to Leah and from Walter to Henry, they seem to promise an intimacy with the dead; but each letter and every image is also a certificate of absence. They are eloquent, but they speak also of everything beyond the picture or the letter that we will never know. For my grandfather, the photos that now tantalise me had a sort of totemic, voodoo power. He always needed a picture of himself – meeting the Queen or Princess Margaret, or chatting to a peer at his club – to prove to himself that it had all truly happened, and truly to him. When they sent through the still of him with the Queen, they gave Henry an image of himself as an ideal

Englishman, to set alongside the snaps from his childhood voyage to Nadworna that fix him as a Galician immigrant. 'It is with great pleasure that I have today received your letter and the enclosures,' he wrote back to Gaumont. 'I am pleased to say that I have been able to identify myself on the negative clipping you forwarded.' Identifying himself in that photo, Henry proved to the world, and to himself, who he really was.

# The Friedman/Freedman, Kanfer, Kaswin, Piechota, Troper and E

Moses Kaswin

Chaje Kaswin = Nuhim Kanfer
?–1913

Moses & Eidel

Illa Kaswin/Rohatyn    Menie Kanfer    Herschel Kanfer    Malka/Millie Kanfer = Fishel Friedman/Freed
1886–1940                              1874–1915

Rifka Kanfer = Joseph Troper

Shulek Troper    Nuhim Troper    Salka Troper    Philippe Troper = Amalia Kiesler
?–1941          ?–1941          ?–1941          1903–1984        1902–1957

Babs Freedman = Morris Feltz    Mick Freedman = Freda Caplan    Ida Freedman = Solly Nemenchins
1915–1994       1913–1963       1911–1995       1915–2003       1909–1988      1904–19

Brenda Harris = Philip Freedman    Frances Waltzer = Michael Freedman    Amel
1939–          1933–              1942–             1938–